Money – The New Rules of the Game

Christian Felber

Money – The New Rules of the Game

Christian Felber
Vienna University of Economics and Business
Vienna
Austria

Translated by Jacqueline Mathewes

ISBN 978-3-319-67351-6 (hardcover)   ISBN 978-3-319-67352-3 (eBook)
ISBN 978-3-319-76383-5 (softcover)
https://doi.org/10.1007/978-3-319-67352-3

Library of Congress Control Number: 2017956749

© Springer International Publishing AG 2017, First softcover printing 2018
Based on a translation from the German language edition: *Geld. Die neuen Spielregeln* by Christian Felber, Copyright © Deuticke im Paul Zsolnay Verlag Wien 2014. All Rights Reserved.
This work is subject to copyright. All rights are reserved by the Publisher, whether the whole or part of the material is concerned, specifically the rights of translation, reprinting, reuse of illustrations, recitation, broadcasting, reproduction on microfilms or in any other physical way, and transmission or information storage and retrieval, electronic adaptation, computer software, or by similar or dissimilar methodology now known or hereafter developed.
The use of general descriptive names, registered names, trademarks, service marks, etc. in this publication does not imply, even in the absence of a specific statement, that such names are exempt from the relevant protective laws and regulations and therefore free for general use.
The publisher, the authors and the editors are safe to assume that the advice and information in this book are believed to be true and accurate at the date of publication. Neither the publisher nor the authors or the editors give a warranty, express or implied, with respect to the material contained herein or for any errors or omissions that may have been made. The publisher remains neutral with regard to jurisdictional claims in published maps and institutional affiliations.

Printed on acid-free paper

This Springer imprint is published by Springer Nature
The registered company is Springer International Publishing AG
The registered company address is: Gewerbestrasse 11, 6330 Cham, Switzerland

Money will determine the fate of mankind.
Jacques Rueff[1]

The real price we pay for our money is that our thinking about it is narrowed with regard to what is possible—money builds a prison for our imaginative power.
YES! A journal of positive futures[2]

On the face of it, the growth spiral of the economy is a so-called snowball system, which is based on the fact that payouts for previous investors come from the deposits of new investors.
Hans Christoph Binswanger (2013, p. 29)

Products were once turned into money in order to make the acquisition of new products possible, now money is turned into goods and the only aim is to turn these into more money.
Christina von Braun (2012, p. 188)

---

[1] In "The Age of Inflation", Chicago, 1967. Cited in Lietaer (2002, p. 360).
[2] Special Edition on Money: print your own, No. 2, Spring 1997, p. 12.

A bank is not an institution for accepting or lending money, it is an institution for creating credit.
Henry Dunning Macleod (1889)[3]

The majority of citizens are of the opinion that they belong to the winners in the interest system.
Helmut Creutz (2008, p. 15)

The total debt in the G20 countries, the 20 most important economies in the world is 30% higher than in 2007, before the onset of the financial crisis.
William White[4]

The situation cannot continue as it is.
Lucas Zeise (2012, p. 7)

It is inevitable that the system will collapse and the question is not whether the system will collapse but rather when.
Dirk Müller (2009, p.105)

The worst crisis since the Great Depression in the 1930s has to date not resulted in science, the trade press and political world being guided towards taking a fundamental look at basic monetary questions and making a reform of the monetary system, a basic component of current financial reforms.
Joseph Huber (2013, p. 34)

The privilege of creating and issuing money is not only a right reserved for the

---
[3] From "The Theory of Credit" (London, 1889), cited in Huber (2010, p. 51).
[4] Head of the OECD Economic Committee in *Welt am Sonntag*, 22 September 2013.

government but can become one of their most creative instruments.
Abraham Lincoln (Cited in Huber and Robertson (2008, p. 13))

Money could only be lent if there is money available to be lent. The banks could no longer over-lend by producing money out of nothing and in doing so creating inflation and booms.
Irving Fisher (2007, p. 19)

Wealth is evidently not the good we are seeking (…) The source of the confusion is the near connection between the two kinds of wealth-getting ["oikonomia" vs. "chrematistike"]; in either, the instrument is the same, although the use is different (…) accumulation is the end in one case, but there is a further end in the other. Hence, some persons are to believe that getting wealth is the object of household management, and the whole idea of their lives is that they ought to increase their money without limit.
Aristotle (1985, 1096a, p. 6) and (2007, 1257b, 31–1258a, p. 5)

Money is in the meantime not the end, but a means to an end.
Friedrich Wilhelm Raiffeisen (Cited in Klein (2008, p. 79))

Economics is just a means to an end.
Thomas Jorberg (Dohmen 2011, p. 203)

Property entails obligations and the use thereof should all serve the common good.
Deutsches Grundgesetz, Art. 14

> *All economic activity serves the common good.*
> Bayerische Verfassung, Art. 151

> *Private institutes and those listed on the stock exchange are not obliged to foster and promote the common good.*
> Alexander Dibelius[5]

> *Those who have money make the rules.*
> Frank Stronach

> *Free financial markets are the most effective control instances of government activity (....) If you like, the financial markets so to speak as "the fifth power" alongside the media have taken over an important watchdog function. If politics in the 21st century in this sense were in the slipstream of the financial markets, this perhaps might not be such a bad thing*
> Rolf-E. Breuer[6]

> *The free financial market paradigm should be replaced by a financial market as infrastructure of the real economy (public service).*
> Philippe Mastronardi (2013, p. 80)

> *I am very satisfied with what we have achieved with the banking union.*
> Wolfgang Schäuble[7]

---

[5] German CEO of Goldman Sachs, cited in Von Braun (2012, p. 120).
[6] Die fünfte Gewalt in *Die Zeit*, 18/2000.
[7] *Frankfurter Allgemeine Sonntagszeitung*, 22 December 2013.

Preface: Money and democracy – an Overdue Wedding

Are you satisfied with the current monetary system? Do you consider it to be fair, democratic, understandable and sustainable?

Do you know how the current monetary system works: how money is created, how the links between the commercial and central banks operate, how a loan is transformed into a bond, what exactly a shadow bank is and in what way a 100 million euro is transferred to a tax haven?

Do you know who has designed the present monetary system? Which body develops it, which commission discusses it, which parliament or sovereign has determined it?

The perplexity which usually occurs when addressing such questions is neither worthy of a living democracy nor of free and empowered citizens. This book would like to end the "reign of money" (Brodbeck 2012) by initiating a public discussion about the reigning monetary system, by recommending concrete and understandable alternatives for all important elements of the reigning monetary and financial system and by outlining a democratic process as to how we could get away from the current plutocracy and financial dictatorship to reach a democratic monetary system.

The author of the book is of the opinion that the current monetary system is not only multi-dysfunctional but that it is also quintessentially undemocratic, which is at the same time the most important cause of the dysfunctionality. The political decisions which have led to the current monetary system do not meet the needs and values of the sovereign. According to a representative survey, between 80% and 90% of the population in Germany and Austria would like a different economic system to the present one (Bertelsmann Foundation (2010, p. 1) and (2012, p. 7)). If there were various alternatives available to choose from, people would definitely opt against the present-day monetary system. If there was for example a democratic vote about whether:

- commercial banks should create money,
- money should be lent to speculators,
- systemically important banks should come into existence,

- these banks should be bailed out with taxpayer's money,
- shadow banks should exist,
- states should go into debt on financial markets,
- movement of capital to tax havens should be free,
- food speculation should be permitted,
- the US dollar should be the commodity currency....

A democratic majority for even one of these present-day applicable rules would probably not be found in any country in the world. However this unspeakable monetary system legally exists within the framework of democratic constitutional states and makes life difficult for us and takes some people's lives. Unfortunately "your money or your life" is often true.

Part of the problem is that the democratically voted representatives are so much under the influence of the most powerful interests, which have evolved from the neo-feudal capitalistic monetary system, that they are not interested in making any decisive changes to the present-day game rules of the monetary system. The government and parliaments also do not have the slightest inclination to question the reigning monetary system, let alone to rewrite the rules of the game. Although a series of reform projects and financial regulation measures are instigated from the G20 and Basel Committee via EU institutions to as far as national states, none of these projects represents a thorough solution and none of these will create an alternative monetary system. This is not at all the objective in these official processes!

Consequently the author is of the opinion that every free, rational-thinking and democratically minded person has no alternative but to disengage himself or herself from the comfortable passivity and shrugging acceptance of a multi-dysfunctional monetary system and independently and cooperatively to tackle the creation of a new monetary system from the grass-roots citizen level.

There are good reasons to motivate us to do so: we are facing the decision: "change by design or change by disaster." It is better to consciously shape and create rather than staggering into the next crisis. We not only owe ourselves, our self-respect and our dignity this "system shift" but also the future generations who we should not passively leave this present "un-system" to.

We should at least make the attempt to develop a fairer, more stable and sustainable monetary system.

A system change or rather a democratic advancement of the monetary system can only be engineered by many people together and decided on by the highest democratic instance, the sovereign. Indirect democracy has fallen victim to the monetary system and its tendency to be corruptly engrossed with blind monetary growth, with finance alchemistical self-referentiality to the "revaluation of all values"[8] and to the unrestricted concentration of economic and political power.

This book therefore recommends the discussion of the new games rules for the monetary system in a participative and decentralized process, to finalize these in delegated or directly elected national conventions and to embed them in the

---

[8]Nietzsche in *Also sprach Zarathustra*.

constitutions via binding referendums. Specifically speaking, a section in the constitutions could be amended, whereby the game rules of the monetary system are firmly embedded, thereby providing parliaments with a clear basis for monetary legislation. The monetary constitution is binding for the legislator but not "cast in stone" forever. It can be amended, however only again by the sovereign, which is the same instance which enforced it. A democratic monetary system can and should be intermittently revised, improved and enhanced by the parliamentary authority.

I would like to direct a personal appeal to those people, who are equipped with exceptional creativity, intelligence and intellectuality—talents which nature has given us. We can use these talents to our personal advantage and we can give these talents back to the community by contributing and playing a part in the development of fairer and more democratic games rules. How many highly talented people today learn the craft of investment banker, asset broker or funds manager? How much creativity is invested today in product innovations within the system? And how much is invested in system innovation? An economic system can only function well, when the rules of the game are fair and accepted. When the "rules of the game" in a company, in a house, in an organization are not consistent, then the whole organization suffers. The present-day monetary system burdens all of society with its multi-dysfunctional rules.

This book advocates a democratic monetary system, which increases freedom for all by (a) having equal opportunities to help shape the rules of the game, (b) the egalitarian impact of these games rules and (c) their tendency towards system stability, distributive justice and sustainability. The more democratic they come about, the more they will be in accordance with the basic values of society, namely human dignity, freedom, solidarity, justice and sustainability. The vision of this book is that money can neither be the objective of economic activity nor can it be a private good, but rather a resource of economic activities and a public good. Money should go from being a weapon to a tool and should serve life, the common good.

References

Aristotle. 1985. *Nicomachean ethics*, Trans T. Irwin. Indianapolis: Hackett.
Aristotle. 2007. *Politics*, Trans T. Benjamin Jowett. Adelaide: ebooks@adelaide.
Bertelsmann Foundation (2010): *Bürger wollen kein Wachstum um jeden Preis*, Survey-Study, July 2010.
Bertelsmann Foundation (2012): *Kein Wachstum um jeden Preis*, Survey-Study, Short Report, July 2012.
Binswanger, Hans Christoph (2013): Finanz- und Umweltkrise sind ohne Währungs- und Geldreform nicht lösbar, pages 19–31 in: Verein Monetäre Modernisierung (2013): *Die Vollgeld-Reform. Wie Staatsschulden abgebaut und Finanzkrisen verhindert werden können*, 3rd edition, Edition Zeitpunkt, Solothurn.
Brodbeck, Karl Heinz (2012): *Die Herrschaft des Geldes. Geschichte und Semantik*, Wissenschaftliche Buchgesellschaft, 2nd edition, Darmstadt.

Creutz, Helmut (2008): *Die 29 Irrtümer rund ums Geld*, Signum Wirtschaftsverlag, Sonderproduktion, Vienna.
Dohmen, Caspar (2011): *Good Bank. Das Modell der GLS Bank*, Orange Press, Freiburg.
Fisher, Irving (2007): *100%-Money. 100%-Geld*, Verlag für Sozialökonomie, Kiel.
Huber, Joseph (2010): *Monetäre Modernisierung. Zur Zukunft der Geldordnung*, Metropolis-Verlag, Marburg.
Huber, Joseph (2013): Finanzreformen und Geldreform – Rückbesinnung auf die monetären Grundlagen der Finanzwirtschaft, S. 33–59 in: Verein Monetäre Modernisierung (2013): *Die Vollgeld-Reform. Wie Staatsschulden abgebaut und Finanzkrisen verhindert werden können*, 3rd edition, Edition Zeitpunkt, Solothurn.
Huber, Joseph/Robertson, James (2008): *Geldschöpfung in öffentlicher Hand. Weg zu einer gerechten Geldordnung im Informationszeitalter*, Verlag für Sozialökonomie, Kiel.
Klein, Michael (2008): *Bankier der Barmherzigkeit: Friedrich Wilhelm Raiffeisen. Das Leben des Genossenschaftsgründers in Texten und Bildern*, Sonder-Edition für Mit.Einander NÖ, Aussaat Verlag, Neukirchen-Vluyn.
Lietaer, Bernard (2002): *Das Geld der Zukunft. Über die zerstörerische Wirkung unseres Geldsystems und Alternativen hierzu*, Riemann, 2nd and special edition, München.
Mastronardi, Philippe (2013): Die Vollgeldreform als Verfassungsinitiative aus juristischer Sicht, pages 61–72 in: Verein Monetäre Modernisierung (2013): *Die Vollgeld-Reform. Wie Staatsschulden abgebaut und Finanzkrisen verhindert werden können*, 3rd edition, Edition Zeitpunkt, Solothurn.
Müller, Dirk (2009): *Crashkurs. Weltwirtschaftskrise oder Jahrhundertchance. Wie sie das Beste aus Ihrem Geld machen*, Droemer, München.
Von Braun, Christina (2012): *Der Preis des Geldes. Eine Kulturgeschichte*, Aufbau Verlag, Berlin.
Zeise, Lucas (2012): *Geld – der vertrackte Kern des Kapitalismus: Versuch über die politische Ökonomie des Finanzsektors*, 3rd revised edition, PapyRossa, Köln.

Acknowledgements

The coffee house sessions with Clemens Guptara were always a buzz of ideas, combining humor, word play and analogies. Clemens is the youngest intellectual in my circle of acquaintances and friends, and this book represents our first joint project.

My thanks to Joseph Huber for his patient support, ranging from emailing to a personal meeting in Berlin, regarding the really not so easily digestible theme of sovereign money. I predict that his work will be the focus of much attention and hope that it will be implemented in the near future.

For inspiring thoughts, critical feedback and reviewing of individual chapters or the complete manuscript, I would like to thank Sven Giegold, Günter Grzega, Gisela Heindl, Ulrich Hoffrage, Elisabeth Klatzer, Karin Küblböck, Nicola Liebert, Helge Peukert, Martin Rollé, Margit Schratzenstaller, Simon Sennrich, Alexandra Strickner, Stephan Schulmeister, Beat Weber, Ralf Widtmann and Albert Wirthensohn.

Thanks to my partner Maga for the affectionate support during the high-production phases and also for support with content-related research.

For the Deuticke Verlag including the Hansa team with Bettina Wörgötter, which has supported me both professionally and as a person with this book, my eighth book which has been published since 2006.

Thanks to getAbstract for granting the getAbstract Book Award 2014 "Business Book of the year" to the German version of this book.

Thanks to the translator Jacqueline Mathewes, who did a great job translating this equally academic and essayistic German text into easy-to-read English.

Thanks to Springer for believing in this courageous text that designs a completely innovative monetary and financial order—which so many humans are longing for.

The last and most important word of thanks for this breathtakingly inorganic theme goes to Pachamama. She holds the natural resources which coins are made of and even provides the raw material for book money.

Biographies

Christian Felber (Author), Austrian, born in 1972 in Salzburg, studied Spanish Language, Psychology, Sociology and Political Science in Vienna and Madrid. He wrote and coauthored more than 15 books and teaches at Vienna University of Economics and Business. He is an international speaker, contemporary dancer, and founder of the Economy for the Common Good movement. He also initiated the Project "Bank for the Common Good" in Austria which is described in this book. His book *Change Everything* has been published in 12 languages: http://www.changeeverything.info/

Jacqueline Mathewes (Translator), is an Irish-born translator who has been based in Germany since the early 1990s, after completing post-graduate studies in Economics and German. Since then, she has been working as a university lecturer and freelance translator, writer/editor for technical and business documentation and publications. Her interests include new/alternative economics, renewable energy, participatory politics, positive money and any sustainable solutions which will get us moving away from the precipice.

Clemens Guptara (Collaborator), is a student of philosophy at Cambridge University.

Contents

1	**Introduction: A Coercive and Intransparent Financial System**...	1
	1.1 The Non-Holistic Evolution of the Monetary System.........	1
	1.2 The Multi-Dysfunctionality of Our Current Monetary System...	4
	1.3 Regulators Wanted...............................	7
	References..	7
	Part I: The Process towards a New Monetary Order.........	9
2	**Tamer Wanted: Who Will Restrain the Global Monetary and Finance System?**..	11
	2.1 G20 and the Financial Stability Board (FSB)..............	11
	2.2 International Monetary Fund (IMF)......................	13
	2.3 World Trade Organization (WTO).......................	14
	2.4 Basel Committee on Banking Supervision.................	15
	2.5 European Union..................................	16
	2.6 United Nations (UNO)..............................	18
	2.7 Independent Experts...............................	18
	2.7.1 Who then?.................................	19
	References..	19
3	**Rewriting the Rules of the Game: The Democratic Monetary Convention**...	21
	3.1 Legitimation and Contextualization of the Convention........	22
	3.2 From Municipal to National Economic Convention..........	23
	3.3 From Local to EU to Global Level......................	23
	3.4 Local Matters....................................	24
	3.5 Core Subject Matters...............................	24
	3.6 Decision-Making Procedure..........................	25
	3.7 Utilization of Results...............................	27
	3.8 Initiated Prototypes................................	27
	3.9 Ten Reasons for a Monetary Convention..................	28
	Reference...	28

4	**The Basis: Money as a Public Good**		29
	4.1	Extended Meaning of "Public Good"	30
	4.2	Values of the Monetary System	33
	References		33

Part II: The Content – Cornerstones of a Democratic Monetary System 35

5	**Who Creates Money?**		37
	5.1	The National Central Bank	38
	5.2	Commercial Banks	38
	5.3	Companies	39
	5.4	Private Individuals	39
	5.5	Political Regional Authorities	39
	References		40
6	**Sovereign Money Reform**		41
	6.1	Creation of Bank Money by Private Commercial Banks	41
	6.2	Sovereign Money Reform	45
	6.3	Benefits of the Reform	47
	6.4	Side Note: Sovereign Money and Hundred-Percent Money	50
	6.5	Amendment of Legislative Texts	51
	References		52
7	**Democratic Central Banks**		53
	7.1	Who Does the Central Bank Belong to?	54
	7.2	Democratic Organization of the Central Bank	56
	7.3	Objectives and Tasks of a Central Bank	57
		7.3.1 The ECB Model	58
		7.3.2 The Fed Model	59
		7.3.3 The Alternative Model	60
	7.4	Monetary Authority	63
	References		64
8	**Solving the Problem of Sovereign Debt**		65
	8.1	Proposal for the Reform of Sovereign Debt Financing	66
	8.2	Benefits of the Reform for the Public	69
	References		70
9	**Bank Lending Regulations**		71
	9.1	Loans for What and for What Not?	74
		9.1.1 Ethical Creditworthiness Appraisal	74
		9.1.2 Speculative Financial Credit?	76
		9.1.3 Regional Priority	79
	References		81
10	**Common Good Oriented Banks**		83
	10.1	Banks Are Historically Common-Good Oriented	83

		10.2 Criticism of Bank Bailouts and the EU Banking Union.	86
		10.3 State Support Only for Common Good Banks	89
		10.4 Common Good Orientation of Banks.	90
		10.5 Prototypes Everywhere	94
		10.6 Systemic Consideration: From the Investment Bank to the Depository Bank.	95
		10.7 Adieu, Return on Investment	97
		10.8 From the Risk Premium/Capital Tax to a Meaningful Return on Investment.	99
		10.8.1 A Hoarding Ban for Cash Millions	100
		References	100
11	**EU and Global Financial Supervision**.	103
	11.1 EU Financial Supervision with an Edge	105
		11.1.1 Splitting up System Relevant Banks	105
		11.1.2 Closing or Strict Regulation of Shadow Banking Activities.	106
		11.1.3 Market Admission Approval for New Financial Products . .	108
		11.1.4 Stricter Equity Capital Requirements	110
		11.1.5 Rules for Funds and Capital Investment Companies.	113
	11.2 Global Financial Supervision	115
	References	117
12	**Derivatives—Close the Casino**	119
	12.1 General Regulation Proposals.	123
	12.2 Shares—Regional Common Good Exchanges	124
		12.2.1 Regional Common Good Exchanges and the "Triple Skyline"	124
	12.3 Close Securities Markets	127
	12.4 Government Bonds—The Use of the Central Bank.	128
	12.5 Foreign Exchange—A New Global Currency System.	129
	12.6 Commodity Markets—Global Commodity Agreement	129
	References	134
13	**Secure Pensions**.	135
	13.1 The PAYG Pension is Easily Financed.	136
	13.2 What Makes Private Provision Better?	140
		13.2.1 Are Private Pensions Less Vulnerable with Regard to Demographic Factors?.	141
		13.2.2 Are the Premiums in Private Pensions Paid More Interest than Social Security Contributions?	142
		13.2.3 Are Private Schemes Cheaper?	143
		13.2.4 Is the Private Pension System Distributively Fairer?.	143
		13.2.5 The Methuselah Conspiracy.	144
		13.2.6 Do Favorable Framework Conditions for the Private Pension System Also have a Favorable Impact on the PYAG Pension System?	144

		13.3 Alternatives	146
		References	146
14	**Global Tax Cooperation**		147
	14.1	Systemic Tax Evasion	147
	14.2	Step 1: Automatic Registration of All Domestic Income	151
	14.3	Step 2: Multilateral Agreement on Information Exchange	152
	14.4	Trust and Cooperation	153
	14.5	From the previous EU Interest Directive to the Sound Capital Income Directive	154
	14.6	World Financial Registry	155
	14.7	Technical Implementation	155
	14.8	Globally Just Corporation Tax—"Entire Group Taxation"	156
		14.8.1 Country of Residence Principle	158
		14.8.2 Unitary Taxation or Overall Group Tax	158
	14.9	A Go-It-Alone by the EU is Possible!	160
		References	160
15	**Income and Ownership Caps—"Negative Feedback"**		161
	15.1	Excessive Inequality	161
		15.1.1 Liberal Argument	163
		15.1.2 System Theoretical Argument	165
		15.1.3 Performance Justice and Equal Opportunities	166
		15.1.4 The Financial Stability Argument	167
		15.1.5 The Health Argument	167
		15.1.6 The Happiness Argument	168
	15.2	Limiting Income Inequality	169
	15.3	Capping of Private Property	170
	15.4	Inheritance	172
		References	174
16	**Currencies—Time for a Bretton Woods II**		175
	16.1	Failure of Bretton Woods I	175
	16.2	Shortcomings of the Current Monetary Order	178
	16.3	Pledge for a Bretton Woods II	180
	16.4	Global Monetary Cooperation	182
	16.5	Adjustment of Exchange Rates according to Purchasing Power Parity	182
	16.6	Epilogues	184
		16.6.1 Planned Economy in Peking und Zürich	184
		16.6.2 End of the Dollar Hegemony?	185
		16.6.3 Local and regional complementary currencies	186
		References	187

Part III: Kick Off 189

17	**The Path to the first Convention**		191
	17.1	Bottom-Up-Strategy	192

	17.2 The Process of a Democratic Monetary Convention	193
	17.2.1 Who Initiates a Convention?	194
	17.2.2 Who is in the Convention?	194
	17.2.3 How is the Convention Implemented?	194
	17.2.4 How does communication and decision making take place?	195
	17.3 Evolution of Contents	197
	17.4 International Cooperation	198
	17.5 From Monetary Convention to Constitutional Convention	198
	References	199
18	**Questionnaire for the Monetary Convention**	201
	18.1 Creation of Money	201
	18.2 Sovereign Money Reform	202
	18.3 Central Bank	202
	18.4 Sovereign Debt	203
	18.5 Banking System	203
	18.6 Commercial Banks	204
	18.7 Financial Supervision	205
	18.8 Derivatives	206
	18.9 Pensions	208
	18.10 Tax Justice	209
	18.11 Restriction of Inequality	211
	18.12 International Monetary Order	213
Index		215

Chapter 1
Introduction: A Coercitive and Intransparent Financial System

Abstract This chapter describes how the monetary system evolved over time and did not follow a master plan. The result is an incoherent, nonsensical complex monetary and financial system which causes wide-ranging collateral damage in society. Although money plays a crucial role in our everyday life today, there is little scientific clarification of the monetary system, with some economists even recommending not to pay too much attention to the phenomenon money. The result is a dense "fog" around money and a high lack of clarity about its various functions. As a consequence of its senseless design and lack of interest in the understanding of its functioning, the current money system is consequently unstable, inefficient, morally corrupting and a threat to democracy and liberty. It is a power structure. Part of its dysfunctionality is that it contributes to the corruption of the political system to a large extent so that re-regulation is not or hardly possible within the current form of democracy.

> *The fact that people neither foresee or completely understand their cultural achievements is one of the fascinating characteristics of mankind.*
> Ulrike Herrmann (2013, p. 247)

1.1 The Non-Holistic Evolution of the Monetary System

It is difficult to allege that our present-day monetary system has been created by a mastermind or according to a master plan. In fact, the monetary system has developed gradually over the centuries or even millennia and has grown into an extremely complex monster.[1] The final result of this development is neither attractive nor good and possesses no democratic structure, no drawn-up ethos and no grounding vision of the system as a whole. The monetary system was never consciously created and set up as a tool for mankind. Each individual step and each additional

---
[1]German Federal President in *Stern*, 14 May 2008.

element would appear to make sense and be advantageous for particular groups; however the system in its entirety does not serve everybody equally and definitely does not serve the common good. This is however not the definition of a public good or a democratic infrastructure, where all are treated equally and all are served.

Of course the current monetary system is far from being completely bad and money brings about a lot of good and makes our daily lives easier with a series of basic functions creating general public advantages, ranging from legal tender to individual bank accounts and to the possibility of taking out a loan. Yet it is precisely these advantages which are worth positioning, identifying, meaningfully designing and democratically determining, and those aspects which are really good will meet wide approval.

However, the present-day monetary system is in too many aspects a source of enrichment for a small group, a casino and a self-service shop for insiders, speculators and gamblers and at times a dangerous weapon. This weapon was also not intentionally designed and planned, but evolved through a gradual joining together of the ever increasing new functions, legislative acts and technical innovations.

The development of the monetary system can be divided into the following phases:

- As we know today from anthropological and historical research (Graeber 2012), prior to money as a medium of payment or exchange, there was credit and debt.
- It was only after this that mediums of exchange with use value came into being, for example, wood and frequently cattle. The "double crossing out sign" on the dollar, pound and yen signs stems from cattle horns (Von Braun 2012, p. 50).
- This was followed by a means of exchange with symbolic value: mussels, bones or certain types of stones. In order for something to act as money and be accepted as such within the community, it had to be rare and uncommon.
- Bit by bit precious metals such as copper, silver and gold caught on and these were quickly taken to the goldsmiths for safekeeping and storage. The goldsmiths became the inspiration for the first deposit banks, which exclusively functioned as storage institutions and not as a money lending business.
- The deposit banks issued a receipt for gold deposits in the form of banknotes or bills of exchange, which were the first precursors of paper money as a means of payment.
- Goldsmiths and deposit banks began to lend the same pieces of gold or gold coins several times—the start of the fractional reserve banking system.
- Legal fractional banking arose from "spontaneous" fractional banking and this resulted in the emergence of commercial banks in Central Europe in the 14th century.
- Private commercial banks established central banks from the 17th century onwards.
- These central banks initially backed national currencies with gold, the gold standard.
- The gold reserve was eliminated in 1971 and the central banks printed paper money without backing, fiat money.
- Computerization has caused the largest revolution to date, namely electronic book or bank money. Money can be created without printing it and with this

1.1 The Non-Holistic Evolution of the Monetary System

book money all money backing has been eliminated. In Europe the base money supply M1 (cash plus current account balances) today consists of, depending on the country, between 5% and 20% of central bank notes and coins and up to 80–95% of book money (Huber 2013, p. 43).

- As a result of double-entry accounting banks can create book money themselves. The so-called "creation of bank money" extends the money supply and leads to inflation—either on the goods markets or on the finance markets—asset price inflations (from the Latin word "inflare" meaning to swell or bloat).
- Securities such as shares, bonds and loans as well as raw materials and currencies are not only traded on the stock exchanges and financial markets, but bets on their future price development are made, these are known as derivatives.
- Along with simple bets (put and call options, futures) a complete universe of new financial innovation has emerged with investment banking, ranging from securitization of loans of variable quality (Collateralized Debt Obligations—CDOs) to insurance against the default of loans or government bonds (Credit Default Swaps) culminating in Partial Return Swaps, Partial Return Reverse Swaps and Total Return Swaps. The globalized financial casino is becoming continually more complex, opaque and unfathomable. In the USA the value of assets of the financial sector was about 450% of economic performance until the 1980s, in 2007 this value had increased to 1000%.[2]
- Banks only disclose a portion of their credit transactions in their balance sheets. A more significant part of these transactions are implemented outside balance sheets via so-called shadow banks, whereby particular legal constructs and tax havens play a central role. In the USA only half of all bank transactions are documented within the realms of balance sheets, 23 trillion US dollars remain in the shadows, where they are brewing the next financial time bombs (Financial stability board 2012, p. 4).
- Computerized securities trading (high frequency trading) drives the turnover volumes to staggering heights, shares and other securities are bought and then resold in milliseconds. According to insider information, high frequency trading accounts for over 50% of the stock trading capacity in New York and Frankfurt.[3]
- Derivatives turnover must be measured in million billions, namely in quadrillions, with such figures being beyond the imaginable, being disassociated from real economy indicators—global goods and services trade amounted to 22 trillion US dollars in 2011 (World Trade Organization 2012), global GDP was 70 trillion US dollars,[4] which was between 1% and 2% of the statistically recorded derivatives volume.

In the course of this "development," money has been loaded with ever increasing functions. Money is no longer only a *measure of value* (for the prices of

---

[2]*Trader's Narrative*, 7 November 2009; *The Economist*, 22 March 2008. Cited in HUBER (2013), 40.
[3]*Financial Times Deutschland*, 14 January 2010. www.ftd.de/finanzen/maerkte/marktberichte/: wall-streeter-unter-ausschluss-der-oeffentlichkeit/50060624.html
[4]World Bank.

product and services) and a means of exchange or better still a *means of payment* in order to simplify exchanges and handling of purchases. Money also has a credit function, is a storage of value (saving, pension provision), is a means of production (companies), is an insurance (crop failure insurance, currency fluctuation or interest rate change), is a status symbol (recognition, a measure of self-esteem and sense of belonging) or it is an instrument of power (intimidation, corruption, bribery, blackmail). Money is also a taxation instrument for the financing of government tasks and functions. There is by no means consensus with regard to everything that money is and which functions it has and this could be the task of a systematic academic study of money, which as far as is known does not exist. Although individual professorships and lecture courses use this title, there are indeed more professorships and courses for banking studies than money studies. The scant regard for money pertains to prominent economists: "There cannot, in short, be intrinsically a more insignificant thing, in the economy of society, than money …" according to, for example, John Stuart Mill (Mill 1909, Volume III. 7. 8). In his standard textbook, Paul A. Samuelson also warns scholars against dealing with the subject of money: "It is only monetary problems that have driven more people out of their minds than love" (Creutz 2008, p. 65).

Helmut Creutz writes: "Even in academic studies responsible for the study of money, money as a theme is still dealt with as a puzzle or copiously avoided" (Creutz 2008, p. 15). Is it a coincidence that there is only very limited academic interest in the functionality of the monetary system, although this is 100% man-made and has such extensive effects on all aspects of life? Is the "fog around money" (Senf 2009) and its game rules part of the power and reign of money? It certainly stands to reason that money can only satisfactorily function for mankind and serve the economy, if we (a) thoroughly understand it and (b) consciously design and shape it—or is this not the case?

1.2 The Multi-Dysfunctionality of Our Current Monetary System

The outcome of the "nonsensical" and "dark" monetary system is a multi-dysfunctionality of the current monetary system, from the economic, ecological, ethical and democratic viewpoint. The current monetary system is:

- Incomprehensible—Try getting an "expert" to explain to you in a comprehensible way and in two minutes how money is created by private banks. In at least nine out of 10 cases he/she will fail to do so. One of the better known money journalists and commentators Helmut Creutz, does not believe in money creation by private banks and says, "If the banks did indeed create loans without deposits, this would be a case of fraud and a matter to be looked into by the public prosecutor's office" (Creutz 2008, p. 175). Dirk Müller, known as "Mr. Dax," did not completely succeed in depicting this in his bestseller

1.2 The Multi-Dysfunctionality of Our Current Monetary System

"Crash Course."[5] In his documentary "Capitalism—a love story," Michael Moore jokingly asked investment and national bankers for a definition of a derivative. The outcome was entertainment without education. Joseph Huber writes, "Sometimes you have the impression that the present-day statistics and terminology relating to money have been especially invented to conceal the true functionality of the monetary system" (Huber and Robertson 2008, p. 11).

- Inefficient—Those who do good and make real-world investments with social and ecological added value are not those who obtain cheap loans, these loans are given to those who promise the highest financial returns, with money flowing into financial bubbles and tax havens instead of jobs and state coffers.
- Unfair—Those who perform the most valuable tasks (e.g. childcare, health or geriatric care) do not receive the highest income, this income goes to those who increase money in the riskiest and fastest way and who already have the most and too much money in any case (hedge fund managers).
- Non-transparent—As the saying goes "one does not talk about money," although it would appear to be the most important thing. Banking secrecy, anonymous trusts, tax havens and the wall of silence of constitutions concerning the question of book money creation all fit to monetary occultism.
- Volatile—There is a systemic tendency towards volatility and crisis due to the fact that private profit interests are given priority over the common good and systemic stability. Short selling, speculative currency attacks, betting on state bankruptcies and increasing food prices, computer-steered high frequency trade, leveraged speculation (leveraging) and the creation of money by commercial banks are allowed.
- Unsustainable—Due to the fact that money comes into circulation as debt, constant growth is necessary in order to be able to repay the interest on loans. The interest system and the general view that capital has a right to multiplication compels it to limitless growth.
- Unethical—Ethical criteria do not play a role in bank lending. Basel I, II and III are all equally ecologically, socially and humanely sightless.
- Ruthless—The current monetary system is virtually an invitation to get rich at the expense of others, to commit fraud by using information asymmetries (insider trading) and to get rich as a result of damage to others (betting on losses). There is a kernel of truth in the saying that "money ruins character."
- Criminal—Ranging from the Goldman Sachs Greece deal to subprime fraud, to Libor scandal and to raw material price manipulation, one criminal case follows the next. JP Morgan paid 13 billion US dollars for a settlement and in the same week paid a further 4 billion US dollars in damages to customers who were cheated. UBS, Royal Bank of Scotland, Barclays and Rabobank together paid a 2.5 billion euro fine for Libor manipulation. At the time of printing of this book,

---

[5]He describes that the *same* 10,000 euro which a bank customer brings to the bank can be spent by two bank customers. This is not correct. Müller (2009), 68.

Deutsche Bank built accruals to the tune of billions of euros in anticipation of a torrent of lawsuits.
- Undemocratic—Individual interest have prevailed everywhere, from the creation of money to product innovation. Money and the complete financial system are today a much too private good and too little a public good. What should be clearly forbidden, for example, "weapons of mass financial destruction," shadow banks or the free movement of capital to tax havens is permitted due to the fact that plutocrats corrupt politics.
- Resistant to regulation—the perhaps largest defect of the current monetary and financial system is that it has led to such a large concentration of power that an effective regulation is no longer manageable. Some individuals, such as Rolf-E Breuer, the former CEO of the Deutsche Bank, welcomed this and he referred to the financial markets as "the fifth power" whose merit is characterized by "controlling the state."[6]

The systemic write-off of democracy comprises of an innumerable amount of small "accidents":

- Financing of political parties and donations to politicians have a powerful influence on the results (formal) of democratic processes. At the end of the 1990s, the advocates of derivative regulation in the US Congress received 1 million US dollars, whereas the opponents received 30 times as much.[7]
- Lobbies beleaguer legislative committees and bring their influence to bear more successfully than penniless citizens. Politicians often openly say that their draft legislation comes from the corresponding industrial sector and for them this represents a welcome reduction of their work load.[8] The finance companies in Wall Street, according to research, paid 5.1 billion US dollars to lobbyists (Weissman and Donahue 2009, p. 15). CEO Jamie Dimon once said that JP Morgan Chase "achieves a good return on investment with the seventh business area of the bank, namely political connections and connections to authorities" (Admati and Hellwig 2013, p. 320).
- From time to time assistance is rendered by bribery and corruption. Austria was considered to be a country relatively free of corruption for a long time, however this has changed in the last 20 years. The former Minister for the Interior and Head of the ÖVP parliamentary group Ernst Strasser offered his political services for 100,000 euros and was sentenced to 4 years absolute imprisonment at the first instance.[9]
- The revolving door effect—the political and business elite form a unit, whereby managers shift to politics and politicians switch to lobbyism for the powerful

---

[6]Rolf-E. Breuer: Die fünfte Gewalt in *Die Zeit*, 18/2000.

[7]http://maplight.org/us-congress/bill/111-hr-977/359058/total-contributions

[8]Lobbycontrol.

[9]At the time of the copy deadline of the German version of the book at the end of 2013, the case was referred back to the first instance by the Supreme Court (OGH).

corporations. Goldman Sachs even appointed several US finance ministers or their deputies and in the USA one in three congress members switch directly to the lobbyism business after their term of office has expired (Reich 2008, p. 183). The doors are constantly revolving between supervisory authorities and finance companies.

- The media is becoming more dependent on powerful advertising customers, which it does not want to lose as a result of critical reporting or it is also the case that business groups actually own the media companies directly and intervene, as in the case of Raiffeisen with the Austrian newspaper Kurier.
- Academics and researchers are afraid to operate outside the mainstream, for fear of losing their reputation and possibly being snubbed by the scientific community and being unable to publish in the relevant journals.

1.3 Regulators Wanted

In view of this systematic undermining and capture of democracy by the money aristocracy, there is little or no prospect of success with regard to a far-reaching reform of the monetary system and a change of the rules of the game by the relevant committees and institutions. Within a functioning democracy governments, parliaments and international organisations would have tackled the game rules of the monetary system after the 2008 crisis or following the 1997/1998 Asian crisis, after the wreckage of the Long Term Capital Management Hedge Fund in 1998 or after the dotcom bubble burst in 2000.

Before I recommend a fundamental alternative, let us first take a tour through the most important institutions on the global political stage that are worth considering for the regulation of the global finance monster. Are they suitable for and are they interested in placing the monetary system at the service of the people and economy? Are they willing and capable of serving the good life and the common good?

References

Admati, Anat/Hellwig, Martin (2013): *Des Bankers neue Kleider. Was bei Banken wirklich schiefläuft und was sich ändern muss*, FBV, München.

Creutz, Helmut (2008): *Die 29 Irrtümer rund ums Geld*, Signum Wirtschaftsverlag, Sonderproduktion, Vienna.

Financial Stability Board. 2012. Global shadow banking monitoring report, 45 pages, Basel., 12 November 2012.

Graeber, David (2012): *Schulden. Die ersten 5000 Jahre*, Hanser, Munich.

Herrmann, Ulrike (2013): *Die vier Krisen des Euro*, Le Monde diplomatique, German edition, 13 September 2013.

Huber, Joseph/Robertson, James (2008): *Geldschöpfung in öffentlicher Hand. Weg zu einer gerechten Geldordnung im Informationszeitalter*, Verlag für Sozialökonomie, Kiel.

Huber, Joseph (2013): Finanzreformen und Geldreform – Rückbesinnung auf die monetären Grundlagen der Finanzwirtschaft, S. 33–59 in: Verein Monetäre Modernisierung (2013):

Die Vollgeld-Reform. Wie Staatsschulden abgebaut und Finanzkrisen verhindert werden können, 3rd edition, Edition Zeitpunkt, Solothurn.
Mill, John Stuart. 1909. *Principles of political economy with some of their applications to social philosophy*, 7th ed. London: Longmans, Green.
Müller, Dirk (2009): *Crashkurs. Weltwirtschaftskrise oder Jahrhundertchance. Wie sie das Beste aus Ihrem Geld machen*, Droemer, München.
Reich, Robert (2008): *Superkapitalismus. Wie die Wirtschaft unsere Demokratie untergräbt*, Campus, Frankfurt a. M.
Senf, Bernd (2009): Der Nebel um das Geld. Zinsproblematik, Währungssysteme, Wirtschaftskrisen. Ein Aufklärungsbuch, 10th revised edition, Verlag für Sozialökonomie, Kiel.
Von Braun, Christina (2012): *Der Preis des Geldes. Eine Kulturgeschichte*, Aufbau Verlag, Berlin.
Weissman, Robert And Donahue, James. 2009. *Sold out. How Wall Street and Washington betrayed America*. Washington/Studio City: Study, Essential Information & Consumer Education Foundation.
World Trade Organisation. International trade statistics 2012, Geneva.

Part I:
The Process towards a New Monetary Order

Chapter 2
Tamer Wanted: Who Will Restrain the Global Monetary and Finance System?

Abstract This chapter discusses which power or which institution could rewrite the rules of the money system. It takes a closer look at each of the already involved regulatory bodies—from the G20's Financial Stability Board and the International Monetary Fund to the European Union and the United Nations. Despite strong rhetoric in favor of tighter regulation and an impressive amount of concrete regulatory projects at all levels, the result of the investigative journey through these institutions is that at this moment in time none of them is willing or capable of fundamentally rewriting the rules of the game of the financial system. Ideological hegemony and power concentration with the consequent regulatory capture have developed too far. Thus a different strategy seems necessary to put the monetary and financial system in line with the fundamental values of democratic societies and make it more stable, just, transparent and democratic.

> *It must now even be clear to every responsible thinking person in the sector that the international finance markets have evolved into a monster which must be reined in and restrained.*
>
> Horst Köhler[1]

2.1 G20 and the Financial Stability Board (FSB)

In view of the high degree of globalization of the financial markets and the high risk of contagion in financial crises an international regulation; a globally democratic monetary system would be the order of the day. The committee that has most apparently taken up the cause of the regulation of international financial markets is the group of the 20 largest and most powerful industrial and emerging economies. However the composition of the group already creates a large question mark: why in particular these 20 from 192 UN members? Why not the UNO directly? These are questions posed by prominent economists in the company of

---

[1]*Stern*, 14 May 2008.

Joseph Stiglitz: "neither the G7 nor G20 represent a sufficiently inclusive global steering group to tackle a global system change. Although the G20 group is more broadly positioned than the G7 group, 172 are still excluded. The organization of any future regulation must ensure the inclusion and appropriate representation of developing nations, including LDC" (United Nations 2009, p. 72).[2] It is a bit steep when technically democratic states come together in a highly exclusive club and assume that their decisions are good for the whole world and that the 172 states waiting outside the door will go along with them. The relative importance of the G20 group in global economic performance is undisputed (85% of world GDP and 80% of world trade), however fact is that democracy is the opposite of hegemony. The G20 group additionally argues with their "openness," as they were after all originally only a group comprising of the seven most important members.

However, the G20 is also numerically a backward step, as in 1944 more than 40 states were involved in the establishment of the World Bank and International Monetary Fund. The economic importance of developing countries has increased since then ... another contradiction. For more than 30 years the ballad of "liberal" globalization with its free movement of people, goods and capital has been sung, and now just about a tenth of all states should look for solutions for problems which apply to all? There is no rational reason why a minority can claim to make the rules for all. The insubstantial outcome of the G20 summit series fits to the undemocratic process. Five years after the onset of the financial crisis:

- there is no global financial regulatory body in sight;
- hardly any too big to fail bank has been dismantled;
- the "too big to fail" nature of many financial institutions is greater than before;
- movement of capital to tax havens is totally free;
- not even one product has been withdrawn from the market;
- with the exception of non-secured short selling in the EU, not even one activity has been internationally forbidden;
- no financial enterprise category has left the world market stage.

Little remains of the promise made at the first meeting in Washington in 2008 "to regulate or supervise all markets, products and players" (G20 (2008, p. 3). The impression which has been created is in fact the opposite of that which should be in place, namely the 20 most powerful nations have come together to protect the "monster" and not to restrain "monster" with joint forces. They *are* the monster. Admittedly not in the sense that the general public in the USA, Germany or Italy are so hell-bent on banks which are too big to fail and insistent on free movement of capital to tax havens, but rather that the financial and economic elite have captured the democratic process in nation states, where decisions are made against the interests of the majority of the population, with the same game being repeated via governments at a global level.

---

[2]"LDC" means the group of 48 "least developed countries," the group of states with the lowest per capita income.

The only success which the G20 could take credit for is the Basel III resolution. However as we will see later on, Basel III will also not be able to prevent the next financial crisis.

The Financial Stability Board (FSB) was initially established by the Financial Stability Forum (FSF) as a consequence of the devastating Asian crisis in 1997/1998.[3] It is composed of the two most important supervisory bodies that is central banks and treasury departments. It can be described as the G20 ground work expert forum and the G20 often refers to the FSB, however both are united to a large extent in inactivity and ineffectiveness. This is also confirmed by prominent sources, as according to the UN expert committee with Joseph Stiglitz at the center, "it is now evident that the reforms recommended by the FSF were not sufficient enough to prevent a larger global financial instability" (United Nations 2009, p. 96).

2.2 International Monetary Fund (IMF)

Although there are 184 member states in the International Monetary Fund, founded in 1944, it does not have any less of a democracy problem than the G20, as it is legally a shareholder company with a majority share of the wealthiest countries. On the basis of its ownership structure alone, it does not represent global interests but rather hegemonic interests. The USA has right of veto, as the only member state, and can prevent any decisions which run counter to its interests. Numerous countries are in contrast fully under-represented and go largely or totally unheeded. The basic voting rights, equally divided amongst all member states, have furthermore historically deteriorated and only account for 5.5% of the voting rights, this was still at 11.3% in 1944 (United Nations 2009, p. 94).

The IMF has acquired a rather bad reputation for a start by forcing structural adjustment programs on the heavily indebted countries in the 1980s, in the form of reduction in public spending, cutting of food subsidies, introduction of debt-based money, privatization and market deregulation. According to Stiglitz, "the market ideologists call the shots and in their opinion the markets on the whole function well, whereas states more or less function badly" (Stiglitz 2002, 239). The prescribed medicine often fails to meet the desired effect—poverty has increased in many of the treated countries. Nevertheless the dubious IMF skill is being applied to EU states, from Greece to Ireland, since the euro crisis. As with former patients, Greece's condition deteriorated after the "therapy" and its economy is in the worst recession of any European country since WWII, with no recovery in sight in the years since the start of therapy. The Troika is therefore increasingly known as "Destroika" and is accused of "Austericide."

---

[3]Members from Germany are the Bundesbank, the Federal Financial Supervisory Authority and the Federal Ministry of Finance. The complete list of members is available at: www.financialstabilityboard.org/about/fsb_members.htm

On the other hand it was the dogmatically blind deregulation, motivated by the fundamental belief of the self-regulatory forces of the market, which led to the severe financial crises, which even the IMF did not imminently foresee before the onset of the crises because they did not fit into its ideological picture of perfectly functioning (financial) markets.[4] In accordance with this, "many of the IMF's economic policy requirements definitely promote global instability" says Stiglitz in his criticism of the IMF. "Instead of serving the interests of the global economy," the IMF "serves the interests of the international finance sector" (Stiglitz 2002, p. 242 und 239).

To the IMF's credit, it should be noted that it has recently actually committed four violations against its own ideological doctrine. Firstly it was suddenly stated, after decades of free movement of capital being the holiest of holies, that limitations to the free movement of capital could possibly constitute a safeguard. Secondly it dawned on the IMF after the total disaster of Greece that saving in a recession might not be the best aid to recovery. Thirdly the IMF experts Jaromir Benes and Michael Kumhof exhumed the proposal of "100 percent money," fully backed with reserves, dating back to the 1920s and dedicated a working paper to this proposal entitles "The Chicago Plan Revisited" (Benes and Kumhof 2012). With the fourth violation the IMF triggered a flurry of excitement in the "Fiscal Monitor" under the title "Taxing Times" because it elaborated the possibility of taxing all bank deposits with a one-off 10% tax, in order to reduce state debts to a pre-crisis debt level (IMF 2013). The IMF leadership however followed up with a hastened clarification that this did not represent the viewpoint of the IMF, but rather represented individual opinions. For the time being, there only remains to be glimmers of hope in a dark organization.

2.3 World Trade Organization (WTO)

The WTO has the poorest cards of all as it represents a breach of continuity on the international community's path of "integration and growing together." After the founding of the United Nations, the proclamation the Universal Declaration of Human Rights (UDHR) and after the institution concert of the UNO had grown member by member, it dramatically stepped out of line in 1995. Ironically, the most powerful trade organization was not incorporated into the UN orchestra and tuned to the existing programs, organisations and objectives, but was founded, as an individual organization, to solely enforce free trade. The reason for this being that the trade interests of transnational corporations should precisely not be aligned with human rights, climate protection, cultural diversity, labor rights or food security and sovereignty. An institution within the realms of the UNO would have had to carry out such alignments

---

[4]Eugene Fama the originator of the theory of efficient financial markets curiously received, albeit together with Robert Shiller who came to very different results, the "Sveriges Riksbank Prize in Economic Sciences in Memory of Alfred Nobel" which is often confused with a Nobel Prize. It was not one of the original prizes specified in Nobel's will, but rather was added by the Nobel Foundation in 1969.

and considerations. Within the framework of the UNO there is actually the "United Nations Conference on Trade and Development" (UNCTAD), which was established in 1964 on the initiative of the G77, a group currently comprising of 130 developing countries, whose aim is not "free trade" but sustainable development. This is precisely why the industrial nations, above all the EU core states and the USA, lost interest in this UN trade organization and relegated it to the political backwater.

The WTO can disregard all considerations and is committed to its blind mission to implement free trade. However trade is not an end in itself, but an instrument for development, freedom and democracy, consequently trade should be practiced to the extent and in the quality required to achieve its objectives. The WTO turns this means into an end, by serving corporate interests. Consequently, it is not at all politically responsible for regulation, namely the restriction, stipulation and shaping of trade, but is exclusively responsible for liberalization and market deregulation. WTO contracts are sophisticatedly drafted in such a manner that regulations are questioned and lawsuits are enabled. In this way it has been possible on several occasions to pursue successful lawsuits at the WTO court of arbitration against national laws in the area of health and environmental protection (ATTAC Austria 2004 and Felber 2006, 165–184).

The WTO General Agreement on Trade in Services (GATS), which also encompasses financial services, is particularly treacherous. In this partial agreement WTO members make claims against each other, especially the EU demands that developing countries lift capital transfer restrictions und banks which operate out of tax havens are allowed access to the market.

In short the WTO does not have a regulation mandate, but rather a deregulation impact. Hoping that the WTO will tame and get a grip on the financial markets would in effect be the same as letting the fox guard the hen house.

2.4 Basel Committee on Banking Supervision

The Basel Committee on Banking Supervision, which was established in 1974 by the 10 most powerful states, developed a third generation of lending rules for member states after the crisis. The "Basel I," "Basel II" and now "Basel III" rules are as a rule converted into national law by the member states, in the EU as rules of equity requirements (Capital Requirements Directive I IV).

The Basel Committee however is not suitable as a global regulatory instance due to the fact that its sphere of competence is very confined and limited to rules regarding equity and lending. Furthermore it does not have any legislative powers but rather carries out activities of recommendatory character and, as in the case of G20, it is a rather exclusive club, but with a slightly higher number of members.

Secondly Basel II along with Basel III, which came into power in 2014, have both been severely criticized, with one important point of criticism being the pro-cyclicality of the rules: companies must be assessed with regard to their creditworthiness and are rated accordingly. However in times of recession creditworthiness of all companies drops and exactly then when they are especially in need of credit facilities. If funds are axed by the banks in a recession, this is then intensified and creates a wave of insolvencies, which is economically exactly the wrong reaction. Conversely, in boom times fuel is added to the fire because the creditworthiness of companies generally improves and encourages the production of bubbles in the capitalist system.

"Basel III" furthermore adheres to the calculation of equity capital for individual assets on the basis of weighted risk factors. Some assets are considered to be more secure or receive a more favorable rating and must therefore be backed with less capital. However, recent years have shown that little trust can be placed in ratings and assets which are deemed to be secure for example government bonds can fail—in Basel II and III these are however deemed to be fail-proof and do not require capital backing. A bank which has specialized in state financing can very quickly find itself in hot water, should a state whose bonds they hold be granted debt relief, a fact which must be known since the situation with Greece.

Thirdly the Basel Committee is not a committee which is representative of all of society. Although the lending decisions made by banks have a massive impact on all sectors of society, there are no ecologists, psychologists, social medicine specialists or neurobiologists on the committee and the ecological, social, human or democratic impacts of a loan are not an issue for the Basel Committee. This perhaps represents the largest qualification shortcoming: the essence does not have to be assessed. The loan can be ecologically destructive, degrading, discriminating and have anti-social impacts. As long as the repayment including interest is assessed as being probable, the loan can be granted. The lending rules are literally "unethical," are monetary autism and therefore dangerous for society. The Basel Committee can be ruled out.

2.5 European Union

Most hopes of a successful taming and regulation of financial markets relate to the European Union and some parties of the wider EU institutions concert give cause for hope. There are some dedicated politicians in the EU parliament, the only directly democratically legitimized body, who are committed to the common good and not the financial lobby. Even if that is far from being straightforward—Sven Giegold, from the German Green Party, who grapples with banks, insurances and funds, reports that for each person representing consumer interests, employees or environmentalists there are 50 lobbyists from the money business waiting at his/her door. It is a struggle of unequal resources. Giegold himself and others founded the common-good oriented NGO "Finance Watch," which is annually supported by the commission to the tune of 10 million euros.[5]

However this is peanuts, in comparison with the billions which corporations and banking associations make available. Some top-level politicians offer their services for 100,000 euros.

---

[5]www.finance-watch.org

2.5 European Union

And even if the parliament hoists the common good flag, its power is limited and it does not even have right to co-decision in many significant policy areas for example taxation policy. In those matters where it has voting rights, it has to come to agreement with the council and national executives (!) and cannot decide anything single-handedly—not even initiate laws. The monopoly for drafting regulations and directives is in the hands of the EU Commission, which is not directly democratically legitimized and more often than not pursues its own agenda. In the case of the financial transaction tax or regulation of hedge funds the parliament had to beg on bended knee to the commission for years, before it reluctantly sprang into action. The EU Commission selects those it listens to and those who advise it. A good example for the commission's ideologically-drenched and interest-driven policy is the composition of the Larosière Commission, which was appointed by Manuel Barroso at the peak of the 2008 financial crisis, in order to develop recommendations for regulation of the financial markets. According to Lobbypedia, the group of eight experts was more than somewhat one-sidedly staffed. Four members of the team have direct connection to the big players in the financial sector: the chairman Jacques de Larosière has been an advisor to BNP Paribas since 1998, Otmar Issing is an advisor to Goldman Sachs, Onno Ruding advises Citigroup and Rainer Masera was CEO of Lehman Brothers, Italy.

Callum McCarthy has been accused of gross failure in his role as Chief of the British Financial Services Authority (FSA). Leszek Balcerowicz, member of the board of trustees of the Friedrich August von Hayek Foundation and member of the Advisory Council of the European Policy Centre is known as a free-market enthusiast and opponent of regulation. Critical perspectives were totally missing in the group and consequently the final report of the Larosière Group did not substantially challenge the self-regulation of the banks.[6]

The following are some samples from the expert group's recommendations: "the role of the IMF in macro-economic monitoring should be boosted" (another fox guarding the hen house), over-the-counter (OTC) derivatives should "be simplified and standardized" (instead of being forbidden) or "off-balance sheet special purpose entities should adhere to stricter rules, as recommended by the FSB. This means that the type and scope of supervisory regulations in force for these special purpose entities must be clarified and if necessary higher equity requirements must be specified. In addition greater transparency must be ensured" (European Commission 2009). In other words, off-balance sheet special purpose entities alias "the shadow bank sector" remain in existence and must only "if necessary" fulfill higher equity requirements and become somewhat more transparent. Shutting down this sector by including all banking transactions in balance sheets is not recommended by the experts.

- The massive besiegement surrounding the delicate seeds of common good in EU institutions does not allow the emergence of effective laws. Although the list of regulatory initiatives since 2008 has been considerable, the legislative texts are nevertheless weak and occasionally a mockery.

---

[6]https://lobbypedia.de/wiki/Dominanz_der_Finanzbranche_in_den_Expertengruppen_der_EU

- Capital requirements for banks (CRD IV package) implemented by Basel III in the EU as of 1 January 2014.
- Insurance Regulation (Solvency II) effective as of 1 January 2016.
- Directive for the regulation of managers of profit-oriented investment funds (AIFMD) was passed in 2011.
- The "Markets in Financial Instruments Directive" (MIFID) was updated and extended in 2014 to MIFID II and MiFIR, and the European Securities and Market Authority ESMA delivered three sets of technical standards in 2015.

Parallel to the diligent pseudo-regulation, the neoliberal project, with European Stability Fund ESF/European Financial Stability Facility EFSF/European Stability Mechanism ESM, fiscal pact, competitiveness pact, banking union, trade and investment agreement TTIP with the USA, is enjoying its high speed development. The EU, in its current status, is not a part of the solution but the crux of the problem.

2.6 United Nations (UNO)

The United Nations General Assembly has positively broken the ranks. After the onset of the 2008 crisis it commissioned an international team of experts with Joseph Stiglitz at its center to develop regulatory proposals for the international financial system. The 140-page final report differs pleasantly from the G20, IMF, Basel Committee documents and from EU directives. The report is in comparison with these downright lucid and recommends the following measures and institutions: a global financial supervisory authority, a global reserve currency with a global central bank and global monetary union, a financial transaction tax, control on capital movement, a global court of justice for debt .... All considered and revised by a UN Economic Council, on the same level as the General Assembly and Security Council—a firework of ideas, proposals and effective measures (United Nations 2009, in particular pp. 70–110).

The problem: the General Assembly did not resolve any of this. The most important reason for this: the G20 governments boycotted the UNO conference in June 2009, Angela Merkel for example failed to attend. If there were something along the lines of a direct mandate of representatives from the sovereign, the Federal Chancellor could as a result of this not make such an important decision autonomously. The main part of this book will deal with the pioneering contents of the Stiglitz Commission in detail, rather than the watered-down EU directives.

2.7 Independent Experts

In the light of political failure some people would prefer if laws were made by independent experts, but as we know today there is no such thing as an independent expert. There is simply no "objectivity" in economics, but rather various possibilities. Every option is "efficient" and "functions" for one or the other stakeholder, every option is more or less "fair," depending on which perspective is taken and how fairness is defined.

Therefore regarding it from the strictly logical point of view, it makes no sense to let economists write the fundamental rules for the economy or monetary system, but rather the democratic sovereign should take over this task, as it alone can set the ethical and political priorities according to which the economy and money is organized. Economists can contribute ideas prior to the democratic decision-making process and afterwards advise the parliament and government with regard to detailed legislation and implementation.

A further problem lies in the question—who would be the "money experts" today? As previously seen, the monetary system has become so complex and unmanageable that virtually nobody has a reasonable comprehensive overview. Although there are numerous money gurus and specialist making the rounds, they all have different approaches—bank analysts, economic historians, central bankers, interest opponents, stock exchange brokers, investment consultants, globalization critics …. They all more or less have their own problem analysis—private money creation, compound interest system, state regulation, deregulation of financial markets, the banking system's greed for profit, lobbyism, capitalism … and other proposals such as deregulation, nationalization of banks, sovereign money, depreciative money, complementary currencies, elimination of interest, amendment of the production model and money-free gift economy. Depending on who is involved in the solution, the solutions look very different.

Various opinions are, on the other hand, not the problem, it is not possible any other way, and there is no "consensus" in any sector of politics, just as there is no consensus among experts. The point at hand is who would select and randomly bring the experts together? If we leave this selection to governments, they usually consult with those who serve the interests of social elites and not with those who are obliged to serve public interest.

2.7.1 Who then?

In view of the failure of governments and their dispatched international organisations and committees as well as the cases which arise with the option of expertocracy and meritocracy, it seems to me at this juncture that the most expedient way to a democratic monetary system is via the sovereign itself.

But how could the general public determine and establish a monetary system?

References

Attac Austria. 2004. *Die geheimen Spielregeln des Welthandels. WTO – GATS – TRIPS – MAI*, Promedia, Vienna.

Benes, Jaromir and Kumhof, Michael. 2012. *The Chicago plan revisited*, IMF working paper, Washington, August 2012.

European Commission. 2009. Brief summary of the De Larosière report, Handout.
Felber, Christian. 2006. *50 Vorschläge für eine gerechtere Welt. Gegen Konzernmacht und Kapitalismus*, Deuticke, Vienna.
G20. 2008. *Declaration of the summit on financial markets and the world economy*, Washington, 15 November 2008.
IMF. 2013. *Taxing times, fiscal monitor*, October 2013, Washington.
Stiglitz, Joseph. 2002. *Die Schatten der Globalisierung*, Siedler, Berlin.
United Nations. 2009. *Report of the commission of experts of the President of the United Nations general assembly on reforms of the international monetary and financial system*, 140 pages, New York, 21 September 2009.

Chapter 3
Rewriting the Rules of the Game: The Democratic Monetary Convention

Abstract This chapter proposes the deepening of current western democracies towards "sovereign democracies" which means that the sovereign body—in a democracy the citizens—should truly become the "highest instance," which is the literal meaning of "sovereign" in Latin. A true sovereign would enjoy "sovereign rights" ranging from the right to write and reform the constitution to the right to legal initiative and referendum. With few exceptions, such sovereign rights hardly exist in any country to date. The first and foremost sovereign right is the right to rewrite the supreme document in a democracy: the constitution. A process how the sovereign could reform the constitution is presented. The process would start in the smallest political units: municipalities or regions. The voting results of local assemblies on the future monetary system would be synthesized on national or international level and finally voted on by the sovereign citizens becoming part of national constitutions and the European Treaty.

> *A good monetary framework is substantially wiser than more regulation and bureaucracy to compensate for the deficiencies of an insufficient framework.*
> Mark Joób (Verein Monetäre Modernisierung 2013, p. 13)

It would be great if the formally democratically elected governments and parliaments took hold of the reins for the design of a monetary system and campaign for it within international organizations. If democracy functioned, as it is described in text books, this would be completely sufficient, functional and efficient. However, as my previously noted reasons state, we cannot rely on this at present and I therefore suggest an alternative to exclusively representative democracy—an innovation of the democratic system itself, namely that all free and independent citizens take the "democratic scepter" in their own hands and decide on the basic principles and elements of an alternative monetary system in decentralized assemblies. The results could be brought together through delegation or direct election in national money conventions and later in an EU-wide and even global economic convention and then consolidated to a multi-optional concept for a democratic monetary system. Using this model all members of the democratic sovereign would vote and the accepted concept would find its way into national constitutions and international agreements.

3.1 Legitimation and Contextualization of the Convention

Some readers will ask themselves how and whether a citizen's convention is legitimate in the first place: is that not precisely the function of the parliament to implement the will of electorate by passing laws and changing the constitution?

It is unequivocally the function of the parliament to pass laws and it is elected for this, however in the case of constitutional changes this is no longer so clear. The fundamental question is: who should ideally write the constitution of a democratic community? From the author's standpoint, this should solely be the democratic sovereign, the highest instance of democracy. This would be in accordance with the Latin root of the word "sovereign," which is "superanus" literally meaning "first and foremost. The sovereign—the general public—is above the government and parliament and is therefore the logical instance for penning the game rules of a democratic state system, which must be adhered to by its delegation, parliament and government.

This would be a logical further development of the principle of separation of powers, which envisages a balanced division of power between the entities of democracy. A wise division of power between the sovereign and parliament (representative body of the people) does not only begin by the sovereign determining the rules of the game, according to which its representatives may "play." "Real sovereignty" in terms of the "highest instance" means that the general public must enjoy a series of rights and privileges, such as:

- rewriting the constitution from scratch,
- amending the constitution on its own initiative,
- calling for or drafting a democratic economic, money, media or common goods convention,
- electing a specific government combination,
- voting a government out of office,
- stopping a parliamentary legislative bill,
- initiating and deciding on a law itself,
- issuing money,
- deciding on an international agreement.

None of these seven basic rights are enjoyed by the democratic sovereign in Germany and Austria at present, the largest share of power currently lies with the parliament. The sovereigns are to a large extent powerless. This is pre-democracy.[1] The first step towards a balanced division of power between the sovereign and parliament is the recognition of the absence of "basic rights of the sovereign" and engagement to secure these in a broad-based citizen's rights and democracy movement. Thanks to the monetary conventions awareness in the general public could be built with the recognition that it is up to them not only to write the rules of the game for the monetary system but in the final analysis for

---

[1]Christian Felber. Prädemokratie und der impotente Souverän, in *Der Standard*, 18 September 2013.

democracy. Ideally following monetary conventions, there could be other thematic conventions and one day the "crown" convention, the constitutional convention.

3.2 From Municipal to National Economic Convention

The first municipal monetary convention will attract a great deal of interest and elicit imitation. The idea is that the monetary conventions take place in hundreds of communities, cities and regions, with the process being coordinated and results documented centrally from one point. This point could be an independent organization such as Mehr Demokratie e.V., the Economy for the Common Good Movement or the pioneer communities could take the reins in the process themselves. A monetary convention "observatory" could be established within the framework of a research project or professorship, scientifically charting all communal and regional processes as well as documenting the results. There is already a basic infrastructure for monitoring communal economic conventions at present in the Economy for the Common Good Movement, which could be expanded or at least used as a starting point for the coordination, supervision and monitoring of monetary conventions.

3.3 From Local to EU to Global Level

In a second phase the conventions could meet at a regional level—at district level, at federal province or as in Switzerland at *canton* level or in Spain at *Comunidades Autónomas* level, which would already be the first EU legal level, as the "Committee of the Regions" is a formal body of the EU institutional structure. Even though it has no legislative competence itself, a resolution from this instance with regard to an alternative democratically constituted monetary system and an EU-wide monetary convention would be a sensational step, which would not be without implications.

There are several instruments and ways within the national states: The Local Government Association or the Association of Cities and Towns in Germany and Austria can pass a resolution. At the federal state level, the Governors' Conference, which already has pertinent influence on the government and parliament, can become involved. If a political willingness were generated at the grass roots level of regional authorities—municipalities, cities, regions—and consolidated beyond the borders of federal states, which could refer to increasing numbers of local and regional monetary conventions, this willingness would gain a huge momentum. This is perhaps easiest in Switzerland, where the sovereign has power to force a referendum on a specific matter, if the initiative is signed by a minimum number of citizens. After a series of recent theme-related initiatives—Minder Initiative, Factor 12 Initiative, Minimum Wage Initiative—the way is paved for money and financial topics and the seeds can germinate quickly as soon as the first tangible experience from Austrian, German, Italian, Spanish and Swiss communities is available.

The municipal and regional conventions can also serve as a delegation basis, from which the federal convention's or higher convention's members could be sent. This would be connected with further benefits such as the development of question formulations and selectable options, as will be shown in Chap. 4.

3.4 Local Matters

An important aspect of the procedure is the fact that the municipality is not the relevant legal level for the matters to be discussed and voted on. Firstly this should however not be an obstacle for the general public to think about the game rules of the global monetary system. Secondly a section of the questions could be formulated in such a way so that they fall within the municipality's sphere of competence, which would lead to a further incentive to deal with the "big" questions— 25% of the questions could apply to municipality matters and competencies. This would include the question of profit or common good orientation of local banks, the introduction of an ethical credit appraisal at these banks, the development of a common good balance sheet, the selection of ethical financial services providers by the municipality, the co-establishment of a regional common good stock exchange, the issuance of a regional complementary currency, the decision to accept this as local tax money and so forth.

The major section, perhaps half of the questions could apply to the monetary system at the democratic nation-state level and a further quarter at international regulation level (G20, Basel Committee, IMF, World Bank, UNO, etc.). The direct democratic mandate of governments through the national sovereigns would for certain result in quite a different monetary regime, an alternative international monetary system. This is especially due to the fact that the sovereigns probably have quite different interests, needs and values to the elite and lobbies, which currently successfully enforce their special interests and turn these into binding laws and international agreements for all.

3.5 Core Subject Matters

These subject matters should effectively form the most fundamental questions with regard to the monetary system:

- Is money a public good?
- Who creates money?
- Which targets should banks pursue?
- Should loans also be granted for purely financial transactions or only for real investments?

3.6 Decision-Making Procedure

- Do loans only need to be assessed according to their financial quality—"creditworthiness"—or on the basis of their ethical quality—and impact—as well?
- Is income from capital permissible (interest, dividends, exchange rate gains)?
- Should there be limits for inequality?
- Should there be a cooperative international monetary system?

It should deliberately only be the formulation of major questions, as detailed work and amendments are the task of the parliaments. In the main section of the book, 47 questions are drawn up, which are then compactly re-summarized at the end and serve as a ready-made basis for a municipal monetary convention. Every "sovereign" is of course free to amend and extend the questions. The modification of the questions including the voting options is a matter of fact part of the tiered procedure from the local to federal to EU or international level. Real democracy means not only does the sovereign have the right to vote but that it can also determine the initial questions.

3.6 Decision-Making Procedure

With regard to decision methods, I would suggest the use of a relatively recent innovation, which has sustainably convinced all those who have used and gathered experience with it. This method, the SC Principle or "Systemic Consensus," was developed by two mathematicians at the University of Graz.[2] This method is employed with sustainable success in the Economy for the Common Good,[3] in the Bank for the Common Good Project[4] and other civil society organizations.[5] The SC method offers two clear advantages over the usual democratic decision-making process: firstly more proposals can be generated for the voting process and secondly the resistance to each of the submitted proposals is measured, instead of approval the proposal with the least resistance wins. The simple idea behind this is that every rule, every law and every norm limits the freedom of a part of the population to a certain extent. At the same time it ideally increases the freedom of a larger group to a greater extent, which is why it is decided. Thus the task is to find the solution which limits the freedom of as few people as possible, as little as possible or to put it another way: the rule of the games are whatever causes the least amount of pain in the population. By way of illustration, on 24 November 2013 in Switzerland a proposal to limit the disparity between the highest and lowest income in a company by a factor of 12 was voted on.

The initiative was rejected by almost two-thirds of the voters and only in North and South Tessin (Locarno and Chiasso) did the majority of the population vote for the proposed limit. The "no vote" means that the status quo remains unchanged that

---

[2] www.sk-prinzip.eu
[3] https://www.ecogood.org/en
[4] www.mitgruenden.at
[5] www.attac.org

is factor 900^6 with the possibility of an endless further increase. Viewed in another way, the Swiss people only had the choice between factor 12 and factor 900 to infinity, with no alternatives in between. This is rather absurd as the current situation is so painful for most of the population that it resulted in the initiative in the first place and a third voted for it—in individual regions the majority. Conversely however the current situation is obviously less painful for the population than factor 12, which is why the majority voted against it. It would however make sense to ascertain the factor which causes the least pain and which is more than likely in between: perhaps it is factor 20, maybe factor 30 or factor 50. In order to ascertain this value these alternatives and others must be an option and not only just two. A mature democracy must be able to endure this degree of complexity and diversity and as a matter of fact enhances it. Human life and evolution in general are a permanent differentiation process.

Systemic Consensus has two basic voting options: the "rougher arm raise option" or the "finer 10-fingers option." With the "arm raise option" the voters have three possibilities to show their resistance:

1. They do not raise their arm, which means that they are basically in agreement with the respective proposal, they do not have to enthuse, and they just do not have anything against the proposal (no resistance).
2. They raise an arm, this is when stomach ache is noticeable or questions arise (slight resistance).
3. They raise both arms, which means they put a veto on the proposal (severe resistance).

This method is clearly visible for all and easy to count. With the "10 point option" the voters score every individual proposal with resistance points between 0 and 10. This measurement process is finer and more differentiated, however it is not visible to the same extent as the "rough process" (unless you use 10 fingers per person). It is a standard method for online voting and is the proposed approach for monetary conventions. All voting options at the end of the book are described with "RP: __ out of 10," RP stands for resistance points.

A further important aspect of Systemic Consensus is the fact that the current status quo in every issue at stake is a "fixed starter" in the proposals and referred to as the "zero option." This is intended to prevent reform proposals, which are clearly ahead but still subject to higher resistance than the old provision—the old provision then remains.

The SC Principle has been spreading globally within the last few years and is a humane high-tech, efficient and future-oriented procedure for decision-making.

---

^{6}The highest salary earned by a manager in Switzerland was earned by Daniel Vasella in 2007 and was 44 million Swiss francs. Divided by the minimum wage demand of 4,000 francs per month or 48,000 francs per year, this results in a factor of 916. The lowest income at Novartis in 2007 is not known by the author. The factor 900 is also used in *Schweiz am Sonntag* in a report from 20 July 2013.

3.7 Utilization of Results

The "local" section of the questions could be implemented directly—a benefit for the municipality, local democracy and self-government. The national and international sections on the other hand must be successively delegated to the responsible higher level in question within the democratic system. The objective is to change the constitution and at present there are only constitutions within the framework of nation states. This would require a "federal economic convention," which would have the mandate to prepare a draft for a monetary constitution, which the public could then vote on and on acceptance could be incorporated into the constitution. On the strength of the monetary constitution, the sovereign could obligate their parliaments and governments to behave in a certain manner and adopt certain positions in the EU, WTO and UNO. The mere prospect that governments and parliaments are no longer permitted to act at their own discretion, and be prone to representing the interests of the elite or yield to pressure from the most powerful lobbies, would be tantamount to a revolution in international relations. Instead of entering into trade and investor protection agreements which are directed against freedom, and perform political work via undemocratic institutions (IMF, World Bank) and committees (G20, Basel Committee), they would have to carry out and implement the democratic mandate assigned to them by the sovereign. After a globalization phase which has been in compliance with corporations, this would be a boost for democratic globalization.

3.8 Initiated Prototypes

The good news is that the practical fundamentals recommended here already exist. In the Economy for the Common Good movement we have developed the "Municipal Economic Convention" concept, which is thought to be implemented in the "Common Good Municipalities," whereby the free and sovereign citizens get together several times within the period of a year in order to ascertain the twenty most important legal elements of a democratic economic system. The results form the basis for an economic constitution section, which should be developed by a federal economic convention. The first common good municipalities started in the course of 2013 in Spain, Italy and Germany and in 2014 we expect the start of the first municipal economic conventions in 2017. Correspondingly "municipal monetary conventions" could also meet within the Economy for the Common Good movement, whereby public citizens develop a monetary system of their choice. The results of hundreds of local and regional monetary conventions could be synthesized into a national monetary convention and edited as a constitutional amendment proposal and in a referendum SC would be used to determine which proposals go into the constitution.

3.9 Ten Reasons for a Monetary Convention

1. The monetary system is technically insufficient.
2. The monetary system is ethically insufficient.
3. The current governments and parliaments are doing absolutely nothing to make any system change, they are themselves part of the ethically insufficient system and are taken in by, instrumentalized and corrupted by the alleged profiteers ideologically, personally as well as procedurally.
4. Changes therefore require another democratic process and other participants.
5. The democratic participatory process will trigger the collective awareness regarding the necessity and feasibility of an alternative monetary system to the necessary degree and thus lead to the result, namely a democratic monetary system.
6. The sovereign is not responsible for the details, but rather the "broad outline," which is precisely what conventions are good for.
7. The detailed work can and should subsequently be carried out by the parliaments, which however have a constitutional framework within which they must operate. Should they violate this constitutional framework, the constitutional court can intervene, as is today the case with every legislative proposal. In addition the democratic sovereign itself can intervene, which in a real democracy can at any time adjust and vote its representatives out of office.
8. If the level of knowledge develops further or the value concepts and priorities of the population change in any way, the convention can re-meet and implement reviews and amendments at regular intervals: a democratic monetary system is not written in stone but is an agile, evolutionary process open to further development.
9. Conventions are inspiration and strengthening exercises for the democratic sovereign, they strengthen the democratic essence, the participation of people in political matters and decisions—the "Res publica," public matters and affairs.
10. Monetary conventions whet the appetite for other topic conventions such as economic conventions, education conventions, media conventions or the icing on the convention cake, constitution or democracy conventions.

Municipal monetary conventions are game changers: they innovatively and democratically reform the game rules of the monetary and financial system. The dream destination of this book is the chance of municipal money, economic or democracy conventions being discussed by at least one person in every municipality: a monetary convention can in principle take place in every community.

Reference

Verein Monetäre Modernisierung (Hg.) (2013): *Die Vollgeld-Reform. Wie Staatsschulden abgebaut und Finanzkrisen verhindert werden können*, 3rd edition, Edition Zeitpunkt, Solothurn.

Chapter 4
The Basis: Money as a Public Good

Abstract This chapter proposes that money, being an equally essential and sensitive infrastructure for modern societies, should become a public good. However not in the classical meaning of economic text books but rather in the meaning that, firstly, the rules of the game of the monetary and financial system should be defined by the sovereign citizens. In this meaning, money would become a "sovereign good." Thus, secondly, the sovereign citizens would become the issuers of money. Operatively, money should be issued exclusively by public central banks and remain in public property, whereas natural and legal persons can only use and "possess" it. The complete financial system becomes a public good which is guaranteed and regulated by the state, although the concrete services such as financial intermediation are operated by private banks. As a consequence, economic freedom is restricted in this sensitive area. Finally, the foundation values of the financial system are proposed in this section.

> *Yes to nationalization of money, no to nationalization of banks.*
> Irving Fisher (2007, p. 20)

One of the fundamental theses of this book is that money should become a public good, a "public service," a modern "commons" and a "Res publica," as is the case or would desirably be the case for the education sector, internet or public safety. In classical economics public goods are those which fulfill the two criteria of non-excludability and non-rivalry. Non-excludability means that nobody is excluded from the use of the good as in the case for example of clean air, street lighting and public security. Non-rivalry means that no conflict emerges in the use of the good. In the case of clean air, street lighting and public security, this is the case. For a swimming pool, it is partly the case and it does not apply at all for a park bench—it is there for everybody, does not exclude anybody, but when it is occupied it cannot be used by others. Public goods are those where both criteria apply and are known as "pure public goods," whereas those where only the first criterion applies are known as "impure public goods" or "commons." Only the first criterion applies for money: whereby one and the same hundred euro note or current account balance can only be used by a certain person and not simultaneously by another, all can use it but not at the same time. The use of money is limited as in the case of the park bench and therefore money is, according to the currently common scientific definition, an "impure public good."

However there is an important aspect of money, which constitutes a pure public good: money creates trust between people who do not know each other. The state establishes and supports the trust in legal tender and the official currency, making this trust a "pure public good"—non-excludable and non-rivalrous. The state puts various measures in place in order to create and maintain this trust:

- it issues money via the central bank,
- it prescribes compulsory acceptance for legal tender,
- it secures a portion of bank deposits,
- it protects private property and bails out banks.

4.1 Extended Meaning of "Public Good"

The state's comprehensive responsibility certainly indicates that money is a public good. However this book recommends a further development of the term "public good" in the direction of "public service" and a "Res publica," in concrete terms there are four identifying features of "money and credit as a public good":

1. The complete financial system, thus not only money creation, but also granting of credit, the banking business and all other financial services will become a public good or "public service" according to Swiss legal understanding. This means providing the economy and general public with money and loans becomes a public duty and the state takes over responsibility for this task, whereby the services provided are for the common good. The "state's guarantee responsibility" consists of two components (Cf. Mastronardi 2013, p. 64.):
   (a) *Fulfilment Responsibility*: The state itself does not have to deliver these services itself and can commission private providers to provide certain bank, insurance and financial services, however in compliance with state regulations. Private and public banks must adhere to a democratically determined catalogue of services.
   (b) *Support Responsibility*: If the private providers fail, the state will intervene in order to maintain the functionality of the basic infrastructure for example bank bailouts, nationalization of banks or saving deposits protection. These burdens will be significantly reduced by the recommendations made in the main section of the book. Firstly there will only be a very low likelihood of bailouts and secondly a sovereign money reform would, to some extent, make saving deposits protection superfluous.
2. Money and Credit will be separated. Money will be exclusively provided by the state and not (simultaneously) by private providers. This is at least the spirit of what is already stated in numerous constitutions:
   - In the German constitution Article 73 states: "The federal government has sole right to legislate on money, currency and coinage system."

4.1 Extended Meaning of "Public Good"

- In the executive legislation with regard to the German Central Bank it is stated in more detail: "The Central Bank has (...) the sole right (...) to issue bank notes."[1] This is a clear statement, however it would be interesting to find out who has the right to issue book money, but there is nothing with regard to this in the statute.
- In the Austrian Federal Constitution it is stated in Article 10 (1) that "legislation and execution in the monetary, credit, stock exchange and bank system is a matter of federal affairs." On the other hand "the monetary, credit, stock exchange and bank system can be directly provided by the federal authorities" (Article 102(2)). This clearly states that a financial system is a "public service": the state does not have to but it can provide financial services. In the executive National Bank Act it is stated, "The Austrian National Bank is, according to the ECB authorization, permitted to issue banknotes in euro denomination. These notes, issued in euro denomination, are legal tender."[2] Here it is also not clarified who can issue book money. It is particularly fascinating that euro denomination banknotes are legal tender, but only these? If there is no mention of book money in the bank act, it is therefore logically speaking not legal tender; however book money is used as a form of payment! Does this therefore mean that book money is lawless? It would be helpful if the bank act dealt with this matter!
- According to the ECB Statute "the ECB has the sole right to authorize the issuance of banknotes within the EU. The ECB and national Central Banks are permitted to issue these banknotes and these are the only banknotes which are valid as legal tender."[3] Great! And again not a peep or a mention of book money!
- In Article 1 (8) of the US Constitution it is stated that, "The Congress shall have the right to coin money, to regulate the value thereof." According to that the Congress has the right to create money; this right was transferred to the private Federal Reserve Bank in 1913 via the Federal Reserve Act. Yet this is peculiar, why does a state relinquish an exclusive right to a private entity? In my opinion the privately-owned nature of the Federal Reserve Bank is in conflict with the state monetary monopoly. In section 16.1 of the Federal Reserve Act it then states that "banknotes are issued at the discretion of the Board of Governors of the Federal Reserve System." One also looks in vain in US legislation for a reference to book money.
- The Swiss Federal Constitution is a further sphinx in the series: "The monetary and currency system is the responsibility of the federal government and it has the sole right to issue coins and banknotes" (Article 99). Does the Swiss Federal Constitution thereby go beyond the basic law? This remains unclear: although "money" is the responsibility of the federal government,

---

[1] German Bundesbank Act, §14.
[2] Austrian Central Bank Act, §61.
[3] Protocol No. 4 of the EU Lisbon Treaty.

its sole right to issue money only involves literally "coins and banknotes." Does the Swiss Federal Constitution deliberately leave open who is entitled to issue book money?

The question whether a state money creation monopoly exists is astonishingly absent or only answered in a strikingly vague manner in constitutions or in the EU Treaty. Consequently the currently commonplace money creation practice of commercial banks is, from the point of view of any constitutional basis, unfounded. Although the constitutions do not explicitly prohibit private money creation, the interpretations of constitutional texts however clearly indicate the opposite—money creation by private entities is unconstitutional, in any case "constitutionless."

3. Money remains a public good in public ownership, even if private entities have a right of disposal and can "own" it. There is a legal difference between an owner (legal possessor) and proprietor (possessor). In the case of private use, including the "possession" of a public good, rules, conditions and limits arise. Although I can possess money, I cannot do whatever I want with it. Money is a "gradual private matter," with the supplying and definition of money being a state matter. Even though the procurement of savings and loans is private, it is commissioned and strongly regulated by the state (Public Service). The final use and ownership of money is the freest, however even here there are conditions and limits. Joseph Huber writes, "Money is a general means of payment and consequently a common good which should therefore also be common property" (Huber 2013, pp. 45–46).

4. The rules regarding the use of money are democratically made, particularly as it is a public good and at the same time—in the case of private use—is the greatest conceivable potential of power concentration. A public good must be designed in such a way that it serves everybody and not just a certain group. It should provide security and stability and not insecurity and crises with the development of the rules of the game being as participative as possible so that the monetary system is a just and liberal as possible in order to prevent its abuse and concentration of power. The result—the rules of the game—should be embedded in constitutions and this constitutes the vision and raison d'être of this book.

Money has a certain analogy to air, energy and water, as all these basic goods should be available to all people. They are a gift of nature and should therefore not at all be considered as private property. In the case of air, energy and water it is not primarily a matter of "owning" but rather using. On the other hand money has no utility in itself, but rather develops its usefulness only when it is used as a method of payment or due to other functions. The "circulation" is the significance of money, as in the case of energy, water and air. The global commons can also be "stored" to a smaller extent—reservoir, rainwater barrel, battery and oxygen cylinder—however these limited supplies are always aimed towards future use. The "essence" of these materials is not their storage but their use and keeping them in circulation, something which the monetary system should pay attention to.

4.2 Values of the Monetary System

The monetary system can only then be a coherent section of the constitution, if the general constitutional values also apply to the system. Therefore all of the following proposals should be examined with regard to the values human dignity, freedom, equality, justice, solidarity, sustainability and democracy. The choice between the individual options then becomes easier. Additionally this book recommends some further values for the monetary system:

- Simplicity and general comprehensibility
- Risk averseness and system stability
- Resilience and diversity

The first two values can be assigned to the value democracy, the second pair to equality and dignity and the third to the value sustainability. The fundamental values for a democratic monetary system must be determined similarly to the rules themselves. These values are an invitation to the readers to "ring freely" reading the book. If the readers find other additional values, which they deem to be capable of winning a majority or being constitutive for the monetary system, we would advise to also let these values "ring freely" and examine whether the proposals in the following main section fulfil these values.

References

Fisher, Irving. (2007): *100%-Money. 100%-Geld*, Verlag für Sozialökonomie, Kiel.

Mastronardi, Philippe (2013): Die Vollgeldreform als Verfassungsinitiative aus juristischer Sicht, pages 61–72 in: Verein Monetäre Modernisierung (2013): *Die Vollgeld-Reform. Wie Staatsschulden abgebaut und Finanzkrisen verhindert werden können*, 3rd edition, Edition Zeitpunkt, Solothurn.

Huber, Joseph (2013): Finanzreformen und Geldreform – Rückbesinnung auf die monetären Grundlagen der Finanzwirtschaft, S. 33–59 in: Verein Monetäre Modernisierung (2013): *Die Vollgeld-Reform. Wie Staatsschulden abgebaut und Finanzkrisen verhindert werden können*, 3rd edition, Edition Zeitpunkt, Solothurn.

Part II:
The Content – Cornerstones of a Democratic Monetary System

Chapter 5
Who Creates Money?

Abstract This chapter considers all potential issuers of money, from the central bank to the citizens. The conclusion is that neither individuals, nor private companies nor commercial banks should be allowed to create money. In the same way, private banks are not allowed to issue cash and bank notes, they should also not be allowed to issue book money. The right to create money should be limited to the public central banks. Additionally, regional political authorities should be allowed to issue complementary currencies with validity only in the region of their authority—should the sovereign citizens of the region wish so. The mandate for the central bank—or a regional issuer—should come directly from the citizens as the issuance of money is a "sovereign right," which has already been the case for monarchies. In democracies the sovereign body is the citizens, which is why they should determine the issuer of all types of money at all levels.

> *It is no coincidence that Faust begins his business activities in the second part of the drama with the act of money creation. In doing so he has the magic key, the duplicate key which can access all safes in the world.*
> Hans Christoph Binswanger (2009, p. 154)

The issue of money creation is central to the monetary system. Who is permitted to create it? Who "creates" the money which serves as legal tender and must be accepted by all members of the democratic community? Who is permitted to control and steer the money supply in circulation—the supply of cash and book money?

The first question alone presents a series of possibilities, which should be kept in perspective and discussed thoroughly and in the following as a first step, we will go through the possibilities with regard to who could create money:

(a) the central bank
(b) commercial banks
(c) companies
(d) all citizens
(e) regional authorities—municipalities, administrative districts, regions, federal states ....

Now let us take a look at the individual options:

5.1 The National Central Bank

Does it make sense for the central bank to create legal tender with compulsory acceptance for a defined monetary area and then issue it—cash as well as book money? It makes sense, as money has to come from some source. If the central bank receives exclusive rights to create money, it can solely control the money supply and the economic situation via the money supply, monetary policy is an important macro-economic management tool. A further advantage of money creation by an official institution is the fact that any profits gained by money creation can entirely benefit the community.

5.2 Commercial Banks

Does it make sense for private banks, in addition to the central bank, to create money? Or even for them alone to create money? It would make sense to do this exclusively, if there were no central bank. However with the emergence of central banks in the 19th century, private banks were prohibited from issuing their own money as a result of the central bank laws (Glötzl 2013, 13.2.3). Despite this ban and indications of various constitutions, that issuing money is an exclusive right of the state; private banks create money today as a matter of course, not cash but book money. This is not explicitly forbidden but not exactly explicitly permitted. The "monetary vagueness" in various constitutions should be tightened by either permitting the banks to do what they are doing, or by forbidding this. Then there would have to be an extensive monetary reform—the fact whether private banks could even create money was contentious for a long period time and has delayed these tightening measures. Today it is clear that they do create money, this can be correctly described as follows. They bypass the money creation monopoly of the central bank by a technical innovation, by using electronic money instead of coins and banknotes. If commercial banks are permitted to create money, this has several consequences. Firstly central banks can no longer solely control money supply and can only do this indirectly via the minimum reserve which banks must deposit at the central bank, as well as via the interest level which is decisive for the refinancing costs of the commercial banks. Due to the fact that the central bank is not the only source of refinancing for commercial bank, this indirect steering lever does not function reliably. Furthermore, the money creation practice of the commercial banks entails dangers of inflation—if they "succeed" in granting more loans with sufficient equity capital, this can lead to inflated bond prices (financial inflation) and to a price increase of everyday commodities (commodity price inflation). Moreover money creation profits become private profits and this does not befit a public good. A portion of the comparably high bank profits can be traced back to money creation.

5.3 Companies

Nowadays companies often make their own money by issuing for example "groupon coupons" or "bonus airline miles." However this money is not a legal means of payment and nobody apart from the company in question itself is obliged to accept these currencies and there is neither risk of enrichment nor inflation attached to these. Companies are not permitted to create legal tender and do not do this. If they printed the official currency, this would be counterfeit money and they would be liable to prosecution. This would also be the case, if private banks were to print money and it is therefore difficult to understand why it is permissible for them to create book money.

5.4 Private Individuals

What would happen if everybody could either print legal tender or book it on a bank account themselves? Everybody would be able to buy everything and this would result in hyperinflation, as a result it would not make sense if private individuals could create money. It is not known that this is the case anywhere in the world and it would also contradict the "public good" principle, which implies that there is a central source of money creation. On the other hand, everybody can issue vouchers, which can only be cashed-in with whoever issues the voucher and these are not legal tender. In exchange/swap circles or time bank systems, people grant each other loans, however these are "covered" by the declared willingness or obligation of the participants to provide or perform services.

5.5 Political Regional Authorities

Would it make sense if municipalities, regions, administrative districts or federal states were permitted to create the official currency? From my point of view this would not make sense, as long as it concerns the official currency, because it would create an overlapping of competences with a danger of inflation. For efficiency reasons alone it would make no sense—issuing money is a "natural monopoly" and it is best if this is carried out by an institution. This institution must be a public one and due to the fact that money is valid in the whole state, it should be a centralized one. In contrast it is definitely worth considering granting small political entities the right to issue complementary currencies, whose validity is locally or regionally limited. Historically, there have been extremely successful experiments with local currencies time and again for example in Wörgl in Tyrol in the 1920s—that would be an argument for its legal approval as official currency.

That was a first brief overview and now let us turn to the question—what would emerge from a democratic vote on the matter? As I see it the majority would (a) grant the money creation monopoly for legal tender to the central banks, (b) revoke creation rights from commercial banks and (c) grant political regional authorities the right to issue complementary currency. Nowadays it is different: "the banks have a de facto monopoly on money," (Huber 2010, p. 75) central banks only react and refinance commercial banks. Municipalities are not permitted to issue their own currency; even it is only within a limited jurisdiction. These alone would already be three substantial changes to the monetary system—concerning the first question! Nevertheless the sovereign should decide.

Incidentally, the issuance of money was one of the sovereign rights in monarchies. This means that if the democratic sovereign does not enjoy this sovereign right, which means that the citizens can decide which instance(s) should issue money, we have taken a backward step from where we were under the monarchy system! Considering that the role of money has not become less important over time, this step backwards is quite unjustified.

The "questions for the monetary convention" for each of the 12 content sections can be found at the end of the book in Part III, Chap. 2 in the form of a compactly summarized service package for decentralized conventions.

References

Binswanger, Hans Christoph (2009): *Geld und Magie. Eine ökonomische Deutung von Goethes Faust*, Murmann Verlag, 3rd edition, Hamburg.

Glötzl, Erhard (2013): *Fragen zur Problematik der Giralgeldschöpfung durch Geschäftsbanken – Banken haben einen ungerechtfertigten Vorteil im Wettbewerb mit Nichtbanken*, working paper.

Huber, Joseph (2010): *Monetäre Modernisierung. Zur Zukunft der Geldordnung*, Metropolis-Verlag, Marburg.

Chapter 6
Sovereign Money Reform

Abstract This chapter describes how money is created today and how this could be changed. Contrary to widespread belief, the electronic cash money we use for our daily purchases does not stem from the central bank, but is created by commercial banks by credit lending and the purchase of assets. As a consequence, the central bank has no control over the money supply and inflationary tendencies can occur at any time. Furthermore, the profit arising from money creation does not benefit the general public, but private banks. This chapter proposes a reform that extends the central banks monopoly to issue money from cash money (banknotes and coins) to electronic money. This "sovereign money reform" would resolve an extensive range of macroeconomic problems, ranging from the decrease of bubble building and financial instability, to secure current accounts, the avoidance of bank runs and the diminishing of private and public debt.

> *The task of the banks is not to supply the economy with the required amount of money or to drain it of money. This is the sole task of the central bank as a monetary instance. It is rather the task of the banks to finance the economy.*
> Joseph Huber (2010, p. 109)

6.1 Creation of Bank Money by Private Commercial Banks

Many people hold onto two persistent notions or "myths about money." On the one hand, they believe that the complete money supply is backed by gold and on the other hand that all the money in circulation comes from the central bank. Only a fraction of both these notions partly corresponds to the reality of the situation, as the gold reserve was abandoned a long time ago. For instance the reserves of the total euro system is 10,800 tons, at the end of 2013 this was valued at about 345 billion euro (European Central Bank 2013a, p. 6),[1] which only amounted to

---

[1] The data on ECB book money have also been taken from these statistics (p. 9).

6.5% of M1 money supply (cash and current account balances) in the Euro system. Quite a few people, the Neo-Austrian School or author Rolf Dobelli consider the decoupling of gold from money to be the "fundamental problem of our current crisis" and hope that "we will at some stage return to a gold standard."[2] However today it would no longer make sense to put only as much money in circulation as is backed by gold—there is too little gold relative to the value of the goods and services supply or in other words: economic output downright exploded in the course of the industrial revolution and consequently outgrew gold backing. As Joseph Huber writes, "The geological lack of gold was ultimately one of the reasons for leaving the metal money era" (Huber 2010, 41). Gold backing is justifiably history.

On the other hand many people believe that the "central bank" is the only source of money. In Germany, it is also called "Notes Bank" as it is allowed to print bank notes. However most of the money in circulation is not cash (banknotes and coins) but rather book money. At the end of 2013 the amount of cash in the Euro system amounted to 951 billion euro or 17.6% of the M1 money supply (European Central Bank 2013b, pp. 2, 4).

Secondly the larger share of book money supply is not created and circulated by the central bank but by private commercial banks. At the end of 2013 the amount of book money issued by the central bank in the Euro system amounted to 245 billion euro or 5% of the M1 money supply. Thus at the end of 2013, about 95% of book money was created by private banks. But how is money created at private commercial banks?

In the classical notion savers "first" bring their cash to the bank and invest it on the liabilities side of the bank balance sheet, this is a current account demand deposit and therefore a current account balance. It can also be directly paid into a savings account or savings bank book. This cash deposit, whether it be in a current or savings account, is booked on the assets side and increases the cash level. This additional cash holding makes it possible for the bank to grant a loan to a company, private individual or to a state—the cash on the assets side is rebooked into a receivable and is paid out. Money supply is not increased in the process; the money already exists and was "first" deposited by the saver.

To put it more concretely: 1,000 € wanders from "outside" into the bank and is deposited on the liabilities side of the balance sheet as a current account balance or as a savings deposit. The bank can thus (subject to sufficient equity ratio and minimum reserve) grant a loan of approximately the same amount (minus cash and minimum reserve). This is booked on the assets side of the bank as a debt claim on the borrower and paid out and "utilized." A thousand in and a thousand out, with the money supply remaining constant due to this possibility of liabilities side loan generation. This can be done like this in the reality of the banks today, it is not incorrect. But it is a—quite unusual—*cash* transaction.

A further possibility, which belongs to the standard repertoire, is the assets-side lending by banks, where a new loan is "first" granted without prior in-payments or

---

[2]*Frankfurter Allgemeine Sonntagszeitung*, 5 August 2012.

6.1 Creation of Bank Money by Private Commercial Banks

savings deposits by booking "out of nothing" on the assets side of the bank balance sheet a (book money) claim on the borrower which is added to the prior assets volume. This claim on the assets side is credited to the liabilities side to the current account of the borrower, also as book money. In doing so the assets and liabilities sides are back in balance, however in this case or rather in this order, the balance sheet in contrast to case 1 has been "extended"—the money supply has been increased.

Not quite yet: the loan here, in case 2, also wants to be "utilized" and it is transferred to an account at another bank (for the sake of example). In this case, a thousand euro "at first" goes out of the bank which has created the money. At the moment of "loan use"—the transfer—a "refinancing" (a replacement of the outgoing money) on the liabilities side of the balance sheet is required so that the balance sheet remains balanced. Roughly sorted, a bank has six possibilities of refinancing: (1) increasing its equity capital out of business profits or by an increase in capital, (2) in payment to a current account, (3) a saving deposit, (4) issuance of bank bonds, (5) borrowing on the inter-bank market, (6) borrowing from the central bank. The thousand euro book money which has gone out can be replaced or "refinanced" on the liabilities side by each of these six sources. With regard to the change in money supply and the question of "creation or non-creation" of money, it depends on where the money comes from and who the banks owes money to and what "type of money" it owes.

If the bank gets into debt at the central bank, the money supply will then increase if the central bank grants more fresh loans than are repaid within a given period of time.

The central bank can in this way help to steer the money supply, in times of recession for example grant more or cheaper loans and in times when the economy is good fewer and more expensive loans. The money which finances the loan is at this point "good" central bank money and the act of bank lending is in this case neutral with regard to the (central bank) money supply. The money is "at first" created by the commercial bank, though ultimately "retroactively" by the central bank.

The situation is somewhat different when the loan is replaced by for example, a current account deposit of a borrower B, who has also received an assets-side generated (created) loan at bank B and in doing so has made, via a current account transfer, a payment to an account holder at bank A. This means that bank A has "recouped" the outgoing thousand euros and has "refinanced" itself. If at the same time borrower A transfers his/her money, which was created at bank A, to an account at bank B, bank B is also refinanced and in both cases without the central bank! The creation of bank money by commercial banks functions in this way and increases the money supply in this example by two thousand euros. (The example could have been shortened as follows: using loan A, the money goes into another account at the same bank and with this the bank would have refinanced via another account customer with the money creation act being completed as well. I have purposely used an example with another bank in order to make the systemic and collective character of money creation of all private commercial banks more visible).

The example is not quite clear-cut—the ability of commercial banks to create bank money is threefold limited by (a) their equity capital (minimum capital requirements under the Basel rules), (b) the minimum reserve (currently 1% in the Eurozone) and (c) the 1.4% cash reserve. In total the money supply can however substantially increase. In the USA money supply has grown twice as fast as the economy since the turn of the millennium, in Germany the economy grew in the period from 1992 to 2008 nominally by 51%, the money supply on the other hand by 189 percent (Huber 2010, p. 75 und 2013a, 40). In Iceland, banks expanded the money supply 19-fold between 1994 and 2008! (Sigurjonsson 2015, p. 11). With these (privately created) loans, consumption is financed and via increasing demand leads to inflation—either to price of goods inflation, if consumer goods are bought with the loans; or to financial inflation if bonds are bought with the created loans.

The analyses of many authors has unanimously shown that the money creation practice of the commercial banks since the 1980s has led to bond price inflation and the creation of bubbles on the financial markets—share, internet, foreign exchange, commodity and property bubbles. In this way private money creation and financial stability are linked.

The profits made by the private banks, which result in the difference between the refinancing and loan interest, are all the higher, the higher the extent of money creation is. In the case of Germany, the money creation profits of private banks are estimated to be 15–25 billion euro annually and for Switzerland between 6 and 12 billion francs (Huber 2013a, p. 49). These profits are not legitimate due to the fact that private players are getting rich on the provisioning of a public good. Joseph Huber argues that the extra profits of the banks can be regarded as a "private tax," which "contradicts our contemporary sense of justice" (Huber Robertson 2008, p. 35) as well as economic thought: "Economists will readily tell you, 'there ain't no such thing as a free lunch'. This does not apply to the financial sector, as special profits lead to a massive and unjustified—free lunch," says Simon Sennrich mockingly (Sennrich 2013, p. 44). The practice of private money creation increases the national economic credit volume and in doing so the systemic debt ratio. It leads to inflation and creation of bubbles on the one hand and on the other hand to systemically excessive debts. The total level of debt of the financial system and national economies is currently the highest it has ever been in history. According to an investigation carried out by the Bank for International Settlements, between 1980 and 2010 the total level of debt (private household debt, private companies and state debt) in 18 OECD states doubled, going from 167% to 314% of their GDP (Bank for International Settlements 2011, p. 1). Japan is in the lead with 456% of economic output ahead of Portugal with 366%, Belgium 356% and Spain with 355%. Comparatively low were Australia with 235%, Austria with 238% and Germany 241% as well as the USA with 268%. The McKinsey Global Institute has further added the debts of the financial sector and therefore comes to even higher figures for 2011: the total level of debt for all four sectors therefore amounted to 665% of GDP in Ireland, 511% in Japan, 507% in Great Britain, 363% in Spain, 279% in the USA, 278% in Germany and 267% in Greece (Mckinsey Global Institute 2012, pp. 13–14).

There is a great deal to explain, not only the prima facie unbelievable discrepancy between Ireland and Greece. Keeping it simple: the composition is very different from country to country—Ireland is in "the lead" with regard to budget before Australia, before Spain with regard to companies and before England with regard to the financial sector. Japan is undisputed leader in government debt.

The Bank for International Settlements considers state debt and private household debt of more than 85% of GDP in each case and company debt of more than 90% of GDP dangerous—altogether maximally 260% of economic output. The Boston Consulting Group considerably "undercuts" this value and recommends a maximum level of debt of 60% per sector, in total 180% of economic output (Boston Consulting Group 2011, p. 5). The OECD states, with an average value of 314% total level of debt, are far away from both these values. It would appear that there is currently a systemic excessive level of debt and therefore numerous insiders, from stock exchange gurus to financial mathematicians, are warning of a big crash: the national economy will collapse under the weight of the inability to service and repay the total debt (Müller 2009, pp. 96–104. Boston Consulting Group 2011, Schachermayer 2011 und Kreiss 2013, pp. 89–92).

6.2 Sovereign Money Reform

How could a stop be put to this private money creation? For quite some time the sovereign money reform proposal has been making the rounds. Sovereign money stands for a fully valid legal tender. In this respect various reform approaches are united which can be summarized as follows: the exclusive right of money creation which is attributed to the state (the state central bank) in many constitutions is extended to book money and at the same time the current defacto money creation monopoly is revoked from private commercial banks.[3] Sovereign money reforms represent a growing movement in German and English speaking countries, they also operate under the term "Monetative" that is alongside the legislative, executive and judicial power there should be an independent monetary power which is conferred the exclusive rights to create money and steer money supply.

These are the most important points of the proposal:

1. The central bank receives the exclusive right to create money, cash and book money. All money in circulation is central bank money, which has been created according to predetermined rules. The right to create money which was never explicitly granted to commercial banks is explicitly revoked.
2. The extension or contraction of money supply will, in the long term, be oriented towards the extension or contraction of economic output, whereby the

---

[3]Prof. Huber argues that money creation is actively initiated by commercial banks and only in part ("fractionally") passively refinanced by the central bank. Nevertheless, both circuits of book money do "never touch": book money from the central bank is only used by commercial banks; and the audience exclusively uses book money created by commercial banks. Huber (2010), 54.

money supply steering instrument will be applied "anti-cyclically": in order to prevent the economy from overheating money supply can be cut back in times of high growth and in order to prevent a depression in times of recession money supply can be increased.

3. The money which is issued by the central bank goes interest-free and debt-free to the state treasury. In doing so, the money creation profit, the original seigniorage (difference between the value of the money and production costs), will benefit the general public directly.
4. Money therefore, via state expenditure, goes to companies and private people, who bring the money to the bank and deposit it there (similar to case 1 with the only difference that it must not be cash but can also be book money). By depositing "sovereign money" it lands on the asset side of the commercial banks, either as a cash or book money claim on the central bank. On the liabilities side a liability to depositors is booked, which is more or less similar to the "myth" which is anchored in many minds today. Reality will be aligned to fiction. This sovereign money is now available as a loan.
5. The current accounts will be excluded from bank balance sheets and set up as "cash accounts" in the possession of bank customers, merely as securities accounts, so the banks cannot additionally create money out of nothing. At present current account balances just as saving deposits are savers' claims on the bank and are a position on the balance sheet. They are legally owned by the bank and in the event of a bank collapse are endangered, from the bank customer's perspective, which is why a deposit protection system is also necessary for current account deposits. Above all however, the current "mixing" of current accounts and savings accounts is a part of the money creation system, whereby a bank books a created loan on the liabilities side as a demand deposit. The accounting separation of "deposits" and "investments" ends money creation by private commercial banks.
6. When lending, sovereign money is transferred from the assets side of the bank balance sheet to the cash account (depot) of the credit customer. From the bank's perspective this is an asset swap on the left side of the bank balance sheet: sovereign money is paid out and rebooked as a claim on the credit customer. During this process the bank's sovereign money balance with the central bank diminishes, it is converted into a credit claim on the credit customer (another balance sheet item on the same side—assets side—of the bank balance sheet). Metaphorically, sovereign money is "passed on" to the public via the assets side of the intermediary commercial bank. The money supply remains unchanged, nothing whatsoever happens on the liabilities side (Cf. Karwat 2009). The only change is that the same amount of (central bank) sovereign money is no longer owed by the commercial bank, but rather directly by the customer—via their cash account. That is also a reason why in the event of a bank's failure the sovereign money depot of customers is not involved, as it is a direct relationship between the customer and central bank. The bank only serves as a depot or (electronic) safe which manages the customer's "cash account," whose content however remains the property of the bank customer and not the property of the bank.

6.3 Benefits of the Reform

7. It is not until a bank customer makes a savings deposit that sovereign money moves from his/her cash account or depot to the assets side (!) of the balance sheet, where it either increases the sovereign money level, a non-cash claim on the central bank, where this is available for lending. On the liabilities side, a customer's claim on the bank is booked, whereby the money legally becomes the possession of the bank and in the event of bank insolvency is at a risk of default. Customers usually take this risk in order to earn interest on their savings, which in the current paradigm compensates for the default risk, and the "restraint in consumption." This is however an investment and every investment is at a risk of default even if the bank minimizes this default risk by "pooling" the loans to all savers. Consequently savings investment protection would also be necessary in a sovereign money system, in the event of this being a wise concept—strictly speaking it is a type of state investor protection. The general public covers the investment risk for savers and this is not market economy. There are also alternatives in a sovereign money system for people who want their money to be 100% secure, to be safer than under their pillows, where it can be stolen and safer than in a savings account where it can be lost in the event of bank or state insolvency—they can deposit it in a cash account, where really nothing can happen.
8. From the perspective of currency, there would only be central bank money that is sovereign money in the sovereign money system. Regardless of whether the money comes from savers, other banks, the state or directly from the central bank, it is always central bank money due to the fact that the central bank is the only instance which can create and circulate money. Today the money supply in circulation, as a means of payment, is exclusively created by private banks. Book money from central banks only circulates between banks, it never reaches the audience, and it is, compared to privately created book money, quite a modest amount.
9. Holding "reserves" (central bank money) would be superfluous because all money is reserve—fully-fledged central bank money and the minimum reserve would be dropped. A 100% reserve, as suggested by others, would also be superfluous for the same reason and the banking business and bank balance sheets would be much simpler.

6.3 Benefits of the Reform

Now moving on from the functionality description of the proposal to the advantages of a sovereign money reform, these would not only be numerous but also relevant:

1. More effective steering of money supply: money supply would solely be steered by the central bank and not in combination with the profit-oriented commercial banks, thereby restoring the sovereignty of the macro-economic steering tool—accuracy increases. Inflation can be kept under better control

by direct steering of the money supply rather than via indirect steering with the key interest rate. This applies to both price of goods and financial inflation.
2. Anti-cyclical steering of the economy: if the extension or contraction of money supply is practiced conversely to the economic cycle, the fiscal counter-cycle of budgetary surplus and debt repayment in boom times and deficits and debt in recession times can be intensified. During the recession the extension of the money supply can be dosed thereby leading to more government revenue providing higher expenditure possibilities, without incurring additional debt. If money supply steering takes place indirectly by lending to commercial banks, which is what the central banks currently do in the present monetary regime (from "quantitative easing" to the so-called "big Berta"), it is possible that the extended money supply does not land in the real economy because the banks reduce lending for fear of defaults and sometimes even to a greater extent than the economy contraction, which results in a pro-cyclical effect of the present form of money supply steering by the central bank. Alternatively the banks prefer to speculate with the cheap money for example by buying government bonds, as they consider these transactions to be less risky or at least see a higher chance of profits than in the "real" lending business.
3. Money would not come into circulation as credit (with the necessity for interest and growth) but rather via debt-free and interest-free public expenditure.
4. The profits gained from money creation—seigniorage—entirely benefit the general public, unlike the current situation where banks skim off a considerable portion of money creation profits by creating money "ex nihilo" and are able to keep the corresponding interest margin profits or capital gains/dividend yields.[4] In a sovereign money system the central bank could raise the money supply in accordance with economic output, on a long-term average by for example 0.5–1% of economic output (particularly as the money supply M1 in Germany and the Eurozone is about half as much as the GDP). In Germany that would be a 13.5–27 billion euro grant to the budget annually (GDP is 2.7 billion euro). In Austria it would be 1.5–3 billion euro annually (GDP approximately 315 billion euro) and in Switzerland 3.8–7.5 billion francs annually (GDP is 500 billion francs, but M1 is larger—almost 80% of GDP). This would drastically relieve pressure from budgets and public finance.

---

[4]Apart from granting loans there is also a second way of creating money by private banks: the purchasing of securities such as shares or government bonds. The securities purchased are booked on the assets side and its financing on the liabilities side for example a sight deposit of the selling person or company. The purchased securities can yield a higher dividend or interest than the costs of refinancing. Or the price gain after resale—difference between purchase and sale—exceeds the accrued refinancing costs. In both cases this is a profitable transaction for the bank. Cf. Glötzl (2013).

6.3 Benefits of the Reform

5. By changing over from the present bank money system to sovereign money, the state would, with a constant M1 money supply, accrue large changeover profits—to the extent of the to-date accumulated money creation by commercial banks in the form of demand deposits. Demand deposits in Switzerland amount to 385 billion francs, which is almost twice the national debt (211 billion francs), the state would be free of debt. In Germany and Austria demand deposits amount to approximately 80% of sovereign debt (Huber 2010, p. 138). In the EU and the USA it is approximately half of sovereign debt (Huber 2013a, p. 58)—this could be halved, which would tremendously alleviate the sovereign debt crisis.

6. In doing so the money supply would remain constant, as the demand deposits of the savings customers on the liabilities side would be transformed into demand deposits of the central banks. Central banks claims on the commercial banks are however not part of the base money supply M1, however the factored-out cash accounts are. With regard to the M1 money supply the demand deposits of the general public are factored out, they are money supply neutral. (The commercial banks' claims on the savings customers on the asset side remain unaffected, until repayment.)[5] Such an "outward transfer process" would be nothing new in money history; private banknotes were discharged from the money system in the course of the establishment of central banks from private bank syndicates. Since then private banknotes have become illegal and are considered to be fake money. Analogously during this "second money nationalization phase" privately created book money would also be factored out. After the transition privately created book money would also be illegal fake money in the same way as privately printed banknotes. The transition process would roughly require a period of up to 20 years—until all outstanding loans have been repaid.

7. The central bank balance sheet total would increase by 50% as a result of the transition (Eurozone), however this would not lead to any inflation whatsoever because only the money supply now already created by the commercial banks—for the first time ever correctly—would be shown in the central bank balance sheet total. In the event of the M1 money supply being reduced by the central bank, the effect on the sovereign debt would be correspondingly lower.

8. In the case of a bank failure the cash accounts are absolutely secure, they are the possessions of bank customers and not affected by the bankruptcy. Savings investments would still be affected in the event of a bank failure and correspondingly at risk. However in a sovereign money system these private investments would be of a more conscious nature, whose national protection is questionable and represents a basic break of market economy principles— the investors do not bear the risk of loss entirely themselves, they share this

---

[5]A very comprehensive description of the shift from the current system of private bank money creation to the sovereign money system is provided by Karwat (2009).

with tax payers. Such a savings deposits protection system could certainly be a democratically decided component of "money as a public good" however should all the more consciously be subject to conditions. These will be discussed in more detail in following chapters.
9. By the clear separation of financial assets, which are solely deposited at banks but not invested and consciously invested capital, the part of the financial assets which is "superfluous" because it cannot be invested in real economic terms can be "pacified" in a conscious manner. Money would not necessarily work and exercise any pressure with regard to return on investment. The complete system would relax on two fronts: the pressure would be removed and speculation risk reduced. The credit lever is turned upside down: not a fraction of the total granted loan volume (balance sheet) is covered by financial assets, but rather a fraction of private financial assets shifts to bank balance sheets and become credit. As a result of the increasing assets surplus (in relation to GDP) it is conceivable that soon only a minority of financial assets will be invested in the economy and the majority as "non-working" bank deposits will only be deposited there—money finally leaves us in peace!
10. The connection between savings investments and bank lending on both sides of the bank balance sheet sides would be restored. It would exactly achieve and correspond to the current generally accepted understanding of a bank.

6.4 Side Note: Sovereign Money and Hundred-Percent Money

Some au fait readers will be familiar with the so-called "hundred percent banking" proposal from the 1930s made by a series of economists from Chicago amongst them the young Milton Friedman. They proposed that all loans granted should be covered 100% by reserves at the central bank. Irving Fisher further developed the "100 percent money" (Fisher 2007). In 2013 two authors from the IMF re-scrutinized the 100% banking plan and presented the results in "The Chicago Plan revisited." All these versions are collectively referred to the 100% reserve, because the active operation of the banks is completely covered by reserves, and they are assiduously confused with one another.

"Sovereign money is technically or rather bank-operatively speaking a completely different system compared to the hundred percent reserve," according to the differentiation of the most important pioneer Joseph Huber from the University of Halle-Wittenberg (Huber 2013b). As a result of the not exactly uncomplicated subject matter, I will only present the differences between hundred percent money and sovereign money here. The overview shows why I clearly favor the more current proposal of a sovereign money reform for discussion in the convention. The 100% money reform has delivered important insights and impulses, but it is outdated and has been surpassed by the sovereign money idea and in doing so simplified it.

6.5 Amendment of Legislative Texts 51

Hundred Percent Money	Sovereign money
Current accounts are part of the bank balance sheet	Current accounts are excluded from the bank balance sheet
Money comes into circulation as credit debt	Money comes into circulation as an endowment to the state
Money comes into circulation subject to interest	Money comes into circulation not subject to interest
Interest seigniorage (indirect) for private businesses	Original seigniorage (direct) for the sovereign citizens
Separate accounting cycle	One accounting cycle
At first a loan is granted, then it is refinanced at the central bank.	At first the central bank money goes to a bank account and then a loan is granted.
Reserve for lending money must be kept	Reserve not necessary, credit (book) money is reserve
Banks must pay interest twice: for the savings investments and for the reserves.	Banks must only pay interest "once"—for savings investment.
Stresses public finances	Relieves public finances

6.5 Amendment of Legislative Texts

De jure only minimal changes would have to be made in various constitutions and respectively in the EU Lisbon Treaty, which contains the ECB statute as protocol 4 for example "The ECB Governing Council has the exclusive right to authorize the issuance of banknotes and book money within the union. The ECB and the national central banks are authorized to issue these banknotes and book money. The banknotes and book money issued by the ECB and national central banks are the only forms of money which are valid as legal tender within the union."

In Germany the law would have to be aligned via the Federal Bank of Germany Article 14: "The Federal Bank of Germany, irrespective of Article 128 Section 1 of the Treaty on the functioning of the European Union, has the exclusive right to issue banknotes and book money within the area of application of this law."

In Switzerland a minor change to Article 99 of the federal constitution would suffice: "The money and currency system is the responsibility of the federal government, which has the exclusive right to issue coins, banknotes and book money."

In the US, the constitution could be amended as follows: "Congress shall have the exclusive right to issue money, to regulate the value thereof." I would certainly prefer this version: "Sovereign citizens shall have the right to issues money, to regulate the value thereof."

References

Bank for International Settlements. 2011. The real effects of debt. BIS working papers 352, von Stephen G. Cecchetti, M.S. Mohanty und Fabrizio Zampolli, September 2011.
Boston Consulting Group. 2011. Back to Mesopotamia? The looming threat of debt restructuring. Studie von David Rhodes und Daniel Stelter, London-Berlin.
Brichta, Raimund/Voglmaier, Anton (2013): *Die Wahrheit über Geld*, Börsenbuchverlag, Kulmbach.
European Central Bank. 2013a. Monthly bulletin, December 2013, Frankfurt a. M.
European Central Bank. 2013b. Euro banknotes and coin statistics. Frankfurt a. M.
Felber, Christian. 2016. Vom Vollgeld zum, Souveränen Geld`. Vorteile und Optionen einer Vollgeld-Reform. Introductory text to the sovereign money reform, 12 pages, 28 April 2016.
Fisher, Irving (2007): *100%-Money. 100%-Geld*, Verlag für Sozialökonomie, Kiel.
Glötzl, Erhard (2013): *Fragen zur Problematik der Giralgeldschöpfung durch Geschäftsbanken – Banken haben einen ungerechtfertigten Vorteil im Wettbewerb mit Nichtbanken*, working paper.
Huber, Joseph (2010): *Monetäre Modernisierung. Zur Zukunft der Geldordnung*, Metropolis-Verlag, Marburg.
Huber, Joseph (2013a): *Finanzreformen und Geldreform – Rückbesinnung auf die monetären Grundlagen der Finanzwirtschaft*, S. 33–59 in: Verein Monetäre Modernisierung (2013): *Die Vollgeld-Reform. Wie Staatsschulden abgebaut und Finanzkrisen verhindert werden können*, 3rd edition, Edition Zeitpunkt, Solothurn.
Huber, Joseph. 2013b. Vollgeld und 100%-reserve. Scientific working paper. https://vollgeld-jh.squarespace.com/vollgeld-und-100-prozent-reserve
Huber, Joseph/Robertson, James (2008): *Geldschöpfung in öffentlicher Hand. Weg zu einer gerechten Geldordnung im Informationszeitalter*, Verlag für Sozialökonomie, Kiel.
Karwat, Klaus (2009): *Vom fraktionalen Reservesystem zur Monetative: eine Darstellung in Bilanzform*, scientific working paper, published on: https://vollgeld-jh.squarespace.com/papers-und-manuskripte-zur-vollgeldreform
Kreiss, Christian (2013): *Profitwahn. Warum sich eine menschengerechtere Wirtschaft lohnt*, Tectum Verlag, Marburg.
Mayer, Thomas/Huber, Roman (2014): *Vollgeld. Das Geld-System der Zukunft*, Tectum, Marburg.
Mckinsey Global Institute. 2012. Debt and deleveraging: Uneven progress on the path to growth. *Study*, January 2012.
Müller, Dirk (2009): *Crashkurs. Weltwirtschaftskrise oder Jahrhundertchance. Wie sie das Beste aus Ihrem Geld machen*, Droemer, München.
Schachermayer, Walter (2011): *Der Rechenfehler der Schuldenbremser*, Kommentare der anderen, Der Standard, 17 December 2011.
Sennrich, Simon. 2013. A review of money issuance concepts in modern economic history. Bachelor Thesis, University of Zürich, 27 June 2013.
Sigurjonsson, Frosti. 2015. Monetary reform. A better monetary system for Iceland. Report of MoP Frosti Sigurjónnson, 110 pages, Commissioned by the Prime Minister of Iceland.

Chapter 7
Democratic Central Banks

Abstract This chapter deals with central banks and the crucial questions such as whom they should belong to, how their governing bodies should be composed and, most importantly, who they receive their mandates from and with which objectives. The proposal is that central banks should be 100% public, that their governing bodies should be composed of stakeholders from all sectors of society and that their mandate should come directly from the sovereign—in analogy that parliaments are elected directly by the citizens. As for the goals, three models are discussed: the European Central Bank model (highest priority is price stability), the Federal Reserve model (price stability and full employment are targeted simultaneously) and an alternative model (price stability, full employment and limited finance of sovereign debt). Finally, the idea of a "Monetative," the development of the central bank to a fourth independent state power is proposed—which would be mandated directly by the sovereign citizens.

> *In the event that the American people allow private banks to control the issuance of their currency, the banks and the corporations growing around them will take all the possessions from the people, firstly by inflation and then by deflation, until their children one day wake up homeless ... the right to issue money should be taken from the banks and given back to the people, to whom it rightfully belongs.*
> Thomas Jefferson (Cited in Lietaer et al (2009))

The central bank is the most powerful individual institution in the complete monetary system. It creates money out of nothing, steers the supply of money; it specifies the key interest rate which provides the orientation for the market interest rate. With the aid of interest and money supply it steers inflation and economic activity, it turns on or turns off the supply of lending for the economy, it can flood banks with liquidity or allow them to dry up, it can finance nations or refuse this finance—it turns the central adjustment screw of the monetary system and in doing so is the most powerful single institution in economic policy.

It is no wonder that the managers of the Fed and ECB are extremely careful with the wording of their public statements; every subtle nuance has implications with words being unlike any other figure of power. Alan Greenspan was referred to as "Sphinx" particularly as he liked to play with the interpretation of his statement and produced "Greenspeak," "I know that you believe you knew what I said in your opinion. But I am not sure if it is clear to you that what you heard is not what I meant." There is a more direct way: on 26 July 2012 it was sufficient for the ECB boss Mario Draghi to sharply defuse the euro crisis which was then escalating with two short sentences: "Within our mandate, the ECB is ready to do whatever it takes to preserve the euro. And believe me, it will be enough."[1] Paul Krugman appraised the effect of this sentence as "without it the euro would have probably collapsed in 2011 or 2012."[2]

Due to this power it is of utmost importance that central banks are (a) public institutions, (b) organized as democratically and representatively as possible and (c) their mandate should be defined as clearly as possible. Their policy must serve the common good and not individual interests disguised as public interests or certain schools of economic thought or ideologies which are currently in vogue in economist or banker circles.

7.1 Who Does the Central Bank Belong to?

The more relevant and the more monopolistic a component of the infrastructure is, the more important it is for it to also be in public ownership. Historically speaking, the central banks were formed out of the largest private banks and initially were predominantly in their possession, which is still partly the case today. The Bank of England was established as a private stock company in 1694 with the initial capital from 1268 persons of independent means granting a loan to the government. It was not until 1830 that the bank notes became legal tender and not until one hundred years later in 1930 that the last private bank, which issued its own notes, was taken over by the Bank of England and in doing so it received a monopoly to issue bank notes—although only in England and Wales. To this day private banks in Scotland and Northern Ireland are allowed to print and issue their own banknotes, which however must be covered by 100% deposits at the Bank of England, which was nationalized in 1946, two hundred and fifty years after it was established.

The US central bank, the Federal Reserve, is still in private hands. It belongs to the central banks of the Federal States of the US and these in turn to the largest private regional banks. Although the seven board members are appointed by the US president, the important open market committee, which makes the monetary policy decisions, contains the presidents of the 12 regional central banks of which 5 are entitled to vote. Joseph Stiglitz criticizes, "The presidents of the regional central banks are elected in a non-transparent and not particularly democratic way

---

[1]Speech by Mario Draghi, President of the European Central Bank at the Global Investment Conference in London, 26 July 2012. Web: https://www.ecb.europa.eu/press/key/date/2012/html/sp120726.en.html

[2]*El País*, 17 November 2013.

7.1 Who Does the Central Bank Belong to?

in which the commercial banks (which are regulated by them) have too much influence" (Stiglitz 2012, p. 326). Such an ownership structure is strange—would we allow the federal police authority to belong to the national police headquarters and this to the most powerful regional private militia and security firms?

Also in Germany the first central bank, the Reichsbank, was founded in 1876 with private capital by several thousand people, although it was a public-law institution from the very beginning. At the start of the twentieth century it obtained independence from the government, however the Nazis brought it back under their control. With the introduction of the Deutsche Mark in 1948, the allies established the "Bank of German States," which in 1957 merged with the regional central banks to become the German Central Bank (Deutsche Bundesbank—alias "Buba"). The Reichsbank was only liquidated in 1961 and the 20,000 shareholders were paid off.[3] In that respect, the Bundesbank did not become a complete public good until the 1960s—well almost.

The path of the central bank in Austria is also a process going from a private to a public good. Until 2006 the OenB, the Austrian Central Bank was 50% privately owned with the full nationalization not taking place until 2010.[4]

There are several suppositions with regard to the reasons for this: on the one hand the social partnership balance was lost in 2006 when the trade union bank BAWAG and the Austrian Trade Union Federation withdrew, which was the reason why the remaining private owns had to relinquish their shares. Another hypothesis purports that the owners of the national central banks will be saddled with the accruing loses of the ECB in the coming years and as a result the private owners are not interested in assuming their proprietor's responsibility in the event of this happening.

From the supervisory perspective, the nationalization is a welcome development due to the fact that the central bank was commissioned to supervise its owners until 2010, which constitutes an unpleasant conflict of roles.

Today the Swiss National Bank is still 48% in private ownership (Swiss National Bank 2017, p. 131). In my opinion this represents a violation against the constitution, as "the issuance of banknotes and coins is solely a right of the federal government." If this right is a "sole" right of the federal government it cannot be performed by an institution which is almost 50% privately owned, including the voting rights. Although about one third of the private joint-owners are legal entities and therefore companies, these are not included by name in the annual report.

---

[3]*Hamburger Abendblatt*, 15 June 1961.

[4]11.93 percent BAWAG, 8.33 percent Trade Union Association (till 2006). 8.73 Prozent Raiffeisenzentralbank, 0.40 Prozent Raiffeisenlandesbank Wien-Niederösterreich, each 0.07 percent Raiffeisenlandesbanken Burgenland, Kärnten, Oberösterreich, Salzburg, Tirol, Vorarlberg; 0.07 percent Kathrein & Co. 8.33 Prozent Austrian Chamber of Commerce; 2.67 percent UNIQUA, 0.67 percent Grazer Wechselseitige, 0.53 percent Niederösterreich Versicherung, 0.47 percent Wiener Städtische Versicherung (Vienna Insurance Group), 0.33 percent Oberösterreichische Wechselseitige Versicherung; 4.27 percent B&C (former Bank Austria); 2 percent Industriellenvereinigung; 0.67 percent Pensionsfonds Niederösterreichische Landwirtschaftskammer; 0.13 percent Bank für Ärzte und Apotheker. Source: APA/OenB, 11 January 2010.

It is particularly curious that 1.52% of the voting rights of the central bank are in foreign ownership, which is not a decisive loss of sovereignty but it does principally contradict the idea of a public good and "public service."

Archaic conditions still prevail in Italy—Banca d'Italia belongs to 60 private banks and trustee savings banks, with the 6 largest holding 50% of the voting rights. Intesa Sanpaola and UniCredit combined own 100 of the 535 voting rights.[5]

From a historical standpoint the most important private banks thus firstly form private or semi-private central banks, which are gradually transferred into public ownership, are independent from the government and after initial coexistence of "private" and official banknotes are given the exclusive right to create money, albeit not yet for book money. This process should be continued in all democracies and with the aid of monetary conventions completed by transferring central banks into public ownership, whereby the complete issuance of money is an exclusive right of the central banks which are organized as democratically as possible and are clearly commissioned on a direct democracy basis.

7.2 Democratic Organization of the Central Bank

Due to the extensive consequences of central bank policy on all sectors of society, it is important for all sectors of society to be able to participate in deciding on the direction of the central bank.

The inclusion of people involved in the decisions is a fundamental democratic principle; however bankers and even investment bankers are predominantly in the central banks and as such are only a small portion and not representative of the whole of society. Further stakeholders would include business people, employees, consumers, unemployed persons, the public sector, future generation and the environment. It would be more holistic if central bank decisions were made by a mixed stakeholder committee in order to form a balance of the most important interests. In the Swedish Central Bank at least the trade unions have a say in the decision making, which shows that a higher extent of diversity is possible.

The independence of the ECB is debatable and is currently de facto a twofold farce. On the one hand there are only central bankers in the committees, who fundamentally represent elitist interests which can sometimes also be divergent. On the other hand the statutory or rather official mandate is so unclear that the delegates from national states can exploit their respective representatives to push through national interests. Such a policy clash has been raging in the ECB since the start of the euro crisis. Some of the Mediterranean countries under the leadership of ECB boss Mario Draghi are in favor of the "fiscal and economic policy" function of the central bank, whereas the "hard core" under the former leadership of the German director Jörg Asmussen, who in turn was standing on the shoulders of the Buba boss Jens Weidmann, are advocates of the "monetary and stability policy" line. Those states

---

[5]Banca d'Italia: www.bancaditalia.it/bancaditalia/funzgov/gov/partecipanti/Shareholders_1.pdf

that see themselves sliding towards bankruptcy understandably want to tap into the central bank as a cheap "lender of last resort," while those states that see themselves beyond the threat of sovereign default are fearful of the role of "transfer payer" and want to safeguard the "independence" of the central bank. Both serve specific interests. While the "tappers" have the easing of their sovereign debt problems in mind, whereby higher inflation would definitely serve them well, the "ECB is taboo" faction is protecting financial assets and financial centers such as Frankfurt in the case of Germany. They fear inflation as the devil fears holy water. The hardliners are however shortsighted, as their rigid position regarding inflation could become a fatal boomerang for the creditors in the coming years as a result of sovereign defaults of the debtor countries, which from my view is a highly probable scenario—this on the other hand does not mean that the Draghi line represents the answer to the euro crisis.

Central bank "independence" is an illusion similar to that of the "objectivity" of science. Every ECB decision is made according to a specific ideological paradigm and serves specific interests. Therefore all large stakeholders should be equally transparent and democratically represented in the supervisory body of the central bank. A multi-stakeholder committee would also not make perfect decisions, but its decisions will be less subject to mistakes and less one-sided than the decisions made by central banks in their current structure.

In any case a mandate clearer than the current one is necessary. The statutory mandates of the ECB contradict one another. On the one hand the Treaty on the functioning of the European Union states that the union "is not liable for the liabilities of member states" and does not "assume responsibility for" these (Council of the European Union 2008, p. 131).[6] If the central bank belongs to the "union" then it can neither be liable nor assume responsibility for sovereign debt. On the other hand the Lisbon Treaty protocol "forbids," via the central bank, only the "direct acquisition of debt securities (from member states) by the ECB or the national central banks" (Council of the European Union 2008, p. 311).[7] Does this then mean that the "indirect" acquisition is permitted? If so, limited or unlimited? Government financing is forbidden, acquisition of government bonds on markets in permitted. With such a contradictory set of targets it is understandable that the bank bodies cannot work reasonably but rather only justifiably quarrel with each other.

7.3 Objectives and Tasks of a Central Bank

The tasks and objectives of a central bank are just as much a law of nature as the monetary and economic system itself. Pursuant to this it is also necessary to have an ideally clear democratic mandate. Nobody doubts the task of money creation,

---

[6]Article 125 of the Treaty on the functioning of the European Union.
[7]Artikel 21 of Protocol No 4 "On the Statute of the European System of Central Banks and of the European Central Bank," of the Treaty on European Union and of the Treaty on the functioning of the European Union.

however with regard to the objectives of monetary policy the opinions of the various schools differ widely and dramatically.

Let us take a more detailed look at the three most important schools of thought—and their practice:

7.3.1 The ECB Model

According to the European Central Bank Charter, monetary stability, hence a low as possible loss in value due to "inflation," should take precedence over other objectives.[8] Other objectives such as the "support of general economic policy of the union" are however explicitly subordinate to the stability objective. What are the most important advantages of "stable money?" A low level of inflation especially benefits private assets, which are protected from devaluation in real terms. Beneficiary is therefore the financial center whose "stable" currency is extremely appealing. The more reliable the promise of the central bank is to ensure a low level of inflation; the more interesting this currency is as an investment currency. The topic of inflation involves the "stability of internal value" of a currency. The "stability of the external value" refers to the exchange rate. There is a connection between both—the more stable the domestic value is, the more attractive the currency is and the more investment influx there will be to this monetary area. The capital influx in turn strengthens the external value that is the exchange rate compared to less attractive (inflation endangered) currencies and financial centers. The exchange rate stems from the demand and supply of a currency: if there is high demand as a result of low inflation, the "price"—its exchange rate rises. What makes the financial investors happy is to the detriment of exporters, the higher the external value/exchange rate is, the more expensive their products are in comparison with trade partners. The vested interests amongst corporations is therefore by no means unambiguous, one could even go as far as to say that when it comes to the topic of "external stability" industry and finance have opposed interests—unless industrial enterprises transform into financial investors and draw only a small share of their revenue from production. The development can indeed been observed—Siemens is described as a "large bank with a small work bench," Novartis as a "large bank with a small pharmacy." Economically speaking the business sector has mutated from being net debtors to net creditors (Schulmeister 1995 und 2007), in other words in total industrial enterprises share the interest of the financial investors and not those of crafts, trade and SMEs.

The consequence of this is the more the central bank pays attention to the external value, the more one-sidedly it serves the interests of banks and large corporations—the "weaker" the euro, the better it is for the exporters. The same applies for the internal value: a slowing down of the economy to prevent higher inflation by means of higher interest rates (the brake cable of monetary policy) leads to a decline in real investment by companies, a reduction in jobs and an increase in unemployment.

---

[8] Article 2 of Minutes no. 4.

While favoring higher interest rates must not necessarily completely lead to a negative impact on the financial success of companies, because the companies have the option of investing on the financial markets and earning good money here, even though this contradicts their purpose. Those looking for jobs have no choice; they suffer as a result of higher unemployment, detrimental working conditions and decreasing income. Here again the central bank's "party position" has diverse impacts on the various groups in society, which makes it more important to (a) as much as possible democratically determine the objectives of the bank and (b) not only have bankers but *all* important sectors of society represented in the decision-making bodies.

7.3.2 The Fed Model

The US central bank, the Federal Reserve, is charted very diversely. Central bank law stipulates the Fed's objective to be "long-term growth of the monetary and credit aggregates at the same pace as the growth potential of production" whereby "the effective promotion of the objectives of maximum employment, stable prices and moderate long-term interest rates" can be supported.[9] Besides supplying credit and low interest rates to the economy, it is committed to two central macroeconomic objects: full employment and monetary stability and in this order. As both of these objectives tend to be at odds with each other, this is an "exciting" assignment. The Fed's board of management can definitely accept higher inflation (higher economic growth, higher money supply, higher flooding of the banks with central bank loans) in order to promote employment and reduce unemployment. The Bank of England also has leeway; in summer 2013 it announced it would maintain interest rates at a low level until unemployment figures were reduced to less than seven percent.[10]

The ECB is not permitted to do this and even has to adhere to a ceiling of 2% for inflation. These are two very different mandates. Who issues such a task to the central bank? The Lisbon Treaty is the initiator in the EU; it is the highest-ranking legal basis of the community. And who implements this treaty? The general public? The Lisbon Treaty was forced on the general public by their representatives in perhaps one of the most undemocratic processes to ever have taken place in the EU. Jean-Claude Junker's opinion about the EU's constitution convention of that time was, "I have never seen such a darker darkroom as the convention."[11] In my view the Lisbon Treaty is null and void because (a) the sovereigns did not vote on it, (b) two sovereigns in referendums had voted against the forerunner treaty, the EU Constitutional Treaty, which the Lisbon Treaty "in substance up to 95%" observes[12]

---

[9]Federal Reserve Act, Section 2A.

[10]*The Telegraph*, 7 August 2013: www.telegraph.co.uk/finance/mark-carney/10227862/Bank-of-England-Governor-Mark-Carney-announces-interest-rates-will-remain-low.html

[11]*Der Spiegel*, 16 June 2003.

[12]The former Austrian Minister for Foreign Affairs, Ursula Plassnik, in ORF-Pressestunde, 21 October 2007.

and (c) the governments purposely broke off the series of referendums because they feared, and rightly so, that further sovereigns would vote against the treaty. Now this treaty is in force and with it the ECB mandate. This was taken over from the Maastricht Treaty where the ruling elite had already stipulated that the central bank should give precedence to monetary stability over full employment. This one-sided mandate stems from the historical compromise between the nation states: the German Bundesbank was famous for its policy of the "hard Deutsch Mark" and the thus accompanying low inflation. Germany was only prepared to give up this position if monetary stability took precedence over all other objectives in the EU central bank. One could argue that Germany imposed its will on all the other European member states, which is not only democratically dubious but it is also, economically speaking, no reasonable basis for a monetary area with 17 member states and for which a uniform central bank policy virtually becomes its fate.

The result of the ECB's "stability focus" was—besides the internal differentiation of lower real interest rates in countries with high inflation such as Spain or Greece and higher real interest rates in low inflation countries such as Germany and Austria—a high real interest rate level in the EU in comparison with the USA for a long period of time and as a result slower growth and a higher unemployment rate. Stephan Schulmeister amongst others presented critical analyses regarding this (Schulmeister 2010). On the other hand, one could argue that slower economic growth was ecologically better than higher growth and the ECB had served climate protection more than the Fed had. However climate protection was firstly not the objective of ECB policy (at best an unintentional side effect), and secondly the primary (perhaps intentional) side effect was the rise in unemployment, risk of poverty and fear. In light of these diverse conflicts of objectives and course of action alternatives of a central bank, it is even more important to precisely define its objectives and priorities when granting it a mandate.

7.3.3 The Alternative Model

In addition to the classical objectives of the Fed and ECB there would be at least one further objective, which a central bank could by statute pursue—limited state financing. State financing? No other topic is more controversial than this. State financing by the central bank is the end of every currency, according to the fears of some. Others counter pragmatically that this is already practised by all central banks. The Fed de facto holds about 12% of all US government bonds,[13] the Bank of England 25% of all British government bonds and even the ECB, which perhaps should not at all, holds over 200 billion euro in Greek and other government bonds, which is at least about 2% of sovereign debts of EU member states.

Quite a few are of the opinion that acquisition of bonds is illegal with the official excuse being: the ECB first intervenes on the so-called "secondary market" and so after the bonds have already reached the "primary market." What is the

---

[13] US Treasury Department, cited in *Frankfurter Allgemeine Zeitung*, 19 September 2013.

7.3 Objectives and Tasks of a Central Bank

primary market and how do the bonds reach this? In the so-called "tender procedure" the national debt agency or the federal financing agency auctions new bonds to a bidder consortium of forty banks in Germany and 26 in Austria.[14] These banks have the exclusive right to acquire newly issued government bonds on the "primary market" or to discard of these. If the interest rate or risk of default is too high, the state agency sits on the bonds—the state loses "access to the markets." As a one-off this would be no problem, however if this repeats itself and the state cannot "refinance" its old debt that is cannot make repayments with newly taken out debts, it is insolvent. Greece, Portugal, Ireland and Cyprus were rescued from sovereign default by diverse EU and euro rescue packages.

Could states then not be directly financed by the central bank? Then the states would be independent of the markets and furthermore the central bank which creates money out of nothing could offer more favorable conditions. Oh, goodness gracious me anything but that—there would be immediate mega-inflation, according to the cries of the stability supporters. They fear that money supply would erratically rise; state borrowing would skyrocket and with it prices. The historical hotspot of their fear is the hyperinflation in Germany in the 1920s, which was triggered, amongst other things, by the loose reins on monetary policy by the Reichsbank. This was on the other hand the reason for the rigid fight against inflation policy ("stability focus") of the Bundesbank after WWII—strategies of fear, according to the rule of once bitten twice shy. Or even better still an anxiety neurosis: if money which must be carried with both hands is no longer worth anything and a handcart and a whole carriage is not enough to haul the trillions necessary for daily food shopping, this is similar to an OCD dream in which people in massive rooms have to count miniature tiles or stones on the riverbank ... Hyperinflation of the interwar era instilled a deep trauma in the collective memory of Germans which is why the paranoid BuBa policy is not ridiculous but rather understandable.

---

[14]Germany: ABN AMRO Bank, Banca IMI, Banco Bilbao Vizcaya Argentaria, Banco Santander, Bankhaus Lampe, Barclays Bank, Bayerische Landesbank, BHF-Bank Aktiengesellschaft, BNP Paribas, Citigroup Global Markets Limited, COMMERZBANK Aktiengesellschaft, Crédit Agricole Corporate and Investment Bank, Credit Suisse Securities (Europe) Limited, DekaBank (Deutsche Girozentrale), Deutsche Bank Aktiengesellschaft, DZ Bank AG (Deutsche Zentral-Genossenschaftsbank), Goldman Sachs International, HSBC Trinkaus & Burkhardt AG, ING Bank N.V., Jefferies International Limited, J.P. Morgan Securities Ltd., Landesbank Baden-Württemberg, Landesbank Hessen-Thüringen Girozentrale, Merrill Lynch International, Mizuho International plc, Morgan Stanley & Co. International plc, Natixis, Nomura Bank (Deutschland), Norddeutsche Landesbank Girozentrale, Nordea Bank Finland, RBC Europe Limited, Scotiabank Europe, Société Générale, State Street Bank and Trust Company (London Branch), The Royal Bank of Scotland (Niederlassung Frankfurt), UBS Deutschland, UniCredit, WestLB.

Austria: Barclays Capital, BAWAG P.S.K., BNP Paribas, Citigroup Global Markets Limited, Commerzbank AG, Crédit Agricole CIB, Credit Suisse Securities (Europe), Deutsche Bank Aktiengesellschaft, Erste Group Bank AG, Goldman Sachs International, HSBC France, J.P. Morgan Securities, Merrill Lynch International, Morgan Stanley & Co. International, Nomura International, Oberbank AG, Österreichische Volksbanken-Aktiengesellschaft, Raiffeisen Bank International, Raiffeisenlandesbank Oberösterreich Aktiengesellschaft, Royal Bank of Scotland, Société Générale, UBS AG.

However fear alone is a poor counsellor. Regarding the situation rationally: does every state financing by the central bank immediately lead to inflation? How much would the ECB balance sheet total enlarge, if the euro member states took out interest-free central bank loans amounting to 20%, 40% or 60% of their economic output? The GDP of the Eurozone amounted to 10.7 trillion euro in 2016; the balance sheet total of the ECB reached its highest level to date in the first half of 2017 with 4.2 trillion (European Central Bank 2017), which is almost 40% of the euro GDP. Thus the balance sheet total of the ECB would not significantly change if the member states replaced a share of their debt, which they have at commercial banks, by interest-free loans at the ECB.

This would have further advantages: the state would issue this money more reliably than commercial banks do so, since commercial banks, as every child in the meantime knows, only pass on an ever decreasing portion of the "liquidity" which they receive at the central bank to companies in the form of loans.

An ever increasing portion goes directly into the global finance casino where bubbles are formed. This means that if the central bank makes liquidity available to the commercial banks and in doing so increases the money supply, this will certainly result in inflation at this stage, albeit not there where it is usually feared that is foodstuffs, energy, water and everyday items, but with securities and financial investments such as shares, real estate, commodities, currencies and derivatives. This inflation is not harmless but represents a *different type* of danger: it does not directly lead to everyday items becoming expensive or non-affordable but to systemic instability—it leads to real estate bubbles, share bubbles, fluctuating exchange rates and speculative attacks on currencies. The central bank fuels "financial inflation" and financial turbulence when it makes money available to the commercial banks via "big Berta" and if they can do what they chose with it.

It would be like raising a child's pocket money without any accompanying measures and hoping that they would buy vegetables and fruit with it....

The figures show to what extent this exactly happens at the central banks and what would happen if they directly financed states (to a limited extent): the balance sheet total of three dozen central banks from industrial and emerging economies doubled, going from 10 to 20 trillion US dollars in the period from 2007 to 2012. The ECB increased from 875 billion to 3.1 trillion, and then decreased as a result of repayments by commercial banks to 2.3 trillion by the end of 2013 and went up again thanks to quantitative easing to over 4 billion in early 2017 (European Central Bank 2017). The Fed increased from 0.8 to 4 trillion US dollars (Board of Governors of the Federal Reserve System 2013, p. 4). Switzerland increased fivefold from nearly 100 billion Swiss francs to 550 billion. In 2013 The Japanese Central Bank wanted to extend the balance sheet total to 60% of GDP.[15] In early 2017, it approached 100%. Measured against GDP, the Bank of England had the smallest balance sheet total in the "big four" group in 2016, with 17.4% at the end of 2016. The ECB had 34.1%, US Fed 24.1% and Bank of Japan 99.5%.

---

[15]*Frankfurter Allgemeine Zeitung*, 2 July 2013.

This is remarkable: inexpensive state financing is rejected with the argument that the accompanying extension of money supply would lead to inflation, but at the same time the central banks finance the commercial banks very reasonably, from which states must then borrow at wickedly expensive rates. Is it possible to be less efficient and more unfair? The accusation that this is not about "sound" monetary policy but rather about creating advantages for the benefit of commercial banks, because their clout at the central bank is (still) large enough, is hard to rule out with such ludicrous facts.

The roundabout is even two levels more absurd: the commercial banks request hefty "risk premiums" from states and at the same time states assume liability for commercial banks when they back the wrong horse. Commercial banks on the other hand hold default insurance for government bonds, however if the commercial banks back the wrong horse they must be rescued by the states which they should actually insure.

In order to get out of this absurd interrelationship in which the general public loses and commercial banks win, an alternative proposal, which will be outlined in detail in the next chapter, is presented in the following. To begin with it is only concerned with the principle commissioning of the central bank with—limited—state financing. If the euro states took out a loan directly at the central bank, amounting to for example 20%, 40% or 60% of their economic output, that would be 2.2 trillion euro, 4.4 trillion euro or 6.6 trillion euro—in actual fact an extension of the ECB balance sheet total but not a very dramatic one. The difference would be:

(a) states could borrow virtually free of charge;
(b) the balance sheet sums of the banks would contract;
(c) the money supply would remain the same.

However what about the risk of inflation? In my view there is no risk: government spending would indeed not soar, states would only finance themselves more advantageously. In doing so there would be savings in debt servicing, these could in turn be used to stop inhumane austerity programs and cutbacks. Inflation will not be generated but rather the current more dangerous deflation, which has been lurking since the onset of the crisis, will be averted.

7.4 Monetary Authority

To clean the air in the relationships between commercial banks, state and central banks the members of the "Monetary Modernization" movement propose a fourth state authority, namely a "monetary authority": an independent public central bank with a clear democratic mandate. This monetary authority stands "for an independent sector of public-law entities responsible for implementing monetary and currency sovereignty independent of other state authority instances and responsible for the availability of legal tender, the control of supply in circulation, national currency exchange management as well as, where applicable, bank supervision

(....) A sovereign state should in addition to its legislative, administrative and judiciary sovereignty have a monetary sovereignty and not be dependent on the weal and woe of commercial credit and investment banks" (Huber 2013, p. 46).

The purpose behind this is a further differentiation of the separation of powers: "The task of parliaments [and the sovereign, author's note] consists of prescribing a rule of law for the monetary system, the banks and financial markets, however not creating money itself or conducting bank business," writes Joseph Huber. And not to transfer the former to private banks, as is the case in the USA, I would like to add. For this reason Huber considers a "monetary authority as a constitutionally embedded fourth state power," as the "more appropriate governance" (Huber 2013, p. 53).

Within the framework of their proposal, the advocates of a monetary authority confirm the idea of central bank autonomy and reinforce it as follows: "It is important that central bankers, once in office are not bound by anybody's instructions. Their autonomy is a functional requirement" (Huber 2013, p. 115). This is in the same manner as the autonomy of the judiciary system. Here it could lead, and does lead, to a conflict of interests—it has "to be absolutely ensured that the government itself does not determine how much money is created" (Huber 2013, p. 22).

References

Board of Governors of the Federal Reserve System. 2013. *Quarterly report on federal reserve blance sheet developments*, New York, November 2013.
Council of the European Union. 2008. *Consolidated versions of the treaty on European Union and the treaty on the functioning of the European Union*, Brussels, 30 April 2008.
European Central Bank. 2017. Consolidated financial statement of the Eurosystem as at 2 June 2017, in Weekly Financial Statement, 6 June 2017.
Huber, Joseph/Robertson, James (2008): *Geldschöpfung in öffentlicher Hand. Weg zu einer gerechten Geldordnung im Informationszeitalter*, Verlag für Sozialökonomie, Kiel.
Huber, Joseph (2010): *Monetäre Modernisierung. Zur Zukunft der Geldordnung*, Metropolis-Verlag, Marburg.
Huber, Joseph (2013): Finanzreformen und Geldreform – Rückbesinnung auf die monetären Grundlagen der Finanzwirtschaft, S. 33–59 in: Verein Monetäre Modernisierung (2013): *Die Vollgeld-Reform. Wie Staatsschulden abgebaut und Finanzkrisen verhindert werden können*, 3rd edition, Edition Zeitpunkt, Solothurn.
Lietaer, Bernard/Ulanowicz, Robert/Goerner, Sally (2009): *Wege zur Bewältigung systemischer Bankenkrisen*, Wissenschaftliche Arbeit für die World Academy of Arts and Sciences (WAAS) in Hyderabad, Indien.
Schulmeister, Stephan: (1995): *Zinssatz, Wachstumsrate und Staatsverschuldung*, WIFO monthly reports 3/95, pages 165–180.
Schulmeister, Stephan: (2007): *Finanzspekulation, Arbeitslosigkeit und Staatsverschuldung*, Intervention 1/2007, pages 73–97.
Schulmeister, Stephan: (2010): *Mitten in der großen Krise. Ein ›New Deal‹ für Europa*, Picus Verlag, Wien.
Stiglitz, Joseph (2012): *Der Preis der Ungleichheit. Wie die Spaltung der Gesellschaft unsere Zukunft bedroht*, Siedler, München.
Swiss National Bank. 2017. Annual Report 2016.

Chapter 8
Solving the Problem of Sovereign Debt

Abstract This chapter presents a proposal to solve the sovereign debt problem once and for all. The idea of granting interest-free loans to the state, from the previous chapter, is developed further and elaborated in detail: central banks could be allowed to extend loans of up to 50% of GDP to states—or a different limit. At the same time, states would not be allowed to become more indebted than this limit, with this limit being anchored in constitutions. States should only be allowed to take out loans for two purposes: infrastructure projects from which future generations also benefit and measures to counteract recessions. An independent parliamentary committee could authorize new debts. If a government exceeds the constitutional limit of 50% of GDP, automatic stabilizers could come into force, proposed here as higher taxes on property and inheritances. This would be an incentive for governments not to exceed the limit—otherwise they would have to take responsibility for potentially unpopular automatic stabilizers. In any case, the sovereign debt problem would be resolved.

> *Due to the opening-up of financial markets, states are not only in competition with other states for global savings but also with private debtors.*
>
> Rolf-E. Breuer[1]

As previously shown, the sovereign debt burden in the USA could be reduced by half as a result of sovereign money reform, in Germany and Austria it would be a good three quarters and in Switzerland it would be completely eradicated. In addition it was briefly discussed that central banks could contribute to state financing by making interest-free loans—to a limited extent available. This statement will be extended to a concrete proposal here as to how sovereign debt problems can once and for all be settled, at least in the EU and industrialized countries.

Why do states get into debt in the first place? Some people are of the opinion that states should not get into debt at all, this is also stated in the constitution: "Federal government and federal state public budgets are to be balanced

---

[1]Rolf-E. Breuer: Die fünfte Gewalt in *Die Zeit*, 18/2000.

fundamentally without revenue from lending."[2] The thought behind this is that every generation should pay for what they consume, which is however exactly the argument *for* national debt, as part of the investments benefit several generations for example hospitals, street infrastructure and stations. According to the generation justice principle, states must be permitted to get into debt to the extent that the benefit of the current investment proportionately benefits future generations, this could be calculated with simple formulas.

State benefits to the current generation ranging from administration, infrastructure, social and public security to the health and education system should be financed by taxes or deferred. If future generations are saddled with the costs of the current generation's consumption costs, the distribution conflicts between those who make use of these benefits and those who pay for these benefits are not resolved but rather postponed: State creditors are served by the tax payers of tomorrow instead of the tax payers who consume these benefits. The resolution of the problem is passed on to a generation who had no say in the matter. This is unfair. The key question is which portion of the current public budget can be attributed to "future investments" and over how many years are they distributed—from this ensues the highest permissible public debt level.

Apart from the matter of future investments, there is also a second good reason why a state should get into debt that is to offset economic fluctuations and in particular to cushion recessions. Then the famous "anti-cyclical fiscal policy" of John Maynard Keynes would come into effect: the state goes into debt in recession times to intercept the downturn and to rebalance the economy. During the boom it saves and repays the incurred debts during the recession period. In the event the "complete" Keynesian proposal is practised, its medium-term impact, spanning the economic cycle, on the state debt level is neutral, it neither rises nor falls. However governments willingly only practise the first part, namely they take on debts in the recession period, but not the second that is the repayment of debts as soon as the economy has picked up. Additionally it may be the case that a recession arises just as the state has reached its maximum debt level and by taking on further debt there would be an exceedance of this debt level. This would indicate that even though anti-cyclical fiscal policy should be permitted and with it the financing of current public benefits in subsequent years. However this course action taken by government and parliament does not lead to an increase in debt level (apart from a small puffer, if need be) and a possible recession must therefore always be calculated into the equation or the proposed consequences, outlined in the following, must be faced.

8.1 Proposal for the Reform of Sovereign Debt Financing

1. States are permitted to take out interest-free loans at the central bank up to a defined limit of their economic output (GDP) for example 25%, 50% or 75%.

---

[2]Basic Law for FRG from 1949, Art. 109 (3).

8.1 Proposal for the Reform of Sovereign Debt Financing

2. The debt right of the parliament is restricted to this limit and furthermore requires that loans can only be taken out if (a) they finance public benefits which will be of benefit to future generations or (b) an economic downturn is to be anti-cyclically cushioned.
3. In order to decide if and to what extent the debt mechanism can be made use of, a "future committee" will be specifically elected and composed of representatives from companies, trade unions, environmental and social organisations as well as other stakeholders, who authorize, amend or reject parliamentary budget committee requests within the framework of the constitutional level of debt.
4. In this manner sovereign debt cannot get out of hand as a result of direct budgetary policy because the debt committee is at the same time obliged to observe compliance with debt limits. Parliament requests which exceed this debt limit will be rejected, unless the general public votes in a referendum in favor of raising the constitutional debt limit.
5. If the debt ceiling is exceeded due to non-fulfilment of the budget plan—lower state revenue, higher expenditure, unstable economy, corrupt government—automatic stabilizers will come into effect, namely debt capping. Unlike an expenditure-oriented debt cap (cutback in state expenditure), I however advocate a revenue-oriented debt cap (increase in state revenue) to avoid making the mistake of cutting or cancelling valuable public benefits, which especially in period of recession have a counterproductive impact—see Greece, Portugal and Spain. An expenditure-oriented debt cap deepens the recession and makes it necessary to implement an even stricter debt cap, which in turn deepens the recession … "In the macro-economy one shrinks to illness never to health," as Stephan Schulmeister put in a nutshellsubsequent decline of interest rates (Schulmeister 2010, p. 95).
6. Higher taxes should in the process be "economy-neutral," those which neither curb consumption nor willingness to work. For this inheritance and wealth tax on large assets would be the most suitable, as they neither have an adverse effect on consumption nor rein in willingness to perform, but rather rein in speculation. Private assets are on average about five times as high as state debt in the Eurozone and about two thirds of the total wealth is owned by 10% of the population. The "automatic stabilizers" would in this way not hit the lower or middle classes but rather the wealthiest, who have such a large amount of assets that they (can) neither consume nor tangibly invest but (must) invest on the financial markets and live from return on investments.
7. Automatic stabilizers only come into effect in an exceptional situation: if the planned budget, which must stay within the range of the constitutional debt limit, gets out of hand which can essentially only happen as a result of a sudden recession. In "normal" weather the government would have to act extremely incompetently and the success of the budget would have to significantly lag behind plan. Then it was ultimately the decision of the sovereign who elected this incompetent government and in doing so put up

with the consequences. The "price" of the poor choice is the temporary increase in taxes. The big advantage—state debts remain independent from government competence within tolerable (constitutional) limits and the costs for state debt remain at zero. That would be a decisive benefit in comparison with today: voters must no longer look on helplessly as governments unrelentingly push up state debt, or how they bring about the opposite effect with expenditure-oriented "debt caps"—a further rise in debt because cutbacks in state expenditure during the recession extend it and increase the deficit.

8. The most common argument against direct—also limited—state financing through the central banks is that it results in an increase in money supply and this would trigger inflation. However as argued in the previous chapter, I do not see any risk of inflation in this proposal, since the only systemic change is that states borrow from the central banks instead of from commercial banks, which for their part finance themselves through the central bank (an unnecessary and expensive roundabout way of doing things) or by creating money: the extension of money supply certainly leads to inflation! The state debt volume would not increase but on the contrary actually sink and with it the risk of inflation. The amount of increase in the balance sheet total of the central bank would be partially or completely conceded by the commercial banks—a zero-sum game. The balance sheet total of the ECB fluctuates between 3 and 4 trillion euro. Fifty percent of the Eurozone economic output, the possible maximum debt level, was 4.8 trillion euro in 2013—not even in a borderline case a substantial change. On the other hand if the euro crisis continues to be managed as it has been to date, the balance sheet total of the ECB will certainly increase to far above 5 trillion euro, possibly even towards 100% of GDP (look at Japan!) with the difference here being that hardly anybody gives two hoots about it—perhaps because the commercial banks are benefiting from it.

9. In the event it were not a zero-sum game—not all government bonds are held by commercial banks and not all bonds held by commercial banks are from their own currency area—and contrary to all expectations if inflation were impending, the central bank still has various instruments at its disposal in order to rein in money supply and inflation, if the worst comes to the worst. It can for example "syphon off" private financial assets by creating its own investment facility for it, thereby allowing money supply and risk of inflation to diminish.

10. The most important point: the right to increase money supply must be revoked from commercial banks, as they cause inflation, although in the current nonsensical system, "only" on financial markets in the form of asset inflation or bubbles. The question of fighting inflation is from my point of view more of a question concerning bank regulation—keyword sovereign money reform plus credit regulations—and less a question of the central bank balance sheet total, if its moderate extension serves the limited and conditional state financing.

8.2 Benefits of the Reform for the Public

Sovereign debt financing through its own central bank would have considerable advantages for the general public:

- Interest savings: In 2012 Germany spent according to calculations 65 or 69 billion euros on total state debt servicing—an unnecessary as well as unfair state expenditure.[3]
- Fairness: The tax money would have been better invested in schools, hospitals, social security, and municipal infrastructure as well as in the ecological upgrading of the economy. In 2014 in Austria it amounted to 7.3 billion euro or 2.2% of economic output. In Spain the government forecasted an unbelievable 33.5 billion euro for interest payments on state debt for 2016, and this with over 50% youth unemployment.[4] 33.5 billion is almost double the amount of the austerity program imposed by the Troika. Spain is being forced to carry out these painful savings not even to repay debts but rather in order to pay interest on debts! Considering the alternatives it is becoming clearer in whose interest the "Destroika" is making policy and why hardly anybody is entertaining the idea that states could refinance themselves with interest-free loans at their own bank.
- Sovereignty: It is actually absurd that autonomous states do not allow themselves to make use of their own—free of charge—source of money and prefer to resort to dependence on the "markets," although these do not possess any form of ethical mechanisms. Market participants are first and foremost interested in profit no matter if this stems from daylight robbery, austericide, speculative attacks or trading with insurances against state default, with which this can be triggered. The decision to finance states through markets is from the democratic perspective a humiliating self-abandonment of the sovereign. Or from another perspective, a coup d'état of parliaments, that are responsible for all these decisions, against the sovereign.
- Stability: In the global finance casino one of the biggest gaming tables would be closed—the government bonds gaming table including the insurance against their default and with that the dubious field of work of assessing sovereign states, namely rating agencies. With this some of the instability factors would be removed from the whole financial system. Since the gaming tables are connected to each other, calm and more stability would also be restored to the

---

[3]The official finance statistics state 72 billion euros for 2012, including actual payments made and derivatives. The national accounts "only" comes to 64 billion euros only the incurred claims in one period are included and derivatives are not taken into account. The highest value was in 1998 by the way, with 70 billion euros, since then it has been declining slightly as a result of the introduction of the euro and the subsequent decline of interest rates. Deutsche Bundesbank (2013), 49–52.

[4]Government of Spain/Ministry of Finance: "Presentación del Proyecto de Presupuestos Generales del Estado 2016," p. 215.

neighboring currency speculation gaming table as speculative attacks on currencies are more enticing if states can go bankrupt.
- With the implementation of the proposal this would be extremely improbable and another party in the finance casino would come to an end. The proposal would consequently make several contributions to systemic financial stability, and last but not least the euro crisis would be over.

References

Deutsche Bundesbank (2013): *Die Entwicklung staatlicher Zinsausgaben in Deutschland*, Monatsbericht September 2013, pages 47–56.

Schulmeister, Stephan: (2010): *Mitten in der großen Krise. Ein ›New Deal‹ für Europa*, Picus Verlag, Wien.

Chapter 9
Bank Lending Regulations

Abstract Loans finance the future. If the economy's goal is the satisfaction of human needs and to increase the common good, and if money is a public good to serve these goals, then the lending regulations for banks should in turn support the achievement of these goals. This chapter proposes that loans should only be used (a) for real investments (b) that do not harm the common good and (c) with a priority for the region in which banks operate. Every loan should be subject to an ethical risk assessment before the assessment of the financial risk for the investor and bank, as the financial risk assessment similar to the ROI does not reveal any reliable information about the impact of that investment, and about the loan which is granted to enable this, on aspects such as the environment, social cohesion, distribution, trust, dignity, gender equality, or democracy. Only if an investment does not diminish these fundamental values, will a loan be granted—the loan will be cheaper the more value it adds.

> *Ideas, art, knowledge, hospitality and travelling should be international. In contrast goods should be produced locally, where ever this is reasonably possible; above all finance in particular should to a large extent remain within the national context.*
>
> John Maynard Keynes

In a democratic monetary system it is not only of fundamental importance (a) who creates money, (b) by what means money comes to credit institutions (ex nihilo created by banks or as sovereign money from the central bank), (c) which objectives credit institutions are given (see next chapter), but also the closely related question (d) for which purposes can loans be granted.

The question as to where money goes to or is poured is decisive for a humane society. It makes a crucial difference whether an organic farmer receives a loan or a factory farm with 100,000 fattening animals in the shed. It makes a crucial difference whether a consumer loan goes to a solar car, a first class rail card or SUV. It makes a crucial difference if a loan is taken out to create worthwhile jobs or whether risky tradeable securities are bought on credit. It makes a difference whether ….

Too much havoc can be wreaked with credit, and this has already happened, to leave this completely to the—only seemingly unbiased—free operation of markets. More accurately: credit creates so much havoc *because* markets are entrusted with the decision whether a loan is "good" (sufficient credit rating) or "bad" and "worthy" or "unworthy" of financing. Markets are not unbiased but rather unduly "biased": the value of all products and services on the market is expressed in money, in many instances independent of their social value and use.

In many cases the price (exchange value) is in radical conflict with the (use) value. Often the most valuable social services, those which contribute to the common good and as a result must be the most valuable economic services with the highest exchange value have little or no exchange value. In contrast "services" which destroy the environment or shatter relationships achieve the highest exchange value (market price) because the system of economic evaluation and measurement of success is currently not matched with the objectives of economic activities but rather with the needs of capital (capitalism). Activities and products which lead to the propagation of capital achieve a higher market price and receive loans the easiest, entirely detached from their ethical content and contribution to the objective of economic activity. What is the objective of economic activity? The Bavarian constitution states that "all economic activity serves the common good."[1] The Italian constitution demands that "public and private economic activity should be geared towards the common good."[2] The constitution states that "property obliges" and it should be used "at the same time to serve the common good."[3] The Spanish constitution envisages that "the total assets of a country (...) are subordinate to public interest."[4] The spirit of these constitutions is clear and unanimous.

If however the common good is the objective of economic activity, then it is more than curious that currently loans are in no respect checked with regard to their contribution to this constitutional objective, or is it not? This is contradictory and ineffective. Everything which serves propagation of capital is financed and credited but whether it serves life, the satisfaction of needs, relationships and the common good is not an issue.

If all economic activity must serve the common good or at least *at the same time* (constitution), this then means that pure capitalism and money-out of-money transactions are unconstitutional: if property at the same time must serve the general public, then this public use must be checked before granting a loan. If the fact that "capital accumulation is not an end in itself applies, but is rather a means of economic development," as is stated in the Art. 157 of the Bavarian constitution, then the purpose must be checked before the means are granted.

"Money and credit as a public good" could mean that (a) loans must serve the constitutional objective of economic activity, (b) when granting loans the contribution to this objective must be assessed and (c) the laws executing the constitution must determine appropriate regulations regarding what loans can and cannot be used for.

---

[1] Art. 151, Constitution of Bavaria.
[2] Constitution of Italy, Art. 41.
[3] Basic Law for the Federal Republic of Germany from 1949, Art. 14 (2).
[4] Constitution of Spain, Art. 128.

Credit differs from money and while the use of money owned by private persons can be relatively free, credit has more of a public character and is "less private" to a degree. One could say that we have a greater freedom to dispose of money which we actually possess, although obligation to the common good is also valid (see constitution), than with the "additional" use of credit, which is a public good. The state carries the responsibility for its supply by commissioning private and public banks to take on the credit business within the framework of constitutional regulations to protect the common good. This spirit is today already to some extent present in the Swiss constitution, "The federal government can, if need be, diverge from the policy of economic freedom."[5] That the complete restraint on the part of the state with regard to credit control has caused enormous and avoidable individual (e.g. eviction, private insolvency) and macrosocial (systemic instability with mass unemployment, hunger as a result of food stuff speculation) damage is reason enough to opt for a soft regulation approach in the form of public responsibility, private implementation and constitutional regulations. Joseph Huber also follows this line of argument, "Money in circulation as well as credit can (…) be considered as a public good similar to the health or mobility of our society" (Huber 2013, p. 67).

Credit is not even "free" today. The Basel rules and the implementation on EU and member state level even very precisely determine under which conditions a loan can be granted and which securities must be furnished. It is just a case of developing ethical loan appraisal and also making this legally binding, in addition to financial creditworthiness which is already legally required.

The total wavering of regulation in the case of ethical loan appraisal is in striking contrast to the rigid regulation of *financial* creditworthiness of every investment project by the Basel rules, which banks moan about and they sometimes even cite these rules as the reason for it no longer being possible to carry out profitable banking business.

Legislators are involved in financial risk determination down to the minutest detail; in contrast ethical loan appraisal does not even take place.

The constitutional values—human dignity, solidarity, sustainability, justice and democracy—are however worthless and invalid if loans are exclusively granted on the basis of financial performance indicators. Today almost *everything*, which guarantees a return on investment, is allowed totally independent of how meaningful, sustainable, ethical or social a project is. "Recovery," becoming whole, is the task of the coming years. It will be a benefit for bankers if they have to take classes in ethics alongside developing economics and mathematical skills. One of these bankers, Thomas Jorberg, GLS Bank Manager, currently considers it as follows: "I see the main problem in our decision matrix for investments and financial investments. The interest rate always decides what happens with the money, based on the same term and risk. What is financed with the money is completely ignored, which is what I consider as the core problem." (Interview in Dohmen 2011, p. 201).

---

[5]Swiss Federal Constituion 18 April 1999 (As per: 1 January 2011), Art. 100 (3).

There are also deficiencies in financial creditworthiness appraisal in the current credit system. Financial creditworthiness appraisal today exclusively evaluates the credit project in question itself in order to minimize the probability of credit default (first risk level) and the accompanied risk of insolvency of the credit institute (second risk level). Whether the use of the loan creates a risk for systemic stability of the financial system (third risk level) is not subject matter of the financial creditworthiness appraisal. Basel II was rightly criticized on the basis that it doubly enhanced systemic instability. On the one hand because in recession times the banks must refuse companies credit as a result of the rigid lending regulations and during a recession company creditworthiness declines in general and a portion of their securities loses value, which is the reason why the same companies with the same security receive less credit. On the other hand, it does this because risky and high risk leverage credits are permitted without restrictions and with Basel III this remains so: there is no provision for appraisal of exposure to systemic stability. Hedge funds for example will not be regulated in future but rather only their managers will be registered (see Chap. 7). An appraisal of the impact of the loans on distributive justice does not take place at all although this distribution is extremely relevant for systemic impacts. The more wealth is concentrated in a few hands, the more "game money" they will have at their disposal which can be wagered at risk that is leveraged. Basel III is blind in the "distribution eye."

Today money goes where the largest return on investment is expected and is totally decoupled from questions of meaning, ethics and objectives. Economically speaking, "credit" as an extremely effective and sensitive steering lever is absolutely disregarded with respect to constitutional objectives and values and therefore has no impact. In a democratically designed monetary system there is one decisive element absent—credit steering.

9.1 Loans for What and for What Not?

We could approach the question of credit steering with three fundamental questions:

1. Should credit projects be subject to an ethical creditworthiness appraisal in addition to financial creditworthiness appraisal?
2. Should loans be granted for "speculative" financial investments or only exclusively for (productive) real investments?
3. Should loans be primarily granted in the region where the bank customers deposit their financial assets?

9.1.1 Ethical Creditworthiness Appraisal

The first question is the core credit regulation or steering question—in the production of what values should money go to and to which line of purpose? Is the

9.1 Loans for What and for What Not?

generation of financial values sufficient? Or is it not equally important, or even more important that use values are created in order to satisfy demands and to increase the common good and in doing so the constitutional values such as human dignity, justice, solidarity, sustainability and democracy? What is the economic objective of investments and loans? If the overall objective of "all economic activity" is the common good, then the instruments of economic activity for example granting loans must serve this objective. From the strictly logical perspective, every loan must therefore be subject to a common good appraisal.

With regard to the money and lending sector, the Bavarian constitution states: "The money and lending sector serves the creation of values and satisfaction of the needs of every inhabitant."[6] If lending must serve the "satisfaction of the needs" of inhabitants, would this by implication mean that loans which do not serve this goal, are unconstitutional, according to the Bavarian constitution? And which values are meant by "value creation"—use or exchange values? Are the needs of the population, are human needs covered with exchange values (money) or with utilizable values (food)? Logically speaking it can only mean utilizable values because they can only "cover the needs." Does this in turn mean that loans that are taken out to propagate money without creating utilizable values and without covering needs are unconstitutional? What does it specifically mean that the federal government can diverge from economic freedom in the lending sector? The democratic monetary conventions do not have to start at zero and can build on a surprisingly solid foundation. However the constitution text requires more precision than it contains to date. Which values are meant? Which consequences do these have? What about loans which in fact cover real demands but destroy human and ecological values for example sweat shops or a shed with 100,000 fattening pigs? What about loans which pass financial creditworthiness appraisal but do not cover demands such as credit leverage for hostile takeovers or casino derivatives?

On the international stage there are already a number of ethical banks, which exclusively grant loans to projects which create a high degree of added social and ecological value. In order to measure this they have developed ethical criteria as a basis for deciding whether a loan is granted or not. The "Bank for the Common Good" is currently being founded in Austria. All credit requests will be subject to a common good appraisal, which has already been developed and premiered in 2017. The common good appraisal ethically evaluates the investment project. Does the product or service to be financed satisfy human needs? Is it compatible with human dignity? What are the working conditions like? Which ecological impacts are to be expected and which distribution impacts? What is the relationship to democracy?

The credit conditions will *also* be oriented towards the results of the appraisal. In the same way as interest increases depend on the risk level of the investment, the loan will be more expensive or cheaper depending on the common good appraisal results. The financial risk will not be disregarded, it is however not the

---

[6]Art. 151 (2), Constitution of Bavaria.

only decisive factor, the credit project must pass both appraisal procedures and if it fails one, it fails completely and no loan is granted. This is the painful experience made by numerous entrepreneurs with financial creditworthiness appraisal. In future companies will also have to verify the "ethical creditworthiness" of the investment in order to receive a loan. Companies with Common Good Balance Sheets will have no further additional expenditure; they "check" the complete company in any case with regard to objectives and values. It will be even easier for ethical companies to receive cheaper loans, the opposite of today. Today an industrial agricultural fattening farm with 100,000 pigs obtains the cheaper loan, the organic farmer's loan is comparatively more expensive, and that is if he/she receives a loan in the first place. In an ethical credit system, loans would be granted to farms with a maximum limit of animals, they would be the most expensive there. The more organically and species-appropriate the animals are kept, the cheaper the loans will be—up to an interest rate of zero or without loan fees. These would then be the "ethical jewels" which provide most benefit for society as they are cross-financed by less ethical companies due to the relatively higher loan costs they incur.

In order to implement the spirit and will of constitutions, a common good appraisal of all investments is therefore necessary in order to prevent investments from infringing the common good. When no wide-ranging values are created loans are not granted and this complies with the spirit of the constitutions. Even though the common good must not be propagated to receive a loan, it should at the same time not be reduced. If a negative contribution to the common good transpires during the ethical appraisal, an "reduced ethical value," then values are destroyed in total and therefore no loan should be granted. The lending sector supports value creation and not value destruction.

9.1.2 Speculative Financial Credit?

A second large matter in economic credit steering is the subject of speculation and their financing by credit ("leverage enhancement"). Firstly a definition is required. What does speculation mean in contrast to investment? What is a financial loan in contrast to a real loan? The meaning of the word is such that every "investment" is a "speculation" at the same time. I "pour money" into the uncertain future in the hope that I can generate the loan amount, its costs and an income. The word speculation comes from the Latin word *speculare*, meaning looking or peering into the future. In the following I will attempt a differentiation between graded forms of necessary/serving the common good and unnecessary/detrimental to the common good "speculation"—"investment."

(a) Real investment: a carpenter who buys a plane or a commercial or industrial enterprise which buys a new machine expects to (hopes to) be able to produce and sell as much furniture or as many industrial products so that not only the working hours are paid but also the procurement costs of the tool/machine.

9.1 Loans for What and for What Not? 77

They hope that the "poured in" investment "yields a profit"—money comes back. This is level 1 of the "speculation" which represents the "real basis" of a monetary economy. There is hardly anything to criticize about this process; the conscience alarm is not being raised.

(b) Credit-financed real investment: the entrepreneur takes out a loan in order to finance this real investment (in production resources) and the repayment of procurement costs is distributed and eked out over many years. There are also no known objections to this. Although the systemic risk is rising because in the case of a false investment ("loss incurred due to speculation") not only the borrowing enterprise is at risk but also the lending bank. However the financial creditworthiness of the borrower is accurately evaluated to minimize the probability of credit default and with it the collapse of the credit institute. The risk is limited and is a part of the "game order" of a free market economy whereby nobody guarantees the success of a private enterprise.

(c) Financial Investment: in this case somebody procures a security for example a government bond or a company shares in the hope (speculation) that the investment will yield a financial gain (return on investment—ROI) or better still a multiple of it. In the case of a government bond this is the interest and in the case of a share it is the dividend. From a private person's perspective this would appear to be a rational decision. If a company behaves in this manner, it could already be classified as a misallocation of resources. Stephan Schulmeister investigated the US share boom in the 1990s and came to the conclusion that enterprises preferred to direct their profits in security acquisitions, especially shares, instead of in real investments and jobs. This trend was so extreme that the complete corporate sector, especially large corporations, went from being net debtors to net creditors. Profits went from the real economy to the financial economy and in this way contributed to systemic excessive indebtedness and instability and as a consequence of the associated decline in real investment to an increase in unemployment.

(d) Credit-financed financial investment: at the height of the "boom" securities were also bought on credit. "Financial investors" naturally only do this when the expected yield from the securities (dividends) are higher than the costs of borrowing (interest). Borrowing to increase equity capital is part of a central strategy of investment banks, institutional investors of all kinds (hedge funds, private equity funds), but also the risk-friendly family offices or investment company of Warren Buffet. Even conservative pension funds maintain their meagre returns with an addition of "alternative investments" or at least fatten them up. Here the fundamental question arises—is it economically reasonable and beneficial for systemic stability that natural or legal entities borrow an amount higher than they can afford from their "real" financial assets to buy more securities?

(e) Financial speculation: here an investor acquires a share, bond or credit default swap not to have a share in the company or to earn interest or an insurance premium but in order to resell the security with profit after a hoped for price increase. Or they enter a bet with specific derivatives on a price slump and if this happens they rake in winnings on their bet. In this case we are already completely decoupled from any real economic link; the investor has absolutely no interest in the enterprise and its products or services. The only objective is to make more money out of money no matter by what means (products, companies, financial instruments). Systemically speaking, "making money out of money" is however impossible—without its own work and performance money cannot become more money. "Nothing comes out of nothing" (Schulmeister 2008). Money can only be propagated by the work performance of other people. The sum of financial values can only grow faster than GDP in two exceptional cases:

1. If a speculation bubble appears which sooner or later bursts with the accompanied elimination of financial, social and human values;
2. Exploitation—one party becomes rich at the cost of another party, who then becomes relatively impoverished—a violation of human dignity and the principle of justice—a constitutional breach.

(f) Leveraged financial speculation: financial speculation on credit is the "highest" level of speculation and "financial alchemy." This strategy also only makes sense if the hoped for speculative profit is higher than the costs of the amount that has been borrowed to finance it. If things go wrong the complete house of cards can collapse, not only the speculators, the money their customers have entrusted to them (e.g. fund bankruptcy), the bank which the speculators "work for" (e.g. Barings Bank) are in danger but rather the stability of the global financial system. This has been the case several times, with the most "famous" case in two senses being the hedge fund LTCM (Long-Term Capital Management). Two professors of venture mathematics who had won a Nobel Prize for their research results, created a hedge fund and collected 5 billion US dollars from people, who were so wealthy that they had nothing better to do with their money than to give it to the award-winning alchemists so that they could do the systemically mathematical impossibility for them—make more money out of money without lifting a finger for it and without producing a real or meaningful product or rendering a real service. The top mathematicians "leveraged" the "equity capital" of their magic fund initially with the support of 125 billion dollar loans from banks—a leverage factor of 25. Thereupon they entered derivative positions valued at 1.25 trillion dollars, then the sorcery of the alchemists failed and they blew the colossal investment. As not only the billions from their wealthy customers were in danger, but also the banks who were involved in the deal with hefty loans and with an impending global chain reaction on the horizon, a number of private banks stepped in under the direction of the Fed in order to prevent a collapse of the global financial system. If the bet had come off, what would its economic value have been? What would have been the collateral profit for the common good?

The LTCM case is no isolated incident—we recall that McKinsey Global Institute calculated a significantly higher national total debt burden than the "BIS" because they also determined the debts of the financial sector. In Ireland this alone amounts to 259% of the GDP, in Great Britain 219% and in Japan 130% of GDP (Mckinsey Global Institute 2012, p. 5).

While the first three forms of investment/speculation—real investment, credit-financed real investment, and financial investment—can be considered reasonable, as far as I am concerned the constitutional conformity, and even more important still the total economic sense and ethical purpose of the last three: credit-financed financial investment, financial speculation and leveraged financial speculation, is for me more than an issue. They could be forbidden in a new monetary system.

Money and credit as a public good mean that the use of loans is regulated within rough regulations. The same rules do not apply to public goods and private property. That is by no means illiberal: loans and financial investments are basically still permitted; just the dangerous excesses and target discrepancies are filtered out. Others are also thinking in this direction. The economist Richard Werner from the University of Southampton proposes, "Loans for transactions which do not contribute to the GDP are simply not permitted. Speculation remains but without the credit leverage."[7]

9.1.3 Regional Priority

A cooperative bank in Austria has deposits of 320 million euro with the volume of loans granted amounting to 140 million euro. The logical consequence: 180 million euro of regional savings and financial assets go out of the region—in the worst case into the global financial casino. Sometimes the credit utilization rate of regional Austrian savings banks and cooperative banks—"primary banks"—amounts to only 50–60%. In other words only half of financial assets are no longer utilized in the real economy of the region, they are passed on to larger commercial banks, to their own central banks or directly to the international financial casino.

The disparity between financial assets and credit demand arises from the fact that private financial assets are growing faster than the real economy (GDP). In Germany in 1970 the annually reported private assets amounted to 70% of the economic output of *that* time. In the first half of 2013 it was 189% of the current GDP or approximately 5 trillion euro.[8] The crisis could pull the growth of financial assets from the fast lane in only one year, namely in 2008. As early as 2009, savings again left the GDP well behind them. Although with increasing income and GDP the savings level, the share of national income/GDP which is put aside and saved must logically continue increasing—the higher the income, the higher the share of income which people do not require for consumption—a sustained

---

[7]*Die Presse*, 17 October 2013.

[8]According to the Bundesbank private financial assets in Germany as per 30 June 2013 amounted to 4992 billion euros, economic output for 2013 was forecasted to be 2650 billion euros at the end of the first half of the year.

growth of financial assets higher than that of GDP is mathematically impossible. To be more exact: the investment and interest payment of ever increasing financial assets is impossible because the real economy cannot absorb investments amounting to a multiple of national income, which is simply does not require.

In other words: there is a structural shortage of investment possibilities for the ever increasing amount of available financial capital. If the propagation of capital is the objective of economic activity this is the largest imaginable problem. Therefore strategic ways forward are sought in capitalism so that capital, although an ever increasing share of it is literally "superfluous," can continue to be completely "utilized" that is invested and propagated with a return on investment. Since capital in the 1970s, after the abatement of the post-war economic miracle, has entered a utilization crisis three "ways out" have been found: (a) privatization, (b) globalization and (c) speculation. However all three of the strategies are only temporarily feasible and as such are not real ways out from the perspective of need of capital to propagate. From society's perspective they are highly dangerous:

– *Privatization*
  A representative investigation of privatizations shows that there are only exceptional cases, selective improvements for some groups of society but never for everybody and in the majority of cases they bring deterioration for the general public. In contrast the new private owners are usually the winners (Jenner 2008, 184–188; Österreichische Gesellschaft für Politikberatung und Politikentwicklung 2003; Reimon and Felber 2003 and Weizsäcker et al. 2006). Under no circumstances should privatizations be motivated by a shortage of investment opportunities for financial assets and a search for ROI options.
– *Globalization*
  Switching to other countries involves chances and risks, worthwhile mentioning are the numerous financial crisis, which were triggered by investment seeking foreign capital (Asia, Russia, Mexico …). The most important is however even if those, who only recognize chances and advocate capital export were right because this triggers development, this could only function temporarily because then it pays off and the poor countries close the gap on the rich ones and want to export their capital—but where to?
– *Speculation* does not provide any solution but only creates even larger problems.

The fact remains that there is too much capital striving for utilization in "mature" economies. The Commerzbank has granted loans of 2.9 billion euro or 5% of its balance sheet total to about 90 US municipalities.[9] I pose the question, whether there are any banks in the USA, where people have savings deposits which could be lent to these municipalities? Is the USA a country with a low level of financial assets? It certainly is not. However US financial assets obviously go to the global financial casino instead of to the municipalities where people who

---

[9]*Frankfurter Allgemeine Zeitung*, 9 August 2013.

possess these assets live. The Austrian Raiffeisen Central Bank lost a loan amounting to 150 million euro in Iceland. The first question: is there no use for this large amount of money in Austria? Is there too much money in Austria? This would apparently seem to be the case. The second question: is there too little money in Iceland? As is well known, the Icelandic banks had balance sheet totals amounting to 10 times the GDP which is a megalomania record only shared by Cyprus and Luxembourg. The balance sheet insanity of the Icelandic banks was financed by Austrian financial assets which find no real use in Austria. The Raiffeisen loan went to the Straumur Bank, which was nationalized and closed by the Icelandic Financial Supervisory Authority on 27 March, 2009.[10]

The following lending regulations could provide a remedy:

(a) Banks should be obliged to lend saving deposits from the region to borrowers in the region. In the USA there is already such a regulation, the "Community Reinvestment Act," which induces banks to regional financing.
(b) With increasing financial asset-GDP relationship banks should "decommission" an increasing share of their deposits that is leave them as "deposits" and not convert them into "investments." This surplus could be deposited in the "cash accounts"—the from the bank's balance sheets externalized current accounts of savings customers mentioned in Chap. 2—and not "work" but rather rest (bank as "deposit site" or deposit bank). This would be extremely advantageous because in doing so the intolerable investment pressure of ever larger financial assets which overwhelms and fleeces the economy would find an end. The ways out of traditional banking and asset management—privatization, globalization and speculation—would no longer be systemically required. At the same time the structurally increasing surplus of financial assets in the event of a bank collapse would be completely secure because the cash accounts would be in the possession of customers and not the bank.

References

Dohmen, Caspar. 2011. *Good Bank*. Das Modell der GLS Bank, Orange Press, Freiburg.
Huber, Joseph (2013): Finanzreformen und Geldreform – Rückbesinnung auf die monetären Grundlagen der Finanzwirtschaft, S. 33–59 in: Verein Monetäre Modernisierung (2013): *Die Vollgeld-Reform. Wie Staatsschulden abgebaut und Finanzkrisen verhindert werden können*, 3rd edition, Edition Zeitpunkt, Solothurn.
Jenner, Gero (2008): *Das Pyramidenspiel. Finanzkapital manipuliert die Wirtschaft*, Signum, Vienna.
Mckinsey Global Institute. 2012. Debt and deleveraging: Uneven progress on the path to growth, Study, January 2012.
Österreichische Gesellschaft für Politikberatung und Politikentwicklung (2003): *Privatisierung und Liberalisierung öffentlicher Dienstleistungen in der EU. Ein Überblick über den*

---

[10]*Der Standard*, 14 July 2010.

Stand der Privatisierung und Liberalisierung von öffentlichen Dienstleistungen in den 15 Mitgliedstaaten der EU, Study Summary, Vienna, May 2003.

Reimon, Michel / Felber, Christian (2003): *Schwarzbuch Privatisierung. Wasser, Schulen, Krankenhäuser – was opfern wir dem freien Markt?*, Ueberreuter, Vienna.

Schulmeister, Stephan: (2008): *Luftschlösser – eingestürzt und ausgebubbelt*, Kommentare der anderen, Der Standard, 23 September 2008.

Weizsäcker, Ernst Ulrich Von/Young, Oran R./Finger, Matthias (Ed.) (2006): *Grenzen der Privatisierung. Wann ist des Guten zuviel?*, Bericht an den Club of Rome, Hirzel, Stuttgart.

Chapter 10
Common Good Oriented Banks

Abstract This chapter is concerned with the function of commercial banks in a common good oriented economy. First, the emergence of profit-oriented banks and banks which are too big to fail is criticized, together with the fact that there is no international supervisory authority. Second, the ideal bank that is a common good oriented bank is described: It fulfills the "conservative" core tasks of a bank such as savings and loans, it does not distribute profits to owners, it applies a common good risk assessment to all loan requests, and it withdraws from the system of interest. Banks that shift to common good orientation could enjoy more preferential legal treatment than profit-oriented banks which could be handed over to the free market thereby losing these benefits. Finally, a solution to excessive private financial fortune is proposed: Money that is not used in the real economy could remain in electronic bank deposits. Capital income could melt down to zero, being replaced by different types of benefits that are in line with the economy's goal.

> *A strictly regulated, small scale financial sector with defined interest rates could replace the current system and remind us of West Germany in the sixties when there was a basic savings rate and no stock market TV.*
>
> Lucas Zeise (Zeise 2012, p. 217)

10.1 Banks Are Historically Common-Good Oriented

The reputation of banks is currently not the very best, which is however nothing new. Bertolt Brecht already asked the question, "What is a bank break-in in contrast to establishing a bank?" in his "Three penny Opera." What is the objective a bank? Is it to propagate money (profit-oriented)? Or is it to finance reasonable investments as cheaply and at as low a risk as possible and in doing so serve the common good? This has slightly fallen into oblivion with most of the bank types in the second half of the nineteenth century being established not as profit-oriented but as common good oriented banks. This applies to the cooperative banks such as Raiffeisen Bank, Volksbank and Sparda Bank. Friedrich Wilhelm Raiffeisen described his bank establishment project as a work of philanthropy, "Our chief director is Jesus Christ" (Quoted in Klein 2008, p. 77). The fundamental values of "Christian solidarity, subsidiarity and regionalism" still form the official foundation of values of the Raiffeisen Association today.[1]

Hermann Schultze-Delitzsch, a contemporary of the token father of the "Volksbank" was also not concerned with profit but rather with a flourishing craft industry. The Sparda banks which were established in the twentieth century pursued the target of granting needy railway worker families consumer loans to be able to cover their daily needs.[2] In the case of "Sparkassen" (savings banks) which partly began as societies, the common good orientation still remains unchanged in the savings banks laws.[3] The banks which we daily read about (have to read about) in the newspapers are not representative of the complete banking landscape. In Germany alone there are more than 1900 credit institutes, but hardly any of them are famous to the extent of the branch leaders listed on the Frankfurt stock exchange, which are daily recipients of (excessive) media attention.

Although profit-oriented commercial banks have been in existence for seven centuries longer than cooperative and savings banks, they are however numerically speaking in the minority. The flagships were always the biggest problem for example the second phase of the great depression originated from the bankruptcy of the enormous Wiener Creditanstalt, whose balance sheet total accounted for two-thirds of the balance sheet totals of all other Austrian credit institutes. The first rescue sum corresponded to 50% of the national budget.[4] The bank was "by far too big to fail."

After the Second World War some regulations took effect so well that relative stability returned for several decades and hardly any financial, currency or bank crises occurred. Not only was the famous Glass Steagall Act passed in the USA, which was annulled in 1999 due to intensive lobbying, but the Bretton Woods Agreement came into force on an international level and ensured currency stability to a large extent for about three decades—see Chap. 12. What many people in Germany can hardly imagine today is that until 1967 savings interest was regulated in Germany by the so-called basic savings rate.[5] This element of a "centrally

---

[1] http://www.raiffeisenverband.at/the-raiffeisen-idea. Retrieved on 19 March 2017.

[2] In the second half of the 20th century the "Eisenbahner-Spar- und Darlehenskassen" (Railway Workers Savings & Lending Bank) was opened for all employees.

[3] For example the Saarland and Rheinland-Pfalz Savings Bank Act, both in §2: "The savings banks serve the common good by means of their task fulfillment." Or the Berlin Savings Bank (Berliner Sparkasse) Act in §4: "The Berliner Sparkasse transactions are to be carried out according to commercial principles considering general economic principles. Attainment of profit is not the main purpose of business operations."

[4] Figures of historian Roman Sandgruber: www.foonds.com/article/13225

[5] The basic savings rate was regulated in the Credit Interest Regulation up to 1967 and was 3%.

10.1 Banks Are Historically Common-Good Oriented

planned economy" could not strangle the economic miracle, on the contrary, the growth rates were at the highest level at that time, the highest ever in history.[6]

However the era of regulated financial markets, of the social market economy and "Rhineland capitalism" petered out with Margaret Thatcher taking office in Great Britain in 1979 and Ronald Reagan in 1980 in the USA. Cutbacks in public services, weakening of the trade unions, privatization, opening up of the markets and globalization climbed to the top of their political agenda, where they are still today which TTIP, the looming trade and deregulation agreement between the USA and EU, proves.[7] The Uruguay Round of GATT, which was heralded in 1986 led to the World Trade Organization (WTO) and the European integration process pivoted from a predominantly political harmonization (peace project, cooperation between nation states) towards the establishment of a free trade zone with primary economic objectives (international competitiveness, monetary stability).

In 1999, two ambitious EU domestic market specialization projects were tackled, namely the euro as a common currency and the single financial market. The second promised a large "free" market but was in its effect however exactly the opposite. The single financial market was a perfect hothouse for banks which are too big to fail. These banks are however the end of the free market. The architects under the single market commissioner Mario Monti at that time successfully managed a historical maneuver against logic, against the market economy, against democracy. They opened an infinite market for banks and financial services:

- No size limits for banks. In this way the colossus could mature unchecked, the banks were openly invited to "become internationally competitive," which means the same as too big to fail. Based on the experience of previous crises for example the hypertrophic Creditanstalt, the legislators should have fed a capping for balance sheet totals of credit institutions into the system in order to prevent ever having to bailout banks again. The opposite was done and history is repeating itself.
- Devoid of market supervision. This was not present nor is it even present in the tiny vegetable market in Salzburg the so-called "Schranne." How should the colossus propagate the common good without a supervisory instance?
- Devoid of all product regulation. This resulted in financial derivatives, termed as "financial weapons of mass destructions" by Warren Buffet, coming into circulation, completely unchecked. This does not occur anywhere else: medicines and chemical are examined prior to authorization, every car has to be checked by the TÜV (Technical Inspection Agency) on a regular basis, on Sunday the police even checks respectable citizens crossing the border between Salzburg and Bavaria. Only the too big to fail investment banks are allowed to bring their "financial weapons of mass destruction" into circulation, and in doing so

---

[6]According to the Federal Statistics Office the German economy grew in real terms by 8.2% in 1951–1960, 1961–1969 by 4.4%, 1970–1979 by 2.8%, 1980–1990 by 2.6% and 1991–2003 by 1.2%.

[7]Christian Felber: Alle Macht den Konzernen, Opinion, *Der Standard*, 20 December 2013.

bring about the collapse of markets. It would be logical for a powerful EU financial supervisory authority to check new products on the basis of their hazard potential for system stability, with authorization only being granted to those who pass this check.
- Free movement of capital in unregulated markets. It has only been since 1994 with an amendment to the Maastricht Treaty, which did not undergo a referendum anywhere, that the movement of capital between the EU and non-member countries is free and as a result of this the EU is not protected against the negative influence of financial crises on other markets.[8] Therefore "financial toxic waste" from the real estate bubble could be freely imported into the EU. The self-gagging of the EU had clear winners—the international financial sector which trades and speculates freely, maximizes profits, creates crises and can pass the costs onto the general public.
- Free movement of capital, also to all global tax havens. With that the EU encourages large EU corporations and wealthy Europeans to transfer profits and private assets to countries that either charge no or next to no taxes. It should come as no surprise that these are also used, if the escape route has been paved.

How can such political decisions be explained? After long analysis, a short conclusion—"There is no such thing as democracy." The current form of democracy is not capable of regulating markets effectively or deconcentrating economic power. It functions the other way round: the regulators are regulated by global players, by systemically important financial institutions and their associations. It is not the sovereign—the general public—which determines the financial and monetary system but rather the powerful minority makes the laws which are then valid for the general public who also has to carry the costs. A new democracy model is necessary for an alternative economic and monetary system.

10.2 Criticism of Bank Bailouts and the EU Banking Union

We are still within the financial dictatorship modus, the same mistakes which were made establishing the "market" and cultivating massive banks are being

---

[8]The Maastricht Treaty from 1992 provided for another course with regard to movement of capital and potential limitations: "For movement of capital between member states and non-member states the EU Commission makes a proposal to the EU Council regarding measures for a step-by-step coordination of foreign exchange policy. The Council enacts directives for this with a qualified majority. It will endeavor to achieve a maximum degree of liberalization. Unanimity requires measures which represent a retrograde step in the area of liberalization of the movement of capital" (Article 70, Maastricht Treaty—7 February 1992). Not until a subsequent amendment, were the rules for movement of capital from Art. 67 to Art. 73 replaced by the updated Articles 73b to 73g, which came into effect on 1 January 1994. It stated at that time that "all restrictions to movement of capital between member states as well as between member and non-member states are forbidden." "Liberalization" comes per regulatory policy ban.

10.2 Criticism of Bank Bailouts and the EU Banking Union

repeated by the EU elite since the onset of the crisis to the present day with macabre consequences:

- The banks were not nationalized, broken up or wound up but instead bailed out by the tax payer. Market economy would be if the owners bore the damages, but the political class chose to protect the owners from the EU financial supervisory authority by establishing a single financial market and now after the big crash they have been protected from responsibility and losses. That is bailout socialism or state-subsidized oligopolistic capitalism and not market economy. Curiously almost all of those who sold us the idea of a single financial market and globalization as a "free market" are noticeably silent with regard to this matter. The rhetoric of the elite on the contrary, still refers to this as market or market economy and often even as "social market economy," the ideological swindle continues.
- Down to the present day not even one large bank in the EU has been wound up,[9] although there is broad consensus that banks which are too big to fail represent per se the core problem: these banks engulf multi-billions of tax money, trigger a crisis in state finances, promote "moral hazard" (a mixture of negligence and ruthlessness), the more so as they rely on state bailouts (this now being legally finalized with the banking union). They enjoy better refinancing conditions due to this implicit state guarantee and an unfair competitive advantage in contrast to small systemically unimportant banks. Furthermore they lower the efficiency of the whole system and undermine faith in the market economy and democracy—it is incredible that this must be argued vis-à-vis parliaments and governments in the first place.
- The bailed out system elephants can continue to carry out their business with and in tax havens and enjoy the boundless worldwide free movement of capital. They can unscrupulously continue their speculation with commodities, shares, loans, currencies and derivatives and the time would be right to demand a common good orientation from these banks as a quid pro quo for the tax money support they have received and continue to receive. The only minute restriction created by the EU parliament was with regard to speculative dealing with unsecured default insurance for government bonds (CDS) and uncovered short selling, a microscopic regulatory success in the still otherwise wide-open global financial casino.
- The "EU Banking Union" is taking shape 6 years (!) after the big crash of 2008—124 mega-institutes with a balance sheet total of over 30 billion euro are to be supervised by the EU. This is the next system error; banks with a balance sheet total of over 30 billion euro should not be supervised but rather reduced to smaller units. For example from the 413 savings banks in Germany that would, according to figures of 2015, involve only one, namely the Hamburger Sparkasse, which has a balance sheet total of 43 billion euro, the balance sheet sums of all the other savings banks are under 30 billion euro.[10]

---

[9]With the exception of the division of Dexia into a Belgian and French group.
[10]Finanzgruppe Deutscher Sparkassen- und Giroverband, Ranking 2016, https://www.dsgv.de – Daten & Fakten, visited on 3 June 2017.

- A discussion about the purpose and objectives of banks, money or lending does not take place at all. The ruling class is so deeply captured by the ideology of the crisis profiteers that there is not even an alternative discussion. A taboo to change the rules of the game dominates the mainstream media and that in the middle of the crisis!

Even worse than the economic systemic importance of a few banks ("too big to fail"), is their *political* systemic importance: "too big to jail." The financial giants are not only too big to be sent to insolvency, they are even too powerful for the legislator to regulate them democratically, split them up or even impose taxes on them. All fines to date are *peanuts*, with the same applying to the fund which the banks pay into in order to finance their liquidation. Between 2016 and 2025 a ridiculous 55 *billion* should be paid into the fund to secure all 124 systemically important EU banks. In the first phase of the crisis 1.6 *trillion* euro of tax money went to the banks, given these ridiculous figures it is really no laughing matter.

Economic systemic importance could "technically" be quickly resolved; however it blocks every change and solution to the problems. Politically systemic important banks constitute a financial dictatorship and literally dictate political direction. They enforced the EU single financial market, they determined the undemocratic and anti-market economy rescue modus, they have written their testament themselves and they are the architects of the banking union. "As nice as it sounds, it still remains perverse, as the new solidarity between the EU member states is of all things related to the banks. It is a bank bailout plan which is aimed at protecting financial assets, also in economically weaker countries," writes Lucas Zeise (Zeise 2012, p. 207).

Suddenly in the midst of the golden age of competition rhetoric when the EU member states are mutually undermining their tax base, refusing mutual debt securities (Eurobonds modelled on the federal government bonds of the USA) and consequently shying away from anything such as a European social insurance or at least an unemployment insurance system, they discover and impose the solidarity of the general public for the too big to fail banks, which are for the most part highly criminal. People should fight against each other and can fall through the mesh of the social safety net, but everybody sticks together for the banks.

Preventing the licensing of oversized banks would actually be the first imperative of a functioning market economy; however it apparently seems to be of no concern to those very people who have always strikingly advocated the market economy system. Their lack of concern for the market economy is the same as their lack of concern for democracy. If this were not the case the people would indeed be asked about the euro rescue system, the banking union or TTIP. Even high-ranking bankers are to some extent publicly stating that the banks are too big. According to the president of the German Savings Banks Association, Georg Fahrenschon, "The Deutsche Bank is very important but it is too big for the German economy."[11] The Deutsche Bank CEO in question, Jürgen Fitschen

---

[11]*Handelsblatt*, 3 September 2013.

defends its position using comparisons to strength and speed: one should not constantly talk about "too big to fail" but rather "too strong to fail" (....) "If you construct a car which travels at 20km per hour, you probably have a safe car, but try to sell it."[12] Does that mean that all systemically unimportant banks are like cars which travel slower than 20 km per hour? What does Fitschen want to say to us? Science is also divided—Max Otte from the University of Applied Sciences in Worms advocates a "size limit for financial service providers" (Otte 2013, p. 46). The bank professor from Zürich Urs Birchler slows things down—"we must divide the large banks into at least 20 smaller banks. I doubt whether these would then pose a smaller system risk."[13] This doubt is justified; however it is not to the point. Systemic giants must be at the same time split up *and* detoxified. That would have been the order of the day directly after the Lehmann Brothers collapse: "the financial toxic waste" should have been factored out to the bad banks, the healthy parts split into small units and the bad banks with exclusive profit participation rights should have been slung around the necks of the owners.

10.3 State Support Only for Common Good Banks

In order to "clean up" the bank landscape market economy wise, and pull capitalism slowly out of the financial system, a second intermediary step could initially be taken which would have the advantage of being universally understandable and would probably be supported by a large majority. The proposal is: all banks are confronted with the decision, either they change to the side of common good orientation and are subject to a binding common good charter or they will be released into the "free market," which means that all state support measures/activities are revoked, which presently benefit the system-relevant speculation tankers:

They receive no access to the central bank. At present commercial banks receive their "raw material" money from the national bank below market price. The state no longer does any business with profit-oriented banks—on all levels including municipal, regional, federal state, national state, EU and UNO—naturally including state debt transactions (see Chap. 4).

- The state deposit protection scheme is dispensed with and with this the trust of private customers in commercial banks, profit-oriented banks must acquire the trust of their customers without backing from the state. (Implementing a sovereign money reform, the cash account deposits would be safe but not the saving deposits; these would still require deposit protection insurance).
- The most important point: when the bank goes bankrupt there is no bailout by the tax payer. The freedom to establish a company and the responsibility to bear the damages if it goes wrong must be reunited.

---

[12]*Handelsblatt*, 20 November 2013.
[13]*Zentralschweiz am Sonntag*, 15 September 2013.

Here I advocate a truly *liberal* and *ethical* market economy instead of the current unethical power economy, which contains more and more capitalism as well as less and less market economy. It should be vice versa: market economy without capitalism, totally ethically and actually liberal instead of rhetorically the case. Liberal means the *same* liberties and rights for all, meaning boundaries to freedom in order to protect against concentration of power and actually ensure equal freedom and opportunities for everybody. Financial capitalism has taken both the market economy and democracy away from us and with that freedom, this must be retrieved.

10.4 Common Good Orientation of Banks

Now coming to the most important section—which criteria could make a bank a common good oriented credit institution and enable it to enjoy the benefits of state support? Here six criteria are proposed:

i. *Common Good Target Setting and Creation of a Common Good Balance Sheet*
The bank defines itself in principle as oriented towards the common good and also enshrines this as its chief business objective in its company articles of incorporation. A "bank for the common good" legal form could be created, whose standard statutes stipulate obligatory characteristic features. The business model must be coherent with this objective; the achievement of all strategic objectives is measured by means of a bank-specific common good balance sheet.

ii. *Conservative Business Model (Separate Banking System)*
The bank does not do business in the global financial casino and stays away from derivatives, funds and securities trading. It limits itself to "core banking services"—current accounts or cash accounts (after the sovereign money reform) with payment transactions, financial investments (savings accounts and savings books) as well as lending which is preferably regional. Prohibiting banks from dealing with derivatives and speculating is also a consideration of others. As Joseph Stiglitz for example writes, banks supported by state guarantees should "keep their fingers away from off-market derivatives" (Stiglitz 2012, p. 348). The German Federation of Trade Unions demands "finally a registration procedure for all types of securities and financial transactions (…) what is not explicitly allowed remains forbidden" (German Federation of Trade Unions 2013). The NGO "Finance Watch" advocates the complete division of securities and derivatives from lending and deposit banking, as otherwise the handling of mixed universal banks would not be plausible (Finance Watch 2013, p. 26).

iii. *Profits Will Not be Distributed to the Owners*
The objective of a bank is not to generate profits and distribute these, as Raiffeisen knew and as is stated in the savings bank law or in the constitutions. Pursuing profit as an objective entices risky speculation, unfair

10.4 Common Good Orientation of Banks

distribution and on the whole leads to an unethical business model. Why should something be right for a bank which is shabby for other infrastructure operations—it would be absurd for a school, hospital or theater to strive for financial profit in order to distribute a part of it to the owners. Banks belong in the same way to the public service of a society and to the fundamental infrastructure of the economy just as education, health, care, social and municipal utilities. The interplay of public goods and services with private companies makes the economy more stable and more democratic. In place of a financial dividend, the utilizable value goes in combination with ethics and co-determination in this direct non-profit business sector, provided the sovereign decides to take charge of utility services itself. The energy provider in San Diego SMUD is for example controlled by the people, the board and supervisory board is directly elected. The company does a good job and enjoys great popularity.[14] The same success can be achieved in the financial sector, in the case of the Bank for the Common Good Project thousands of cooperative members, who are not concerned with return on investment (there is none), but rather on purpose and the common good are standing in line.

iv. *Withdrawal from the Interest System*

The interest system is a prime example how seemingly enlightened and educated "knowledge-based societies" can be collectively and permanently mistaken. Ninety percent of all participants lose in the current interest system and nevertheless defend it. From the systemic perspective, interest exerts unnecessary growth pressure on the economy and is in the long term mathematically impossible—however almost every wealthy society is adamant about this *system error*.

What is missing is the critical information about the systemic impact of interest and possible alternatives. Perhaps the largest problem with the interest system is its distributive effect. Ninety percent of the population accommodates a small winner class of perhaps 10% with interest. However they are not aware of this because only the *savings* interest which we receive is disclosed on paper. The credit interest which all consumers pay on the products and services from daily purchases remain invisible and is not disclosed anywhere. Therefore hardly anybody does the self-evident calculation whether he/she pays more interest or receives more. Only by doing so, would we know if we belong to the net interest recipients or net interest payers. There are currency calculators, tax calculators, net salary calculators and savings interest calculators but no "net interest calculator"—we should actually be presented with this by the banks on World Savings Day. If the banks do not enlighten us, then at least the central bank should do so, as a "public service" to its citizens. However if the central bank does not do this, then at least the universities and scientific research institutes could enlighten citizens on such fundamental systemic interrelationships. To all intents and purposes there is

---

[14] www.smud.org

virtually only the calculation made by Helmut Creutz available, which is ignored by the academic research community (Creutz 2008, p. 83).[15]

Companies which via lending rates finance the savings interest calculate these borrowing costs completely into the products and services (along with all other costs) and consumers pay these costs in full. If all people consume the same and save the equivalent amount the interest system would be a distributively neutral roundabout. However surprise surprise! This is not the case, as the bulk of the population earns so little that they have to spend almost all of their income (for convenience only—they have an average propensity to consume—APC—of 95% and a savings rate of 5% of their discretionary income), while another group has such a high income (employment and capital income) that it can save the bulk of it (for convenience only—APC of 5% and savings rate of 95%). That part of the population which spends or must spend the bulk of its income, can accumulate no or very limited assets and thereby gain no noteworthy investment income. It gets worse: 95% of the employment income which has already been taxed at a high rate is again burdened with another approximately 20% tax by value-added tax—a real double taxation of real output revenue.

In contrast those who enjoy such a high income that they cannot spend the bulk of their money are systemically twofold rewarded. Their assets are propagated via interest and other capital yield without any further performance. To boot they are spared double taxation, as value-added tax only affects 5% of their income, 95% remains tax free. Capital gains tax in turn does not affect the saved (not consumed) income—the 95%—but rather only the additionally accumulated assets, the on-top achieved capital income (no double taxation). The rich also win.

– An incredibly effective redistribution mechanism from about 90% to about 10% of the population via this double asymmetry of highly different consumption and savings rates is created out of interest, which so many people are pleased to receive, even in the smallest amounts. It is an undisclosed "private capital levy" which is not redistributed to the rich by the state but rather by the market.

The proposal here: savings interest should be totally phased out, it represents an unnecessary redistribution and financial disadvantage for 90% of the population. Instead of the lending rate, a loan or bank charge could come into effect via which banks could finance their operations including the costs for credit defaults and company investments. With the cancellation of savings interest, dividend payments and bonuses would be credit charges—on average only to the extent necessary for the bank to be able to cover its operational

---

[15] According to calculations done by Creutz, 80% of the population are the net interest payers and 10% the net interest recipients. 10% results in distribution neutrality. As wealth distribution in Germany has become more unequal since the calculation in 2000, according to the German Institute for Economic Research (DIW), I presume that the figure of 90% net interest payers and 10% net beneficiaries is correct.

expenses and credit losses. In the case of medium-sized banks, this could be achieved with average credit costs of 2.5% which would significantly defuse interest as a growth driver or even neutralize it. For all borrowed money more money would still have to be repaid, however if
- the credit sum accounts for example 200% of GDP,[16]
- the average lending rate is 2.5%,
- 1.5% of credits fail,
- there is 2% inflation,

the credit system would be growth neutral and there would no longer be systemic growth compulsion stemming from the interest system.

v. *Common Good Appraisal of all Investment Schemes*

In the previous chapter it was argued why all credit applications, in an ethical market economy, should not only be checked with reference to their financial creditworthiness but similarly with regard to their ethical creditworthiness, their wide-ranging added value and their contribution to the objectives of economic activity. The currently sole practical test for credit projects within the exchange value logic of the system should be extended to comprehensive utilizable value logic, to include all values—purpose, dignity, justice, sustainability, democracy as well as the general objective of economic activity, namely satisfaction of needs and the common good. An appropriate common good appraisal could become part of the obligatory credit appraisal. Some alternative and ethical banks have already developed initial approaches to such a common good appraisal, which must be completed and fine-tuned to a legal basis. Considering *beyond ideology* financial creditworthiness appraisal is also an "ethical" appraisal—the "value" being evaluated here and deciding on whether a loan is granted or rejected is the monetary and economic viability. This apparently "objective" or "mathematic" criterion however conceals a massive load of values whose implementation leads or does not lead to the monetary economic objective—ranging from human and social interaction to respect for law and tax ethics as well as short term and long term ecological effects. This is why it is incomplete, not transparent and dysfunctional to hide ethical appraisal behind financial creditworthiness appraisal when granting loans. Ideally loans with the best financial creditworthiness are ethically impeccable. However there are also cases where the investment is both highly profitable and worthwhile as well as ecologically and socially destructive, which is why all investment projects must be subjected to two appraisals and only when both have been passed will the loan be authorized and money will flow. This would have three positive effects:

- Loans which represent a far too high financial risk will not be granted.
- Investment projects which do not pass the ethical appraisal will not be financed.

---

[16]According to BIS the total of all loans to private companies and households is 221% of GDP—on average of the OECD states, see Bank for International Settlements (2011), 24–25 (Table A2.1 and A2.2).

- Investments which are ethically speaking particularly valuable such as future-oriented technology, a social innovation, a public or community good and which narrowly fall short of the profitability limit can be realized using various funding instruments—eco-social risk capital, ethical companies or start-up financing, structural policy investment funding, interest-subsidized or subsidized loans from special bank funds and others.

vi. *The Common Good Oriented Use of Profit*
   Here the wheel does not have to be reinvented: typical Sparkasse saving banks do not distribute their profits to private people but rather to social and cultural community projects where they do business. Many cooperative banks on principle do not pay any dividends due to the fact that other objectives are more important for example the increase of equity capital, subsidizing loans for investments with exemplary ethical added value, support of regional common good in the form of social, sport, cultural and education institutions, ethical start-up support in regional common good hubs, direct participation in companies via regional common good exchanges. There are so many good uses for financial profit that nothing else simply remains for the owners but purpose, use, values, happiness and co-determination ….

These six above mentioned criteria and others could be required from the banks which further enjoy public infrastructures, refinancing, guarantees and contracts. If the state or a democratic society extensively "upholds" the banks, they must in turn uphold society. Within the framework of "public service" the state can leave the implementation of "provision with financial services" to the private sector, having said that in return for fulfillment of ethical requirement specifications or a catalogue of services—a "Common Good Charter."

10.5 Prototypes Everywhere

These thoughts are not utopian—in the last 40 years ethical banks, which serve the common good instead of maximizing profits, have been founded worldwide. The Triodos Bank was established in Holland, in Germany the GLS, the "Ethics Bank" and the "Environment Bank" in Switzerland the Alternative Bank and the Freie Gemeinschaftsbank, in Italy and in Spain Banca Etica.

In Austria the globalization critical movement Attac called for the establishment of a "democratic bank."[17] The project has developed in recent years and is now a cooperative with more than 5,000 members that started its financial services in early 2017.[18] Thirty-six alternative and ethical banks have joined together in the Global Alliance for Banking on Values.[19] The European Union, in cooperation

---

[17] http://www.attac.at/fileadmin/_migrated/content_uploads/Demokratische_Bank_02.pdf
[18] www.mitgruenden.at
[19] www.gabv.org

with this association, could develop the criteria catalogue for common-good oriented banks which benefit from state support. One further step would be the founding of a separate EU-wide banking association of common-good oriented banks, which would then no longer be reliant on conventional banking associations— start-up projects must currently incorporate themselves into the existing auditing and deposit protection associations. This association could be open to all banks which sign the Common Good Charter and comply with these standards, with the accompanying legal advantages.

Furthermore the first banks in Germany and Austria, the Sparda Bank in Munich, the Raiba Lech am Arlberg and the Sparkasse Dornbirn have begun to compile a common good balance sheet, which has been developed by the ever expanding Common Good movement since 2010.[20] They are concerned with a new route and a new identity or also a "back to the roots" approach with regard to the founding values of the cooperative banking sector. The Common Good Balance Sheet would be an important part of the Common Good Charter for banks and perhaps the first step in this direction.

10.6 Systemic Consideration: From the Investment Bank to the Depository Bank

A core problem of the current monetary system has already been broached several times and will now be dealt with here in more detail—private financial assets are growing faster than economic output. Until about 1980 private financial assets were smaller than the respective GDP of the leading industrial countries, but since then they have gone their own way. According to investigations carried out by various consulting and financial service companies, the global financial assets of private households' amounts to several times the global economic output. The Global Wealth Report 2013 of the Boston Consulting Group comes to 135 trillion US dollars or 190% of the global economic output (Boston Consulting Group 2013, p. 4). According to the McKinsey database, global financial wealth actually reached 225 trillion US dollar or 312% of the world GDP (Mckinsey Global Institute 2013, p. 14). Credit Suisse calculated for 2012 a gross total wealth of private households of 264 trillion US dollars (Credit Suisse Research Institute 2012, p. 3), which would be 3.7 times the global economic output of 72 trillion dollars. With regard to financial wealth of private household the BCG comes to the same result as McKinsey, namely 1.9 times global GDP. The problem with growing financial wealth is that the economy, as previously argued, cannot absorb a growing multiple of itself in real loans, there is simply no demand, no investment possibilities and certainly no principal repayment capacity with interest markup. Moreover insolvency risk increases acutely when the total debt-equity ratio is above a certain level. As previously illustrated, the Bank for International Settlements situates this threshold

---
[20]Specifically Sparda Bank München: https://www.sparda-m.de/gemeinwohl-oekonomie.php

with 260% of GDP and the Boston Consulting Group with 189% of economic output: both calculate with loans to the extent of 60% of GDP to each the corporate sector, private households and the state (Boston Consutling Group 2011, p. 5). Now if one of these figures, 180% or 260% were to become a key performance indicator, this would be to some degree arbitrary and hard to defend with historical corporate and budget insolvency waves or national insolvencies. However the 60% ceiling for sovereign debt, which became law in the Maastricht and EU Lisbon Treaties, and if exceeded is safeguarded by contractual penalties, is an equally arbitrary limit. The fear behind it is that states which exceed this threshold and as a result have repayment difficulties would not be able to afford to service their debts. The fact that the Eurozone has been exceeding an average sovereign debt level of 90% of economic output in recent times, thus more than 30% above the contractually permitted maximum, not only shows that states are heavily indebted but also that there is a great deal of too much private wealth present, which on the one hand is searching for investment and on the other hand exerts political influence to further increase debt! If debt was cancelled or even only halted, investment possibilities and return on investment would be gone. In a national and global economy, where real investment possibilities in relation to investment and assets in search of yields become less and less, this is a more disastrous and distorted situation. Debt is necessary in order to provide investment for assets, here the systemic tables have literally been turned. As the debtors were desperately at times seeking creditors in the post-war years, today creditors are more desperately seeking debtors—thus enforcing the strategies privatization, globalization and speculation. The euro states throw themselves here into the breach for the wealthy making themselves available as courageous debtors in the system. That will naturally not go well for too long for two mathematical reasons:

1. From a certain threshold, perhaps not at 180% and also not at 260%, but probably at the latest at 300–450% (100–150% per sector), economies are so heavily indebted that it results in insolvency in one or several sectors, or debt relief and the accompanying creditor wealth loss, the assets are in any case destroyed. Therefore it would be better, also for the well-to-do, if financial assets were specifically curbed by taxes and re-dimensioned before ending in crisis-related uncontrolled destruction. When speaking about a "debt cap," its twin sister wealth cap should also be included in the discussion, for the sake of honesty.
2. If financial wealth is as big as GDP, a return on assets of 10% means that one tenth of national income flows as "private capital tax" to the wealthy. If financial wealth accounts for 3.1 times GDP, as it does today, it would be almost a third of annual economic output. If financial wealth grows to 10 times the economic output, then the complete national economic cake baked in one year would have to be distributed to the owners of financial wealth, as a private capital tax. Everybody else would come away empty-handed.

The bigger financial wealth is in relation to the national economy, the more difficult it will be to maintain high interest and even just to offset loss in value as a result of inflation. In the case of 100 times, 1% interest would not even be possible, because with it the complete national income would have to be used for debt servicing—all working people would be without an income.

Absurdly, exactly this fact namely when interest on capital is under the rate of inflation, has been commonly termed "financial repression" in the discussion in recent years.[21] The perpetrator-victim spear has been turned by 180 degrees: it is not the expropriation of the general public by the hunger of owners of financial wealth for returns—legitimized by a rentier ideology which equates capital ownership with performance—which is termed "financial repression," but rather the fact that capital returns are lower than currency devaluation. From reading the daily newspapers you get the impression that interest on capital, at least at the rate of inflation, is considered a basic right, which is violated by useless politicians and central bankers. At the same time nobody explains who should then generate this basic right—a universal basic income for the wealthy! You cannot create something out of nothing. Every income must be worked for, if not from the recipient of income him/herself then from others whose effort is partly skimmed off and flows to owners of capital. Remembering that even with financial assets which are five times as big as economic output, interest of 3% would yield a "basic income" for the wealthy to the volume of 15% of economic output. Anyone suggesting a basic universal income of 15% of economic output for those who really require it is defamed as a utopian, pseudo-economist or socialist. "Capital socialism" is de facto what really exists at present—all together for capital.

10.7 Adieu, Return on Investment

A possible way forward would be a downsizing of return on investment towards 1% and later zero. In the case of small or short term savings deposits this trend can already be observed (albeit more due to the politics of the cheap central bank money than the glut of saver's capital). However in the case of sizable assets it is still going in the opposite direction—from 1993 to 2009 the assets of the Forbes 400 grew on average by 10% annually (Valluga AG 2010, p. 13)—10%! What is the reason for this daylight robbery returns on investment, which are economically and in the long term impossible? There are two mechanisms: aggressive redistribution and professional speculation. Thanks to professional asset management and ruthless behavior of institutional investors towards the boards of management of corporations, the value-added profits which other people have generated flow to the shareholders. At the same time the professionals in the asset management business (funds, investment companies, and family offices) know how to use information so well that they achieve double-digit returns on investment. The "small investors"

---

[21]The term can be allegedly traced back to Carmen M. Reinhart & M. Belen Sbrancia, The Liquidation of Government Debt, BIS Working Paper No. 363, November 2011.

are gladly called "plankton" by the financiers. The result of both strategies—disparity is growing.

A solution to the ever increasing unfavorable relationship of financial wealth to the real economy would be the immobilization of "superfluous" assets, so that they no longer face debts and no financial returns accrue. This could take the following form: financial assets are "deposited" in the already described cash accounts, which stay in the ownership of savers and do not represent any claims on the bank, they are literally *deposits*. Only when the saver wants to consciously make his/her deposits available to a credit project (via direct or automatic instructions) is the money deposit transformed into a savings investment and is entered into the bank balance sheet.[22]

In this scenario it would not be the slightest problem if financial assets were five times as big as economic output. Then assets amounting to for example 300% of GDP on current accounts could "redundantly" lounge around, where they exert no investment or return on investment pressure and do not generate debts, while two-fifths of the assets amounting to 200% of GDP enter bank balance sheets and finance investment or consumer loans.

Naturally inflation would be gnawing at the deposits ("financial repression") and somewhat less also at investments which would be earning low interest in the transition period. However the slight asset devaluation for the average citizen is a comparatively slight loss in contrast to the resulting profit in the form of a secured workplace, the tendency towards full employment, high social security and a good life with sufficient work income. The *system error* is that a large part of the population identifies ideologically with a capitalist elite that lives from capital returns and shares their interests, which are against their own material interests. Adversely, the "good life" for all including a large middle class is thereby only feasible if no relevant share of economic income is going to a wealthy minority as private capital tax, as is the case today. As previously seen, for 90% of the population every tenth of a percentage point of interest is a financial loss. The large majority would get a better deal if there was no interest on savings, regardless of whether there is inflation and how high this is. This is perhaps hard to believe for some people, but as we have seen it is easy to recalculate.

Ninety percent of the population would do better if there was no redistributive interest system. The fact that 10% of the population fight for the interest system and defend this with various arguments (risk premium, consumption cut, and lending fee) is explicable by their material interests' situation ("net interest winners"). However it is more difficult to explain that a much larger part of the population deems interest to be justifiable and fair, although it suffers damage and is made poorer as a result—they do not know that they are the "net interest payers" and as a result belong to the losers in the interest system.

---

[22]In the sovereign money system on the liabilities side of the bank balance sheet as savings and on the assets side as sovereign money claim on the central bank. In the current bank money system as savings on the liabilities side of the bank balance sheet (the same as in the sovereign money system) whereas on the assets side as book money claim on the saver.

If "only" 200 % of economic output is granted as loans (to companies and households) and these savings investments received low interest, the large redistribution would continue to persist, however the extent would be kept in check—for example, if interest on savings could be capped to 0.5% or at most 1%, as it was in West Germany until 1967 in the form of the savings basic rate which was legally regulated. Then "only" 1–2% of national income went to the wealthy—still redistribution from the general public to a minority but a lower one and less radical than is the case today. To illustrate the fact that this would still be blatantly unfair, here is a small example calculation: if a person has financial assets of 50,000 USD, then this person would receive an annual income from interest of 500 USD, with a savings interest rate of 1%. An individual with 100 million USD would receive an unemployment annual income of 1 million USD, an individual with 10 billion in the bank (the wealthiest people and families own 50–80 billion USD), receives 200 million USD annually. The interest "creates," even with the lowest interest rates, a gigantic redistribution because income disparity is so enormous.

10.8 From the Risk Premium/Capital Tax to a Meaningful Return on Investment

Alternatively it can be argued that if saving investment received at least 0.5% or 1% interest, this would be an incentive to transform deposits in cash accounts which are not in the bank balance sheet into reportable savings deposits—to invest the money. Interest could be regarded as a risk premium for the share of financial assets which in the case of a bank collapse becomes a part of the insolvency assets and is partially endangered, in contrast to the cash accounts which in the case of insolvency are not endangered at all as they do not belong to the bank. While depositors remain the money owners, investors are the creditors of the bank. However the "risk premium" argument, as explained several times, is devoid of purpose for 90% of "premium recipients" because via their daily purchasing they not only pay for their own risk premium but also for those who do not consume as much and above all have a higher level of savings than they do. This argument in favor of interest does not sustain logical analysis, for 90% of the population risk premium alias savings interest is in the final analysis not an income but a tax on capital.

Another argument against interest as a risk premium is that the risk of loss of savings investments in a common good oriented bank system is close to zero because of the (a) state deposit guarantee, (b) the conservative business model of common good oriented banks and (c) the increased equity capital requirements (see next chapter). For zero risk there is also no risk premium, based on the "old" logic.

Savings interest gravitating close to zero is also justified by the ever stricter "competition" of financial assets for the "supply" of savings investment. If only every second, third or fifth euro gets a chance, because only a smaller amount of financial assets are required for credit financing, the downright decline of financial returns on investment is in line with market demand. There is one "consolation," savings investments, although not earning interest, have big advantages for savers which are today perhaps not yet appreciated in their full depth and scope. They benefit others; enable investments and the creation of workplaces, which is of economic benefit to everybody.

Financial returns on investment are replaced by a system benefit and meaningful returns on investment, which perhaps may sound like dreams of the future for some people, but they are components of a paradigm change—this will be described in more detail in the following chapter with the "triple skyline" and as a result will become perhaps more plausible than it would initially appear.

10.8.1 A Hoarding Ban for Cash Millions

Finally some will ask what the incentive would be to deposit cash in the bank against hoarding it in a pillow or in the bedroom safe. Apart from the physical impossibility of stuffing 10 million euro in a pillow or a billion in a basement safe, for a start it would economically not matter whether the private cash disposal sites are at home or in the bank. The only difference would be with increased hoarding at home the issued cash supply would have to be increased, which could be addressed by banning cash hoarding, which was at least the case in history (the more so as there was only cash and no book money) (Huber and Robertson 2008, p. 72). An element of money as a "public good" is that over a certain threshold (of allowed cash money) it must either be used for consumption or deposited at a bank to efficiently use the cash in circulation—a "common" good used by those who actually require it at that moment. (As seen in Chap. 2, the supply of cash in the Eurozone amounts to 950 billion euro or only 10% of economic performance). Similarly, the park bench is not available for everybody who is *not* currently using it. It is only possible for citizens to "possess" the bank, but not to own it and exclude others from its use. In this way private ownership with regard to the use of the public property "banknote" and "hard cash" could be regulated.

References

Bank for International Settlements. 2011. *The real effects of debt.* BIS working papers 352, von Stephen G. Cecchetti, M.S. Mohanty und Fabrizio Zampolli, September 2011.

Boston Consulting Group. 2011. *Back to Mesopotamia? The looming threat of debt restructuring.* Studie von David Rhodes und Daniel Stelter, London-Berlin.

Boston Consulting Group. 2013. *Global wealth 2013.* Maintaining momentum in a complex world, Boston.

Credit Suisse Researche Institute. 2012. *Global wealth report 2012*, Zürich.

Creutz, Helmut (2008): *Die 29 Irrtümer rund ums Geld*, Signum Wirtschaftsverlag, Sonderproduktion, Vienna.

References

Finance Watch (2013): *Europe's banking trilemma: Why banking reform is essential for a successful Banking union*, verfasst von Duncan Lindo und Katarzyna Hanula-Bobbitt, Brüssel, September 2013.

German Federation of Trade Unions/Deutscher Gewerkschaftsbund (2013): *Auch Trennbanken können gefährlich sein*, Klartext 13/5 April 2013.

Huber, Joseph/Robertson, James (2008): *Geldschöpfung in öffentlicher Hand. Weg zu einer gerechten Geldordnung im Informationszeitalter*, Verlag für Sozialökonomie, Kiel.

Klein, Michael (2008): *Bankier der Barmherzigkeit: Friedrich Wilhelm Raiffeisen. Das Leben des Genossenschaftsgründers in Texten und Bildern*, Sonder-Edition für Mit.Einander NÖ, Aussaat Verlag, Neukirchen-Vluyn.

Mckinsey Global Institute. 2013. *Financial globalization: Retreat or reset? Global capital markets 2013*, New York, March 2013.

Otte, Max (2013): *Wie die Staaten aus dem Würgegriff der Finanzmärkte herauskommen*, opinion piece, Format 24/2013.

Stiglitz, Joseph (2012): *Der Preis der Ungleichheit. Wie die Spaltung der Gesellschaft unsere Zukunft bedroht*, Siedler, München.

Valluga AG (2010): *D.A.CH.-Vermögensreport 2010*, Vaduz.

Zeise, Lucas (2012): *Geld – der vertrackte Kern des Kapitalismus: Versuch über die politische Ökonomie des Finanzsektors*, 3rd revised edition, PapyRossa, Köln.

Chapter 11
EU and Global Financial Supervision

Abstract This chapter proposes that every market level should be equipped with corresponding financial supervision. Today, there is still no such supervision on a global scale, although financial markets have been liberalized globally within the World Trade Organization WTO and other trade and investment agreements. Furthermore before the onset of the 2008 financial crisis, there was also not even a supervisory authority at EU level. Within the aftermath of the crisis, three authorities have been established in the EU, however they are toothless. They cannot split up banks that are too big to fail nor will they check new financial products prior to launching nor can they apply ambitious capital requirements for the financial dinosaurs. Additionally, a supervisory instance on a global scale is proposed which could also coordinate international tax policies as already proposed by other authors. Furthermore, an Economic Coordination Council at the United Nations could round off the new picture of global governance.

> *There is no evidence that the sharp rise in the size and complexity of the financial system which has taken place in the rich developed world in the last 20 years has ensured increased economic growth or stability, and it is more than likely that the financial sector has siphoned off surpluses from the real economy instead of creating values itself for the economy. We have to radically question some of the assumptions of the past thirty years and also contemplate radical political measures.*
> Adair Turner (Admati and Hellwig 2013, p. 345)

In Chap. 7, I argued that the EU financial supervisory body, in a consistent manner, should have been present at the start of the single financial market and which core tasks it should have had. The fact that governments deliberately refrained from doing so is a clear sign of the lack of democracy in the EU, in general and in particular with regard to the monetary system, which is the reason for this book. After the big crash in 2008 there was a slight movement in the matter, at a superficial level. In 2009 three supervisory authorities were founded, one for banks in London (Europan Banking Authority, EBA), one for insurance companies in Paris (European Securities and Markets Authority, ESMA) and one for stock exchanges in Frankfurt (European Insurance and Occupational Pensions Authority, EIOPA). In addition the European Systemic Risk Board (ESRB) was also established. This sudden institutional establishment fervor is a clear admission of the previous failures; however the same mistakes are being made in diluted form, the three authorities are toothless. The London supervisory authority was a complete flop, it will not be supervising the banks but rather the ECB will be doing so, although this creates a conflict of interest and a "Chinese Wall" between the monetary policy department and those involved in bank supervision. The Systemic Risk Board was in contrast splendidly overstaffed, with more than 60 members certainly having lots of fun trying to find a common position. "The new EU institutions were nothing more than a coordination committee which should take action in the event of conflicts (…) they are in any case not an EU-wide financial supervisory authority," writes Lucas Zeise (Zeise 2012, p. 204). The financial sociologist Helge Peukert from Erfurt comments, "There are neither uniform global nor European supervisory bodies with national intervention rights" (Peukert 2012, p. 549).

The completion of the regulation failure of EU institutions is becoming evident with the developing banking union. The failure consists of the fact that the systemically important banks, which were bred along with the EU financial single market, will be "supervised" rather than being split up. According to the latest plans of the banking union, in contrast to the "era prior to 2008" only bank bailouts and recapitalization with taxpayer's money are now included in the law. This is even doubled, once with tax money from the states where the insolvent giant banks originate from and should this be insufficient, additionally with tax money from all other euro states via the ESM. This is quite surprising considering that after the first bailout in the aftermath of the Lehman Brothers collapse; the mantra stated that a bank would never ever be bailed out with tax money again. Five years later EU law stipulates the tax payer's legal liability for insolvent systemically important banks. Jeroen Dijsselbloem, Chief of the Euro Group explains it as follows, "If a bank wants direct capital injection from the ESM, then it must fulfill a series of very strict conditions. One of these conditions is: the bank must first have involved all it shareholders and creditors in the losses."[1] This statement is more than downright preposterous. In a (real) liberal market economy the owners (shareholders) and creditors bear the losses entirely themselves in the event of insolvency. In 2009 it was solemnly pledged that this would be rapidly restored after the knock out of the market economy in the form of state bank bailout. This is now valid as a "very strict condition" for future state bank bailouts, if the owners and credits are "involved" in the losses and with this the EU is carrying out a conscious departure from the market economy and replaces it by an authoritarian state oligopolistic capitalism as an economic model. Along the same lines one could for the future consider a "very strict condition" for constitutional amendments by governments whereby the population must be consulted beforehand instead of leaving the decision to the government itself. The reinterpretation of all values is forging ahead.

---

[1] Interview Wir müssen mehr Klartext reden in *Handelsblatt*, 22 November 2013.

The picture becomes "more coherent" if we read what Lucas Zeise wrote about the fact that the plan for the banking union originates from the same person and lobby responsible for the single financial market, namely Josef Ackermann and the Institute for International Finance IIF (Zeise 2012, p. 209). Once again the EU proves itself not to be a project for its citizens or at least for their benefit but rather as the politic lever of the monetary industry. Zeise then comes to the resigned conclusion that "the interests of the decision-making figures in our society are such that an effective regulation of the finance section is currently politically impossible" (Zeise 2012, p. 223). Pre-democracy—it is therefore high time that the sovereign got hold of a better lever than voting for a party every four or five years. It is high time that we had democratic monetary and economic conventions.

11.1 EU Financial Supervision with an Edge

If a powerful and functioning EU financial supervisory authority is equipped with logical expertise, not from the Josef Ackerman and the systemically important bank association perspective but rather from the perspective of critical reason and common sense, then the following tasks and areas of responsibilities are literally a must:

i. splitting up of systemically important financial institutions,
ii. closing or strict regulation of shadow banking activities,
iii. market admission approval for new financial products,
iv. stricter equity capital requirements,
v. rules for funds and capital investment companies.

11.1.1 Splitting up System Relevant Banks

This matter was previously mentioned, with the EU financial supervisory body being the suitable institution for splitting up the banks. The German federal government in particular is against a powerful supervisory body at the ECB in order to protect the Deutsche Bank and the Commerzbank. It would be better to ask the sovereign instead of allowing the Schäuble-Merkel tandem decide this matter. This has probably less sympathy with the national champions than the closely associated head of government. One can still surely discuss about the threshold, however the thirty billion threshold is one which the EU proposes itself. Larger banks are evidently so "systemically important" that national supervision is no longer sufficient.

In order not to present the smaller EU Banks with competitive disadvantages compared to larger foreign banks, the single financial market would have to be protected against larger banks from outside the EU. This is a legitimate and non-discriminative regulation comparable to environmental, labor and tax regulations, which are valid for all domestic and foreign companies operating in the single market.

It is often argued that the USA could react against these "protectionist" measures with "counter-protectionism" and retaliation measures. On the one hand this is not ensured and it remains to be seen whether the US government will punish the EU sovereigns for not granting US banks in the EU more liberties than domestic banks. Perhaps even the opposite effect will occur, namely the EU sovereign's self-confidence will encourage the US government or even better still the US sovereign to do the same as the EU—to split up their banks. The liquidation practice indicates this, as barely 40 banks were closed in the EU up to December 2013, in the USA 488 were closed.[2] There are also no known surveys stating that US citizens are ardent fans of J.P. Morgan, Bank of America or Citigroup. In any case potential sensitivity of a trading partner should not represent an obstacle for the EU regulation of its own single market in compliance with the values and priorities of its sovereign. Democracy comes before trading interests.

However let us consider the "worst case" scenario—the USA over-reacts and closes off the US market for EU banks. Would that be the end of the world? Hardly, just as little as the US banks entry to the EU single market provided an improvement in financial services and the banking business, it was quite the opposite, is it just as necessary for the basic supply of bank and financial services for US citizens to be implemented by EU banks on US soil. And if so, then nobody should deprive the USA of its right to voluntarily refuse this.

Consequently the EU should revise the WTO General Agreement on Trade in Services which regulates free trade in financial services. Although this was ratified by the parliaments under international law, the sovereigns would however not be sovereigns if they could not correct the decisions of their representatives. Thinking one step further the unfair globalization of governments and parliaments for the benefit of corporations could be altered by the rightful sovereigns step by step to a globalization of people and their values. The first step in this direction, the limiting of the size and power of corporations would be a high point of democracy.

If the EU as the first economic area dares to limit the size of banks, other democracies will also take heart from this with regard to taking the first step. The freedom of the first sovereign will trigger the freedom of the next.

11.1.2 Closing or Strict Regulation of Shadow Banking Activities

According to estimates by the Financial Stability Board (FSB), a quarter of all financial transactions worldwide are carried out "in the shadows" bypassing bank balance sheets. These are various financial companies such as money market, hedge and private equity funds in addition to "vehicles" such as "conduits" or "special purpose vehicles" (SPV), whose "special purpose" is for example to purchase

---

[2] www.start-trading.de/liste-der-pleitebanken-usa

11.1 EU Financial Supervision with an Edge

incredible loan packages from banks who own these. The FSB defines shadow banking as "the system of credit intermediation that involves entities and activities outside the regular banking system" (European Commission 2012, p. 3). In the USA the share of bank transactions which takes place within the shadow banking system is considered to be the same as the number of transactions which take place within the regular banking system. In the 24 investigated industrial countries, it was found that on average the shadow banking business is half as big as the sum of all bank assets. The shadow banking "sector leader" with the highest dark business in relation to its economic output is Hongkong (520%), followed by the Netherlands (490%), Great Britain (370%), Singapore (260%) and Switzerland (210%). In 2011 shadow banking business worldwide reached a record high with 67 trillion euro and was with this equally as big as world economic performance. Ten years previously this volume was still at 26 trillion euros (Financial Stability Board 2012).

In the first five years after the crisis there was no regulation impact and I ask the question whether the absence of the will to supervise and regulate the banks can be made more clearly than by the fact that the currently valid balance sheet regulations for credit institutions do not even stipulate that they must include all their activities in their balance sheet.

From "forgetting" of the EU financial supervision when establishing the single financial market, to the missing size limit for banks, the state bailout of systemically important financial institutions, the legally determined liability of the tax payers for super banks to the super lax equity capital and balance sheet regulations—it must be the *politically* systemically important financial institutions which control the government and determine the laws, otherwise something like this could not happen. No reasonable legislator with a heart and mind could bear the responsibility for the fact that half the banking business is not even included in the balance sheet. He must be prevented by massive means from using his common sense, intelligence and conscience from doing what is appropriate and right and instead of this maintaining the giant banking black market business within the legal realm.

The Waldviertel regional shoe manufacturer Heini Staudinger is being pursued by the Austrian Financial Market Authority because he finances his photovoltaic systems with customer loans amounting to approximately three million euro.[3] 67 trillion in the shadows are currently being "researched" by the FSB. Hedge funds, with a volume of 100 billion euro must be registered in the EU according to the AIFM directive from 2011, private equity funds not until there is an amassed capital of half a billion. The proportions here are completely out of sync.

A powerful supervisory body must, after amending the accounting regulations, shut down all bank transactions outside of the balance sheet and banks which carry out such transactions and do not include them in their balance sheet must incur stiff fines or have their licenses revoked.

We could indeed also say that particularly dangerous experiments in the chemical industry are not subject to the chemicals act, because … well, the reasoning

---

[3] www.w4tler.at/geaneu/fma-vs-gea/pressemeldungen

here is really difficult! Or that income from certain types of economic activity does not need to be declared to the tax office ....

Not to be duly unfair, but there appears to be some movement in the matter. The EU Commission publicized a "green paper" in 2012 on the subject of shadow banking, nevertheless it was still five years after the Lehman Brothers collapse. However there is a high level of understanding for shadow banking evident in this green paper—"Shadow banking performs important functions in the financial system (...) Shadow banking activities can constitute a useful part of the financial system" (European Commission 2012, p. 2 und 5). The G20 Financial Stability Forum is still researching and collecting data without any sense of haste and curiosity—in the area where there is no invasion of privacy but rather where it would have been highly necessary, the authorities looked the other way. Nevertheless it envisages the first regulations for the near future ....we are dying of curiosity!

11.1.3 Market Admission Approval for New Financial Products

Economic freedom can be restricted to limit the risk for the general public, this is the case everywhere. For example pharmaceutical companies cannot simply launch new medicines on the market and promote these. New chemicals in the EU are subject to a registration, appraisal, and authorization and restriction process (REACH) before being brought into circulation.[4] Every car must be checked by the TÜV (Technical Inspection Agency) not only before its use in public transport areas but also at regular intervals. Life endangering risk products such as weapons are furthermore subject to personal assessment checks. Ironically only "financial weapons of mass destruction" are free of all regulation. New financial products must neither be ethical nor comply with system stability criteria or any other requirements for that matter.

That is just as absurd as legislators trusting in the fact that only "useful" weapons are created and are used "responsibly" and due to this any form of regulation is waivered. People are not directly harmed by financial weapons,[5] however more so indirectly. A simple example is the speculation with regard to rising foodstuff prices which can lead to an increase in starvation and famine (Oxfam Germany 2012). Another example are real estate loan derivatives—does it make sense for a

---

[4]However this—anyway weak—regulation is in (deregulation) danger by TTIP because the USA has lower regulation standards and in TTIP the "mutual recognition of standards" is included. US companies would have access to the EU single market by adhering to US standards.

[5]In August 2013 the media reported that a 21 year old intern of a US investment bank worked himself to death. The reports stated that not only night shifts until 3am were usual but also magic roundabouts, which means that taxi drivers were waiting outside the front door while the people were showering and changing clothes for the next shift. With the same lack of empathy that investment bankers show for themselves and their bodies, investment banking and the professional industry of making more money out of money impacts other people, all of society and the environment.

mortgage bank which has granted a real estate loan to sell this to an investment bank, which then bundles loans with various creditworthiness to form a "CDO" (collateralized debt obligation) which is then "graded" by a rating agency to subsequently sell it on to investors, who never set their eyes on the persons who took out the loan and *can* therefore not at all estimate their "creditworthiness"—they are subject to the grading of the rating agency, whose employees know the borrowers just as much and subsequently *cannot* at all estimate the risk! Does that make sense? As we have seen, these derivatives caused gigantic economic and human damage because all economic and commercial rationality, all professional liability and all human sense of responsibility and empathy got lost in this "structural irresponsibility" system (Honegger et al 2010). This consists of the mortgage bank (taking a risk and selling), the investment bank (exponentiation of the risk), the rating agency (incorrectly classifying the risk and thereby misleading millions), brokers (general public funds or banks, which ill-advise public authorities) investors (avaricious purchase of products whose risk they can by no means evaluate) und the refurbishers (the tax payers). Sometimes it is also a hedge fund with a return on investment chain which already knows that it will go wrong and even bets on the price collapse and earns a fortune on the idiots.

A financial market supervisory body which promotes a "system of responsibility" would plainly not allow such derivatives onto the market. Responsibility could mean that the mortgage bank must maintain the mortgage on its own books because (a) it is the instance which has generated the risk and (b) the instance which can best evaluate the risk and therefore ultimately earns its bread and butter with it. As a result it would act accordingly cautiously when lending and the probability of a bubble would sink to close to zero. The EU legislators took action on this matter after 2008, but they have also impressively demonstrated their failure in this matter. According to the EU regulation, 95% of loans can still be sold.[6] The collection of illusory regulations is richer by one more regulation. This example also speaks in favor of a direct vote by the sovereign. It could commission a EU financial supervisory authority, with extensive powers, to check financial products, to evaluate them and only to authorize them after passing a system-risk evaluation, which is the procedure demanded by a series of organisations and experts, ranging from Attac to Wilfried Stadler (Stadler 2011, pp. 145–146).

Similar to the exclusion of hypertrophic banks, an assertive EU financial supervisory body can prevent access to the EU single market for financial products from non member states, which are not authorized in the EU. The free movement of capital is no end in itself let alone sacrosanct, but is an economic policy instrument, whose objectives it serves for example financial stability. The import of hazardous financial waste represents a massive danger for financial stability and it must therefore be possible to selectively restrict the free movement of capital.

---

[6]Directive 2009/111/EC ("CRD II"). In June 2013 the CRD IV package replaced CRD I, II and III.

In the Bretton Woods system this was common sense and also within the EEC, as Jörg Huffschmid writes, "the time at the end of the 1960s and the start of the 1970s was dominated by increased movement of capital controls by member states"—"Movement of capital controls contributed to the protection of the post-war development in individual countries against disruptive movement of capital" (Huffschmid 1999, p. 109). It was not until the 1990s that the doctrine of undifferentiated free movement of capital was enforced. However the logic of specific differentiation of cooperation with non-member states also functions in other policy sectors. In this way the EU for example fundamentally cooperates with the USA with regard to the extradition of suspected criminals.[7] However no extradition takes place, where the USA does not share fundamental values which are valid in the EU or violate these values for example if the extradited person is threatened with the death penalty or an unfair trial for example before a military court. This is a specific and differentiated restriction to cooperation in police matters. Similarly conditions must be prescribed to the free movement of capital which is subsequently subject to restrictions should they not be complied with. Currently the EU Lisbon Treaty apodictically stipulates that "all restrictions on the movement of capital between Member States and between Member States and third countries shall be prohibited."[8] Exceptions are only permitted if "movements of capital to or from third countries cause, or threaten to cause, serious difficulties for the operation of economic and monetary union," and even in this case only "for a period not exceeding six months if such measures are strictly necessary." A long-term import ban for "financial weapons of mass destruction" is illegal according to the Lisbon Treaty. It is certainly high time that the sovereigns of the EU member states decide on a more reasonable treaty basis here, which will offer them a larger scope within the realm of monetary, financial, taxation and trade policy. Democratic monetary conventions are good instances for the disclosure and correction of weak points and undemocratic content of the current EU treaties.

11.1.4 Stricter Equity Capital Requirements

The topic of equity capital is one of the few topics which receives relatively broad media attention, at least the bank bailouts first and foremost comprising of "recapitalizations" from "under capitalization" that is money institutions equipped with too little equity capital. The issue at hand is how much own financial wealth (equity capital) must a bank provide in relation to its lending business. Equity capital is on the liabilities side of the bank balance sheet, and is a liability due to the fact that it is in substance a "claim" by the owners on the bank. There are three

---

[7]Resolution 2009/820/GASP (Common Foreign and Security Policy) of the commission dated 23 October 2009 on the conclusion of an agreement on behalf of the EU on extradition between the EU and the USA and the agreement on law enforcement between the EU and the USA.

[8]Art. 63 Treaty on the functioning of the European Union (TFEU).

11.1 EU Financial Supervision with an Edge

things which are unsettling about the current rules including their revision in recent years.

1. On the one hand it is unclear with regard to financial assets how much they are actually worth. In short, there are two possible assessment approaches: the conservative lowest value principle according to the German Commercial Code[9] and the modern "mark-to-market" procedure, according to which the current market price of an asset for example a security is used in the evaluation calculation of assets. It is not difficult to guess that this latter principle leads to high fluctuations in assets and therefore equity capital of the banks, as in times of turbulent financial markets the asset prices are subject to severe appreciation and devaluation thereby resulting in variable levels of equity capital. Wilfried Stadler describes the problem as follows, "market value-related increase in the value of investments triggered apparent increases in equity capital items. This facilitated in the usual ratios of equity capital to balance sheet total an extension of the leeway for debt without having been accompanied by the materialized value increase. In a long pro-cyclical market movement it caused, gauged on real, liable equity capital, excessive increases of external funds leverage and to the emergence of dangerous debt bubbles. The inflation of the balance sheet sums in relation to an even thinner cover of real equity capital led to an all the more intense consumption of equity capital during the crisis" (Stadler 2011, p. 142). If balancing of accounts was implemented according to the lowest value principle, the banks would not be able to extend more loans only on the basis that the securities they hold have increased in price.
2. The rules of Basel II and III, which are implemented in the EU with the regulation regarding equity capital requirements (Capital Requirement Directive—CRD IV) stipulate that the various asset items, depending on their risk, must be covered by equity capital set at varying levels. Assets which are classified as low risk for example AAA rated securities are covered with lower capital, loans to small and medium-sized enterprises and securities with lower rating must be covered with relevantly more equity capital. The problem is that the ratings are anything but reliable but lead to very different equity capital requirements. In 2009 for example the Deutsche Bank had a policy-compliant equity capital level of 10.9%, while its equity capital gauged on its lending business amounted to just about 1.8% (Sinn 2009, p. 160). At the end of 2011 the values were 14% and 2.5%, with the latter being only 2.1% at the end of 2013 (Admati and Hellwig 2013, p. 272).[10] Lehman Brothers slid into bankruptcy with a Basel-compliant equity capital ratio of 11% (Huber 2013, p. 37). In the light of this discrepancy between "official" (risk-weighted) and actual (pro rata) equity capital ratio it does not sound reassuring to hear the Bundesbank analysis at the end of 2013: "The results of these new requirements can in the meantime be very clearly measured in figures. Thus since the Lehmann collapse for instance the core capital ratio of the 12 largest internationally active German banks has risen

---

[9] HGB (German Commercial Code) §253, Section 3 und 4.

[10] *Die Welt*, 22 December 2013.

from 8.7% to 15.3%."[11] In contrast according to Helge Peukert, "the relevant non-weighted balance sheet equity capital ratio of significant German institutes was and is in mid-2011 still to a large extent under two percent" (Peukert 2012, p. 391). Risk weightings are so dangerous because risks (a) change and (b) cannot be reliably evaluated, which is what the current procedure suggests. Government bonds are a notorious vulnerability, as they are considered to be fail-proof and must therefore not be covered with equity capital at all, although in the past there was a high incidence of national insolvency—Germany and France 8 times each, 7 times in Austria, 5 times in Greece and 13 times in Spain (Reinhart and Rogoff 2008, p. 32). In 2012 in the Eurozone the first debt relief took place in the case of Greece and there was therefore a failure of government bonds, it was certainly only the first case (Cf. Felber 2012).

3. Various experts such as Martin Hellwig, Anat Admati, Wilfried Stadler or Helge Peukert therefore demand that solely the "balance sheet" equity capital ratio should be applicable. Basel III actually includes for the first time, in addition to risk-weighted equity capital ratio of a lean 7% from 2018 onwards, an actual minimum equity capital ratio of 3%, which must be gauged on the total and not weighted lending business—"Leverage Ratio." Yes that was correct, 3%! Also after the complete implementation of Basel III in 2019, which is already much too late to prevent further crises, banks may finance up to 97% of their lending business via debt. With an equity capital of 3% of their balance sheet volume, a value loss in assets of 3% would drain total equity capital, which is indeed not a wall of defense against the next crisis. "That Basel would be so weak was the result of an intensive lobbying campaign carried out by the banks against every noteworthy tightening of regulations. "This campaign is still ongoing," according to Admati and Hellwig (Admati and Hellwig 2013, p. 157). In the nineteenth century when the owners were still completely liable for bank losses, equity capital ratios of 40–50% were not unusual. Around 1900 there were still in the region of 20–30% in many countries, before the onset of sustained descent (Admati and Hellwig 2013, p. 275). This is the reason why not only a few authors are in favor of clearly higher equity capital ratios than those stipulated in Basel III. The former chief economist of the IMF Simon Johnson proposes 15–25%; the financial market theorist Eugene Fama proposes a point-blank 25% ratio.[12] Martin Hellwig and Anat Admati recommend 20–30% and have filled a complete book with arguments in favor of this (Admati and Hellwig 2013, p. 276). In "Post Bailout Financial System," Helge Peukert from the University of Erfurt advocates a "balance sheet unweighted core equity capital" of 30% (Peukert 2013, p. 391). The former CEO of Investkredit Wilfried Stadler deems "more than 10% equity capital in the unweighted balance sheet total" appropriate (Stadler 2011, p. 159). While such levels for systemically important financial

---

[11]German Bundesbank: *Fünf Jahre nach Lehmann. Wie eine Bankeninsolvenz die Bankenwelt verändert*, 18 September 2013.

[12]*The New York Times*, 14 January 2010; *Frankfurter Allgemeine Zeitung*, 17 October 2013.

giants appear to be utopian, at the end of 2013 large US banks were at 4.3% and the rest of the world at 3.9%,[13] local cooperative banks have almost always been fulfilling these requirements. In Austria equity capital ratios of 15–30% in the primary sector of the Raiffeisen and Volksbank Association are not seldom. Switzerland proves that there is also more leeway for the large banks: so that the taxpayer does not have to take on owner obligations against his will again in the future, the two financial giants UBS and Credit Suisse must hold 19% in future. Since 2015 large banks in Denmark must have minimum equity capital ratios of eleven to 13.5% depending on their level of system relevance.[14]

An EU financial supervisory authority could increase system stability and minimize the risk of a chain reaction by stipulating (a) a return to the lowest value principle, (b) the task of risk weighting in the equity capital securitization requirements as well as (c) equity capital ratios between 20% and 30%. This would disrupt the dividend payout orgies of banks for a longer period of time and as argued above, banks are in the opinion of the author not there for distributing profits. After so many years of instability, permanent crisis and record dividends, it is now the turn of security and system stability. This opinion is also shared by Admati and Hellwig, "Profit payouts are a means by which banks increase their debt (…) the core objectives of bank regulation and supervision must be to safeguard the security and solidarity of the financial system in the interest of the public" (Admati and Hellwig 2013, p. 268 und 336).

11.1.5 *Rules for Funds and Capital Investment Companies*

A small part of the shadow banking system deserves special attention—private equity funds and hedge funds, both of which have caused a lot of commotion and discussion in recent years. Hedge funds are specialized in the asset management of extremely wealthy individuals, who on the one hand can afford higher risk than annuity savers and on the other hand over a long-term average achieve a higher than average return on investment. In the period from 1994 to 2007 this amounted to 11.1% annually after fees.[15] Small savers can only dream of such returns on investment. Hedge funds produce results in propagating the wealth of individuals, who already belong to the wealthiest class and possess more wealth than they require, by propagating their wealth at a faster rate than the wealth of all others. Hedge fund managers earn the highest income worldwide for this "service." In 2009 25 of the most successful hedge fund managers pocketed 25.3 billion US dollars.[16]

---

[13] *Frankfurter Allgemeine Zeitung*, 5 November 2013.
[14] *Frankfurter Allgemeine Zeitung*, 11 October 2013.
[15] *Emagazine der Credite Suisse*, 31 March 2008.
[16] *Süddeutsche Zeitung*, 7 April 2010.

John Paulson earned the highest income of all times in 2010 with believe it or not 5 billion US dollars.[17]

Hedge fund strategies are partly very highly questionable, they can speculate on rising commodity prices, on corporation or even state bankruptcy, on the basis of good information against the market or with complex and systemically risky derivatives. Criticism with regard to the practices and influence of hedge fund managers is always played down with the reference to their low volume of only about 2 trillion US dollars. However this is only the amassed capital, hedge fund managers move far bigger volumes with credits and derivatives. The most illustrative example for this is the previously mentioned example of LTCM fund, which with just under 5 billion US dollars equity capital took out bank loans to the value of 125 billion and formed derivative items of 1.25 trillion US dollars (Lowenstein 2000, p. 191).

Due to public pressure and after the EU parliament had begged the Commission for several years to take regulatory actions—the initiative monopoly for laws lies in the hands of the Commission—it reacted with a shameful regulation proposal. The AIFM Directive (for Alternative Investment Fund *Managers*), as its name states, regulates not "alternative investment funds" but their managers. This directive is a further illusory regulatory product in order to suggest to the EU population that "all markets, products and participants" are regulated, as the G20 announced at its first meeting after the 2008 crash (G20 2008, p. 3). However one element of the directive is worse than the next:

- If a manager is authorized in one EU country, he can also manage funds in all other EU member states. It would appear that Great Britain is generously authorized and those with authorization may work in the whole of the EU.
- Managers from non-EU states are not registered and therefore fully unregulated funds can also enter the EU market.
- Funds with a volume of up to 100 million euros are excluded from regulation—if they take out loans, they are unregulated up to an amount of 500 million euros: a legal reward for leveraging!
- Equity capital of 300,000 euros or approx. 0.1% is stipulated for a fund volume of up to 250 million euros—the regulators have surpassed themselves!
- Limitations to manager salaries are not planned (European Parliament and European Council 2012).

This is already a considerable list of poor regulatory performance; the largest weaknesses in the directive are however in the fact that the funds themselves are hardly regulated and with this the large problems are not addressed. An effective regulation of funds could contain the following measures:

- A credit raising ban: zero "leverage" or investments and transactions only with equity capital—then no minimum equity capital ratio is required;
- Full transparency with regard to ownership structure, management and all investments.

---

[17] *The Wall Street Journal*, 28 January 2011.

- A ban on hostile takeovers of companies;
- Uniform taxation of all funds—capital income must be taxed at a higher rate than labor income—in the case of funds which do not come from the EU, reporting obligations regarding all tax-relevant information (see Chap. 7);
- Limiting of bonuses: for example maximum 50% of fixed income and not only for good financial performance but rather for good ethical performance—measured with an obligatory common good balance sheet.

Funds would still move within the old paradigm of a capitalistic market economy with these regulations. In the next chapter the end of all capital income will be proposed and with this the logic of funds would radically change, they would no longer create monetary return on investment pressure, but would support meaningful economic activity and an ethical return on investment. Bonuses would be connected to ethical key performance indicators and customer's money would be invested according to the criteria of sense, value and ethics.

11.2 Global Financial Supervision

Being strictly logical there are two sensible constellations as to how global financial transactions and their supervision could be politically organized:

Option 1: International markets are created by a series of international treaties as is currently the case—from the EU Treaty (free movement of capital to non-member states) to the WTO Services Agreement GATS and in addition the special WTO Financial Services Agreement to TTIP, which is currently being negotiated. In this case a global regulation and supervision of these transactions is logically required. Markets devoid of regulations and supervision do not function and create damage.

Option 2: No international markets are created and consequently no global regulation, supervision and controls are also required—the national and for example EU-wide rules and institutions are sufficient for national or continental markets.

Both variants are logical and justifiable. However at present there is a gaping open contradiction between globalized markets on the one hand (option 1) and the total lack of global regulation and supervision on the other hand (option 2). Global economic freedom and markets are not faced with any global control whatsoever which is an inacceptable disparity. In addition nothing has changed in this respect since the 2008 crisis. The minimum which should now happen is the expansion of the EU supervisory body by a similarly authorized global institution. As we have however seen, the political elite refuse to implement this minimum cohesion. At present the EU supervisory bodies are just doing some catching up with reluctance, in a diluted form and with teething problems.

Therefore in the current situation *only* the sovereigns could oblige their governments to create a global regulation and supervisory structure. However if we tread the direct democratic path, the sovereigns must also be able to decide on both fundamental options—either to continue following the globalization path and establishing a global regulatory body (variant 1) or revoking of the globalizing of financial markets and discontinuing WTO, TTP, TTIP or CETA negotiations (variant 2). These alternatives are at least for the EU zone so plausible that they have also been brought to paper by Deutsche Bank Research—"As could be observed, financial institutes live globally, but die nationally. Consequently we have a choice between either maintaining an integrated financial single market in the EU, and creating a corresponding supervisory framework at EU level—or allowing the re-fragmentation of European financial markets" (Deutsche Bank Research 2011, p. 1).

In a democratically clean approach the sovereigns would have to be asked whether they want to decide in favor of a completely globalized variant or against global financial markets. In the second case the WTO agreements which the parliaments decided on without the consent of the sovereign would have to be cancelled. Should the sovereign decide in favor of international financial markets, governments are obliged to establish global supervisory bodies. Concrete proposals are already in existence with regard to these. The previously mentioned 10-strong working group of Joseph Stiglitz[18] has compiled an extensive list of regulations for the global financial system on behalf of the United Nations General Assembly, which were however not even ignored by most governments. Amongst the proposals there is a series of new international institutions on the basis of the same considerations which have been listed here:

- To coordinate the economic policy of UN members the authors propose a Global Economic Coordination Council GECC, which should take care of the cohesion of political objectives and measures of the community of nations. As an initial step, an international panel of experts based on the model of the UN Climate Protection Advisory Council IPCC could be established and could warn at an early stage about global systemic risks of economic, social and ecological nature—a task in which the IMF has spectacularly failed. In the long term the GECC should be positioned at the level of the UN Security Council and General Assembly and also be placed in charge of the IMF and World Bank as well as the WTO, which were established outside the UN system, and formally integrate these institutions into the system. I have been making this proposal since 2006 (Felber 2006, S. 165ff) and am now receiving prominent support with regard to this.
- The report then proposes the establishment of a global financial supervisory authority ("Global Financial Authority.") This should coordinate the various regulation efforts and be equipped with its own skills set and responsibility for example the combating tax evasion and money laundering (United Nations 2009, 96ff). This authority could absorb the Basel Committee (equity capital regulations) as well as IARS (accounting rules) and also the finance stability board FSB, which to date has delivered no convincing results. In this way some ineffective and tenuously legitimized institutions would be done away with again.

---

[18]Experts from Egypt, Barbados, Malaysia, Ecuador and Tanzania were members of the task force.

- Thirdly there is talk of an "International Tax Agreement" (International Tax Compact—ITC), which on the one hand combats detrimental tax practices and tax competition and on the other hand should support poor countries to establish an effective taxation system in order to enhance their national finances and public services (United Nations 2009, p. 84). This could also advance the implementation of "Unitary Taxation" for corporations—this will be dealt with in Chap. 7.
- Finally in the footsteps of the 1971 failed Bretton Woods System, a new world monetary system with a global reserve currency, a global reserve bank and a global reserve union is proposed—this will be dealt with in Chap. 7.

This is not a small number of new supervisory and regulatory bodies. The authors admit this but argue, "While we understand the worries with regard to the increase in international institutions and the hesitation to establish new bodies, the necessity for such a GECC is urgent" (United Nations 2009, p. 87ff). I agree with the experts—it is in fact the globalization of the markets which makes the establishment of international institutions necessary. "Globalization" contains not only economic freedom with new markets but also new institutions to supervise and regulate these markets to assure the responsibility and ethical behavior of business. Additionally in a countermove, as proposed, some ineffective and tenuously legitimized panels could have their mandate democratically revoked. It is enticing to speak of institutional clearing out after all the regulation failure and numerous feigned regulations of recent years.

From the strategic perspective the implementation of the Stiglitz Commission proposals, as with other international agreements, it would not at all be necessary to wait for the participation of all states. Every sovereign would only need to equip his representative with a clear negotiation mandate. If the EU or the USA started, then a large number of other states would follow on immediately—based on experience, it is indeed the EU and the USA which together block the further development of the UN system in terms of mankind's objectives.

Apart from this, the example of direct mandating of governments by their sovereign would probably set a precedent—if the sovereign in some democracies manage to charge their representatives with the co-establishment of a global financial authority and the achievement of a tax justice treaty, then the sovereigns of other states would also perhaps suddenly want this—states which currently do not have the necessary democratic laws or have not even taken the liberty to date to even consider such a step. It would be the starting point towards a democratic globalization.

References

Admati, Anat/Hellwig, Martin (2013): *Des Bankers neue Kleider. Was bei Banken wirklich schiefläuft und was sich ändern muss*, FBV, München.

Deutsche Bank Research. 2011. *Financial supervision in the EU. Incremental progress, success not ensured*, EU Monitor 84, 4 August 2011.

European Commission. 2012. *Green paper shadow banking*, COM(2012) 102 final, Brussels, 19 March 2012.
European Parliament and European Council (2011): Richtlinie 2011/61/EU über die Verwalter alternativer Investmentfonds, 8 June 2011.
Felber, Christian (2006): *50 Vorschläge für eine gerechtere Welt. Gegen Konzernmacht und Kapitalismus*, Deuticke, Vienna.
Felber, Christian (2012): *Retten wir den Euro*, Deuticke, Vienna.
Financial Stability Board. 2012. *Global shadow banking monitoring report*, 45 pages, Basel, 12 November 2012.
G20. 2008. *Declaration of the summit on financial markets and the world economy*, Washington, 15 November 2008.
Honegger, Claudia/Neckel, Sighard/Magnin, Chantal (2010): *Strukturierte Verantwortungslosigkeit. Berichte aus der Bankenwelt*, Suhrkamp, Berlin.
Huber, Joseph (2013): Finanzreformen und Geldreform – Rückbesinnung auf die monetären Grundlagen der Finanzwirtschaft, S. 33–59 in: Verein Monetäre Modernisierung (2013): *Die Vollgeld-Reform. Wie Staatsschulden abgebaut und Finanzkrisen verhindert werden können*, 3rd edition, Edition Zeitpunkt, Solothurn.
Huffschmid, Jörg (1999): *Politische Ökonomie der Finanzmärkte*, VSA-Verlag, Hamburg.
Lowenstein, Roger. 2000. *When genius failed: the rise and fall of long-term capital management*, New York.
Oxfam Germany (2012): *Mit Essen spielt man nicht. Die deutsche Finanzbranche und das Geschäft mit dem Hunger*, brochure, 60 pages, Berlin.
Peukert, Helge (2012): *Die große Finanzmarkt- und Staatsschuldenkrise*, 4th revised edition, Metropolis, Marburg.
Peukert, Helge (2013): *Das Moneyfest. Ursachen und Lösungen der Finanzmarkt- und Staatsschuldenkrise*, Metropolis, Marburg.
Reinhart, Carmen M. and Rogoff, Kenneth S. 2008. *This time is different. A panoramic view of eight centuries of financial crisis*, National Bureau of Economic Research Working Paper No. 13882, Cambridge, March 2008.
Sinn, Hans-Werner (2009): *Kasino-Kapitalismus: Wie es zur Finanzkrise kam, und was jetzt zu tun ist*, Econ, Berlin.
Stadler, Wilfried (2011): *Der Markt hat nicht immer recht. Über die wirklichen Ursachen der Finanzmarktkrise und wie wir die nächste vermeiden können*, Linde Verlag, Vienna.
United Nations. 2009. *Report of the commission of experts of the President of the United Nations General assembly on reforms of the international monetary and financial system*, 140 pages, New York, 21 September 2009.
Zeise, Lucas (2012): *Geld – der vertrackte Kern des Kapitalismus: Versuch über die politische Ökonomie des Finanzsektors*, 3rd revised edition, PapyRossa, Köln.

Chapter 12
Derivatives—Close the Casino

Abstract This chapter is about the breathtaking development of financial derivatives. It shows how they contribute to instability, how much they are concentrated in the hands of very few investment banks and the key role they play in financial alchemy and the casino. "Table by table," alternatives for the current "gaming practices" are proposed. As for shares, local common good exchanges that follow a different logic than capitalistic stock markets are proposed. With regard to government bonds, a concrete proposal has been presented in a previous chapter. Securities, composed of bank loans, are deemed as unnecessary—mortgage banks should bear the risks they create. Commodities are very sensitive both in terms of human rights and ecology—therefore democratic bodies not markets should determine commodity prices. Around these "main tables" of the global financial casino, some general proposals to stabilize and ethically develop the financial system are offered, such as the linkage of voting rights to a minimum holding period of assets.

> *If we want to support financial innovation, we cannot establish regulations which hamper this.*
> Alan Greenspan[1]
>
> *The only useful thing banks have invented in 20 years is the ATM.*
> Paul Volcker[2]

The sector of global financial markets which has by far experienced the most innovations is without a doubt the world of derivatives. Derivatives are commonly bets on future prices of their underlying values such as shares, securities, credits, real estate, commodities and currencies. These bets can be won or lost and if such bets are made based on taking out loans, the profits and losses are correspondingly higher. The "leverage" of derivative bets supported by loans explains the spectacular profits made by hedge funds and the billion incomes earned by their most successful mangers. Derivatives can assume various forms for example bundling of

---

[1] Greenspan, Alan. 1997. Fostering financial innovation. The role of government. In James Dorn, ed., *The future of money in the information age*, Cato Institute, Washington, 1997, 48.
[2] *New York Post*, 13 December 2009.

loans to a bond (CDO) or insurance against credit defaults (CDS). The derivative universe is expanding at the speed of light and is as unclear as it is voluminous—while global economic performance in 2012 amounted to 72 trillion US dollars, the total of all registered derivative contracts in the best available statistics of the Bank for International Settlements constituted 633 trillion US dollars (Bank for International Settlements 2013, p. 1). According to estimates, OTC (over the counter) derivatives which are private to private in nature constitute four fifths of all derivative transactions, one-fifth are carried out on supervised exchanges. In total the derivative transaction volume is therefore ten times as big as the global economy. The incurred items are resold, four to five times on average, so that derivative trading volume amounts to several quadrillions, a size which is hardly imaginable for anybody and soon to amount to 100-times the global GDP.

The largest part of the derivatives cake in the BIS statistics are the interest derivatives (490 trillion US dollars), followed by currency derivatives (67 trillion) and credit default insurances CDS (25 trillion).

The figures make one dizzy along with the gigantic extent in relation to "real" economic performance and their torpedo-like development. At the beginning of the 1990s derivatives did not play any meaningful role but since then they have dominated the global financial casino unlike any other influencing factor. The destabilizing impact which derivatives cause can be documented by an impressive series of examples in the meantime—the tradition-steeped Barings Bank from Great Britain fell victim to the use of financial derivatives as did the French Société Générale or the Francfort-based Metallgesellschaft AG. The Californian District Orange County lost through speculation, as well as Amaranth Hedge Funds, the Bear Sterns investment bank or the Austrian Trade Union Bank BAWAG. As illustrated, in 1998 the global financial system was standing at the edge of a precipice because two Nobel Prize winners for risk mathematics Myron S. Scholes and Robert C. Merton went to the wall with the legendary "Long-Term Capital Management Fund" (LTCM). As is common knowledge today, the "sinner" in the US sub-prime crisis which grew in a chain reaction from a house bubble to a bank crisis to a national debt crisis and now to the euro crisis was derivatives—house loan derivatives. Warren Buffet must therefore not have had a particularly emotional moment when writing to his investors, "Derivatives are as I see it financial weapons of mass destruction which are, now latently, potentially deadly."[3]

All types of derivative transactions have one characteristic in common—no real economic production takes place, no commodity is manufactured and no personal service is rendered. Derivative transactions are purely money out of money transactions. The baseline of this book is if the propagation of money becomes an objective, the sense, use and ethics of economic activity is over. Money goes from being a tool to a weapon if it no longer serves life and the creation of *utilities*, but

---

[3]Buffett, Warren. 2003. To the Shareholders of Berkshire Hathaway Inc., Letter to the shareholders, 21 February 2003.

rather its own propagation. Financial capitalism should be fundamentally forbidden and the global casino should be closed down.

Let us now take a more closer look at the individual game tables of the global financial casino—where is the meaningful source of the activity and where does doing business shift to being self-referential and senseless? Where does it break away from the objective of economic activity, namely the production of goods and services to satisfy needs?

(a) *Shares:* private individuals participating in companies appears meaningful as the companies receive the necessary equity capital and become viable, in contrast *trading* with shares on a (conventional) exchange is not. Interest shifts from meaningful joint ownership (A) and participation on the performance of the company (B) to financial profit from the difference between the purchase and sale price (C). With derivatives (e.g. put options) or short selling (sale of shares which the speculator does not even possess), the "owner" is even interested in even falling prices and the potential damage to the company (D). High-frequency trading (E) makes use of technical advantages in trading and is the highest form of monetary autism—in 2008 the holding time of a share had decreased from 10 years to 3 months since 1980. While holding shares increased by 11-fold, the trading volume increased by 390%.[4] Thanks to HFT the period in recent times has, according to insiders, fallen to 22 seconds—an absurd value.[5]

(b) *Loans:* borrowing money in order to build a house to live in appears reasonable to a lot of people. It makes sense that a bank which has experience in appraising the necessary securities for lending grants this loan. If it holds this loan in its own books it will be careful when lending and not take any reckless risks, whereas if it sells the loan for example to an investment bank which then bundles this with other loans of varying creditworthiness in order to sell the mixed bundle on to "international investors" it loses meaning. In the end somebody who does not know the house builder and thus *cannot* estimate the credit default risk at all is liable for the loan. Nothing changes due to the fact that a third instance, a rating agency, rates the risk because in doing still no direct contact occurs between the risk generator and risk bearer. It would be as meaningful as for example a German regional bank granting a loan to a US citizen without knowing him/her or without doing any risk appraisal and relying solely on a third party, who also does not know the house builder! The holding of loans should remain reserved for the banks which grant these and generate the risk together with the borrower—according to common sense. The "free world market for financial services" does not make the traditional mortgage lending process of any better.

(c) *Government Bonds:* as long as a state is reliant on financing by private individuals, it is reasonable for me to buy government bonds and live from the interest. The "sense" is that I consciously lend the state money to finance public—ideally democratically legitimized—tasks at an agreed price. However where is the sense

---

[4]World Federation of Exchanges: Annual Statistics Reports, Annual Query Tool.
[5]Börsen-Entschleuniger in *Die Zeit*, 26 February 2013.

in selling this bond? If I sell the bond at a price which is higher than the purchase price (or vice versa with the help of derivatives), I am not interested in financing meaningful state services but rather in making more money out of money—here the sense gets lost and the speculation merry-go-round starts turning. If I go a step further and insure against credit default of the government bond (CDS) this perhaps has a positive effect for me as a result of a negative one, namely that speculative investors start to massively buy up these insurances in order to manipulate the market by simulating an imminent state default and speculate that they trigger a trend by which they can sell the insurances for a higher price at a later date. *That* is their economic damaging objective. "Ideally" a state default is looming (from the perspective of CDS speculators) because then the CDS can be auctioned at the highest price to the holders of government bonds.

(d) *Commodities:* purchasing raw materials for productive use is naturally expedient. A mechanism to ensure against price fluctuation is also essential for producers and processors because otherwise stable planning would not be possible. Trading with raw materials without self-interest is already questionable, even more questionable is trading in raw materials derivatives. The Deutsche Bank has a license for sugar trading, the bank is neither an industrial company nor is it connected to one and its primary interest can only be in making profit from rate differences and derivative transactions. In 2009 Goldman Sachs earned 5 billion US dollars with raw material trading, without even growing one crop (Peukert 2012, p. 423). In July 2010 the London based hedge fund Armajaro bought 7% of the global cocoa harvest, the price per ton exploded to 2,700 pounds per ton which had been the highest price in 33 years. After the speculation became public, the price crashed and cost 1833 pounds on 8 October.[6] Speculators are increasingly dominating the floor—on the Chicago raw materials exchange CBOT, the share of producers of total commodity trading between 1998 and 2011 was halved from two thirds to one third (Oxfam Germany 2012, p. 16 und 43). Capital invested in commodity funds increased by 30-fold between 2003 and 2013, going from 13 to 430 billion US dollars. In the USA in 2012 60 million tons of wheat were produced and futures amounting to 4.4 billion tons were traded.[7]

(e) *Currencies:* when a tourist buys local currency in the country of destination to pay for expenses, this without any doubt makes sense. It also makes sense when an exporting company sells in the currency of the country of destination and in doing so generates foreign currency revenue, which it then exchanges back into its own national currency. However does it make sense for a trader in a foreign currency department of an investment bank to buy a foreign currency and resell it 10 minutes later in order to profit from a minimum exchange rate difference? Does it make sense for somebody to take out a loan in a foreign currency based on the supposition that the exchange rate for this currency will decline making the loan cheap and repaying it with a fat profit? Does it make sense that a hedge fund or an investment bank can make billions

---

[6]*Kurier*, 9 October 2010.

[7]Barclays Capital (2013): The commodity investor.

in profit by winning a bet with derivatives on a rising or declining euro or dollar exchange rate? The crux of the matter—is the objective behind currency transactions a real economic activity (import, export, investment) or is the objective to make more money out of money (speculation)?

Since money out of money transactions neither contribute to the real objective of economic activity nor can "out of nothing" economically become anything, the baseline proposed here is that money out of money transactions should basically not be permitted. I share the opinion with Lucas Zeise that "the most urgent regulatory aspect of the financial sector is its shrinkage." What now follows are concrete alternative proposals for the individual game tables: how corporate financing, commodity prices and exchange rate stability or the financing of public debt can be carried out in a different and better way than today.

12.1 General Regulation Proposals

Beforehand I will summarize the most important proposals of the regulatory discussion, which would be valid across the breadth of all derivative categories or pertain to individual aspects. They can be individually implemented independent from the following large alternatives:

- Authorized derivative transactions must take place at supervised exchanges and be covered by a high amount of equity capital, which is determined by the financial supervisory authority (Admati and Hellwig 2013, p. 352).
- Derivative transactions outside supervised stock exchanges (OTC) are either forbidden or their judicial protection is revoked. Jakob von Uexküll writes, "Gambling debts are debts of honor which are not enforceable. As soon as this is also valid for financial bets, the market will quickly shrink to a small fraction of its present volume. Then there will no longer be the need to forbid specific speculative transactions" (Von Uexküll 2010).
- Werner Rügemer argues that in order to weaken the power of the rating agencies, it would be an easier and more plausible step to ban them legally and from public institutions—"from the national and international policies and laws, from the IMF and the Bank from International Settlements, from the Security and Exchange Commission (SEC) from the German Federal Bank and the Federal Financial Supervisory Authority (BaFin) and from the European Central Bank etc" (Rügemer 2012, pp. 183–184).
- Voting rights for shares could be coupled to a minimum holding time of 5—10 years as well as stipulating a minimum holding time of 1 year. The first proposal is also supported by the Swiss management expert Fredmund Malik, "They have a right only to be interested in short-term returns but they cannot steer the company in the wrong direction."[8]

---

[8]*Die Zeit* 51/2002.

12.2 Shares—Regional Common Good Exchanges

I previously stated that financial wealth is becoming ever larger in contrast with real economic performance, the "supply" of investment or financial capital is on the increase. Therefore its price on functioning markets would have to constantly fall, however the price relations are power relations and supply and demand are power factors. If for example a relevant number of owners of a stock company enforce a specific return, it is unimportant whether there is a twofold or threefold of demanders for this share. The share of profits which are distributed to the owners is often determined by a minority of powerful owners. A Siemens employee related that a return of 16% is the minimum standard for new product developments. He himself developed an innovation in the area of renewable energy which would have yielded a financial return of 15%—it was not authorized because the financial returns were too low. Would other owners have been prepared to accept a return of 5%, if Siemens had shifted the focus more towards renewable energy sources? We do not know because the present and not the potential owners call the shots. Large shareholders are usually "institutional investors"—pensions, hedge funds, private equity funds or state funds—that share a very homogenous attitude to returns on investment. If it then means that the "markets" demand 17% return on invested capital, then it is the cartel-like opinion of large investors whose task it is to propagate their client's wealth with the highest possible financial return. It is no longer concerned with sense, satisfying needs, quality of life or the common good, the actual objectives of economic activity, but rather money out of money—financial capitalism. If the constitutions of democratic states say that the economy serves the common good, then this "real existing" capitalism is unconstitutional.

12.2.1 Regional Common Good Exchanges and the "Triple Skyline"

An alternative to the capitalistic exchange is the regional common good exchange. It would—analogously to the banking sector, which ideally brings financial wealth from the region in the form of loan capital to regional companies—lead equity capital from the region to regional companies. With two decisive differences: 1. The company shares cannot be traded, there is no stock exchange price, the speculation regarding increasing or declining prices comes to an end as does the old style share option which rewards managers for achieving a particular price target. Company shares can only be returned and not at all times but only under predetermined conditions such as sufficiently available company equity capital or by providing a successor. 2. There is no financial return on investment, which would be a groundbreaking change to the flow direction of money. Financial return on investment is the most outstanding investment motive, the decisive allocation factor. Money is however only a means of economic activity and a return flow of funds as investment objective is not a meaningful motive. Which motives could replace financial return on investment? A "skyline" could supersede the "bottom line" position of the financial return flow, a "triple skyline":

1. Sense—If I no longer receive any financial returns, I will only invest my money in companies whose existence is especially important for me: drinking water, renewable energy, organic seeds, social and educational institutions, common-good oriented banks .... I facilitate the existence of these companies with my equity participation.
2. Benefit/Satisfaction of Needs—I can then make use of the output of these companies. Without my "generous" investment, there would then be no seeds, no drinking water, no solar energy, no senior citizen care, no software, and no current account at a "good bank" (Dohmen 2011).
3. Ethics—With the thawing of financial returns, "ethical returns" would in contrast gain more importance: other values flow back. The more human, cooperative, ecological and democratic a company behaves and organizes itself, the more attractive it will become for common-good oriented financial investors. The Common Good Balance Sheet also serves as an appraisal for the "ethical performance" of a company and measures how much a company lives the most common constitutional values of democracies—human dignity, justice, sustainability, solidarity and democracy. The better the Common Good Balance Sheet result is, the more capital the company will attract. This makes sense—ethical companies have an easier time of gaining access to money—exactly the opposite case of today!

This "triple skyline"—sense, benefits, ethics—is like silver, gold and diamonds. They incorporate the objectives and values of economic activity not the means! They are the values which the Bavarian constitution as well as the German Basic Law is committed to create, which stipulate the common-good obligation for property.

To this triple non-financial return on investments also comes, as is the case today, a fourth advantage, namely co-determination because as a co-owner I can co-shape the company—this is no change compared to today. Despite this abundance of advantages, some individuals will probably due to force of habit think: how naïve is it to believe that people will invest their financial wealth in a company and do without financial returns? Here are some answers:

- A company should fundamentally not be a money investment but rather an organization which satisfies needs (the target of economic activity), which does not return production means to the investor in a larger amount but rather quality products and fulfilling work! That is its intent and purpose supported by the constitutions. Many economists are of this opinion for example Stephan Schulmeister, "Economic activity is no end in itself but rather should tend towards improving the conditions for a 'better life'" (Schulmeister 2010, p. 115).
- In contrast to the depiction of the capitalistic idea of man which is common in economic faculties in the universities of this world—economics students behave more egocentrically than the average population in experiments because

they have adopted the "homo oeconomicus" ideological image of man[9]—many people act in a more sense-oriented than return-oriented way and are prepared to forgo financial returns, if their investment generates meaning and if they generate quality products and gain co-determination rights in the company. Today the member banks of the "Global Alliance for Banking on Values" have already around 10 million customers in 24 countries. In Germany alone experts estimate a potential 8–12 million people, who are prepared to invest their money alternatively and meaningfully (Dohmen 2011, p. 7 und 216).

- It is sufficient for a fraction of financial assets to be made available to companies as return-free equity capital, as financial wealth is always a larger multiple of the real economy and therefore constitutes the maximum necessary equity capital. This fraction is becoming even less. In the transition phase from the current extreme returns to the return-free common good economy, financial returns can slowly melt, this process is supported and encouraged by the Common Good Balance Sheet.
- That companies in the long run and systemically return the production means money to investors in larger amounts ("return on investment") than they have poured in ("invested") is not possible because not all financial wealth can be propagated if it constitutes an ever larger multiple than the economic output. To believe *this* would be naïve.
- If there are no investment alternatives with financial returns, anywhere, "freedom of ownership" takes on a new meaning: the more so as I do not receive financial returns anywhere, I allocate my financial assets to places where it makes most sense and generates the most ethical added value. I decide that this company in particular is supported and not another one. The most meaningful and ethical companies receive money the easiest in this manner, whereby it is easier for them to be profitable or remain so, although they would impose higher costs on themselves than less common good oriented companies. In capitalism things go differently: the company which creates the best returns receives the money the easiest, no matter what activity it is engaged in and how it carries this out.

The regional common good exchanges would fulfil a threefold function and supply services:

- They maintain a complete list of companies who want to raise equity capital and present these in a standardized manner (capital market prospectus). Investors receive comprehensive—including ethical—information about all companies in the region who are applying for equity capital.
- They support companies in compiling the prospectus in order to minimize costs. Today the prospectus required by the Capital Market Act represents a high and in some cases an insurmountable obstacle, as the case of "Waldviertler" in Austria shows. The all-time-healthy company received no loans from the banks

---

[9]Frank, R.H., Gilovich, T., and Regan, D.T. 1993. Does studying economics inhibit cooperation? *Journal of Economic Perspectives* 7(2): 159–171.

and borrowed 3 million euros from customers in order to install photovoltaic panels. As the loans in the "savings society" earned 3% interest, the project was subject to the Capital Market Act and should have required a prospectus, whose costs are currently in part prohibitive. When editing this book, there was no "light prospect" for SMEs in the EU.

- All decentralized regional exchanges can collaborate in the financing of large international corporations. Whoever for example would like to finance a global software company, which develops free software, can partake in this through the nearest regional common good exchange. This would be a sort of crowd funding for particularly valuable global projects. In contrast global companies, which create no recognizable value, would receive no financing. Who would invest in Monsanto, the Deutsche Bank, Blackwater or ExxonMobil, if there were no financial returns on equity capital? Small daily bribery and moral corruption would have one less facet.

The exchanges could be jointly operated by the municipalities, by common good banks of a region or could be established as independent companies or cooperatives.

12.3 Close Securities Markets

Credit derivatives are an extremely new phenomenon in economic history and have emerged as a result of the liberalization of financial and capital markets in the 1980s and 1990s. They are concerned with the transformation of loans into securities: bank loans are bought up by investment banks and bundled to securities, "securitized" and after the evaluation by rating agencies they are sold to international investors who then inherit the credit risk. These are profitable investments in boom times when there are few credit defaults, however when there is a downturn or a bubble bursts or both together then losses are impressive and a global morning-after feeling breaks out. Investors are sitting on bad loans whose starting position they knew nothing about. Credit default swaps (CDS) were invented so that investments do not make a loss if there is a default with a credit derivative or government bond and represent one of the newest and fastest "innovations" in the global financial casino.

The market for credit derivatives emerged in the USA in the 1980s and in Europe in the 1990s. The global trading volume in 1998 was at a languid 350 billion US dollars (Weed and Lipke 2003, p. 36). Up to 2007 the volume had rocked to 45 trillion US dollars (Hirtle 2007, p. 1)—123-fold! Such a growth cannot be healthy, in 2008 the bubble burst—for the first time.

The first generation of credit derivatives was limited to a handful of investment banks, after central production however half the world was flooded with the "financial toxic waste." The credit default swaps (CDS) are today even more highly concentrated—worldwide 10 banks are involved in more than 70% of all contracts.[10] In the USA just four banks are involved in 93% of all derivatives!

---

[10]Andreas Dombret: Globale Derivatemärkte im Umbruch, in *Börsen-Zeitung*, 2 August 2013.

(Office for the Comptroller of the Currency 2013, p. 10) The economics journalist Ulrike Herrmann writes, "The so-called 'financial markets' have absolutely nothing at all to do with 'market', as the competition is completely eliminated."[11]

The argument in favor of the development and bringing into circulation of these derivatives is that the risks which the banks take on can be "more widely distributed." However as the world spectacularly experienced, the risk was not minimized by this but rather exponentiated and grew in concentric crises—real estate crisis, banking crisis, state debt crisis, euro crisis—into the current financial crisis.

Wiser than the global fine distribution of "financial toxic waste" would be to stipulate that the bank that has granted the loan and generated the risk together with the customer holds the credit. This would significantly improve the quality of the credit business and credits, a proposition which is supported by Admati and Hellwig. They are of the opinion that "the quality of mortgage loans in the new system (of securitizing and trading) was worse than in the old (…) fraud cases are on the increase, also payment delays and defaults. With mortgages which were not securitized there were by far fewer quality problems" (Admati and Hellwig 2013, p. 103).

The "free global market for financial services" alias financial casino does not bring any improvement here. Therefore the proposal: the game table in the global financial casino, the market for credit derivatives should be closed. If credits are not traded, there is no necessity for CDS and no ratings for CDO, thus saving another game table and a reduction in financial red tape.

Covered bonds are an exception in shifting the credit default risk from the bank to third parties. These are however issued by the mortgage bank itself and are so tightly regulated in Germany that according to Lucas Zeise "since over one hundred years no covered bonds have defaulted" (Zeise 2012, p. 83). Guarantees should also still be permitted; this involves people who are personally known to the borrower or people who are highly interested in the investment coming about and are prepared to enter a highly personal risk. In contrast to CDOs the guarantors here know the credit customer; the motive behind the transaction is not money out of money transaction, but rather a supportive friendly turn.

12.4 Government Bonds—The Use of the Central Bank

A more compelling proposal to state financing through credit was made in Chap. 7. The market for government bonds could also be closed. Many parties criticize that:

- it is forbidden for the ECB to finance states while cheaply refinancing banks which are technically insolvent—also without employing risk premiums!
- states have to borrow from this these banks, which have technically bankrupted themselves by speculating and are extremely cheaply refinanced by the state central bank,

---

[11]Ulrike Herrmann: Erpressen und Auspressen, in *taz*, 7 December 2013.

- banks that are technically bankrupt hold insurances against the bankruptcy of the same states which rescued them from bankruptcy by means of recapitalization with tax money and public guarantees.

Such a system is an insult to everything which can be insulted, its sole objective is to serve the interests of for-profit banks and I therefore advocate:

- free of charge direct financing of states through the public central bank,
- limiting this in order avert devil-may-care spending and inflation (automatic debt capping),
- decoupling of all non-common-good oriented commercial banks from the central banks as step one—step two: obligatory common good orientation of all banks,
- as a result, the focused fulfillment of core bank business by the commercial banks: secure administration of cash deposits and saving investments, granting of real and mainly regional loans.

A second function of the rating agencies becomes no longer necessary with the disappearance of government bonds from the global financial casino. With the end of state debt rating there is no longer the possibility of speculative attack on states. A noticeable systemic easing of tension is to be expected.

The only "disadvantage" which is often tabled is the concern with regard to how pension provisions can be made if there are no longer government bonds which can be invested in for retirement provisions. The argument is indeed strange—the state should go into debt so that the basic right of capital return can be enforced. The result is that in Germany annually almost 70 billion euros in interest is redistributed from the tax payer to state creditors, this cannot be the duty of the republic—but more about this in the next chapter.

12.5 Foreign Exchange—A New Global Currency System

The number one standard textbook example for legitimizing financial derivatives is fluctuating exchange rates. The reason is understandable, "real economic" participants such as exporters or importers want to ensure themselves against rising or falling exchange rates in order to be able to plan reliably. This is understandable and justified in a system of freely fluctuating exchange rates that is where "prices for foreign exchange" are created according to supply and demand. However do currencies have to fluctuate? As is the case with almost everything there is also an alternative here, namely stable exchange rates within the framework of a global foreign exchange cooperation, which will be presented in Chap. 7.

12.6 Commodity Markets—Global Commodity Agreement

Safeguarding farmers against fluctuating commodity prices is the number two standard textbook example for legitimizing derivatives. If a grain farmer calculates on the basis of a specific acceptance price and a particularly good harvest leads to market price deterioration, this can lead to his/her ruination. Therefore many farmers try to ensure themselves against this risk with commodity derivatives. There are no objections to this apart from the fact that it requires the creation of opposite standpoints—somebody must bet on rising prices, "the speculator." Alternatively an insurance system could distribute the risk amongst farmers and distribute it over years; in this case farmers would also receive the profits instead of passing them onto speculators.

Both variants, ensuring with derivatives or with insurance, both presume that agricultural commodity prices must be determined on markets, but this is not necessarily the case. A fundamental alternative would be stabile commodity prices, determined by a democratic committee. There is currently massive resistance to politically determined prices. The advocators of the "free market" argue that supply and demand represents the best form of price regulation, thereby resulting in the "most efficient resource allocation." However this poses the question—which efficiency is being discussed here? If commodity prices are determined by markets this results in a series of grave disadvantages:

- The prices are often subjected to extreme fluctuations depending on weather, harvest, stability of the supply infrastructure—the producers as well as the purchasers have to permanently cover themselves against risk at a high price with derivatives.
- The distribution basically goes wrong: the commodities neither flow into the most meaningful sectors nor to the neediest people, but rather to the purchasers with the strongest purchasing power, regardless of what they do with these.
- Conversely market prices fall to such a low level when there is a supply glut of agricultural commodities that the producers cannot live from or not deservingly live from their farming or are forced to extreme rationalization (e.g. dairy sector or cotton sector) which occurs at the expense of nature and meaningful work.
- Commodity scarcity is not continually or proactively priced but is done too late and too abruptly—when the supply is near to exhaustion levels and an economic transition without extensive failure is no longer possible.
- Ecological burdens as a result of raw material extraction or agricultural production are without political intervention not priced at all.

Markets fail repeatedly with price determination for commodities and therefore an alternative system should at least be tabled. At this point I would like to present a new paradigm which is based on the values of sustainability, human dignity and fairness. Truly "free" economic activity can first evolve when these fundamental values are ensured. The consideration is: raw materials are a present from nature. Mankind neither invented coffee or the cocoa bean nor gold, iron ore, aluminum or copper. The "wonder of nature" of the free existence of these resources should be safeguarded with the largest possible mindfulness, appreciation and reverence. (Schweitzer 2013). At present mankind, which did not create these resources, is acquiring these natural resources of the earth with such negligence, recklessness and ingratitude that a new paradigm in dealing with the limited and ecological sensitive resources of the earth is necessary.

12.6 Commodity Markets—Global Commodity Agreement

One could say, natural mineral and agricultural raw materials are, similar to money, a global public good which may only be produced, processed, distributed and consumed and returned to ecological cycles in compliance with specific rules. In doing so there are four central aspects: the ecological extraction limitation, price determination, globally just distribution and ecologically compatible recycling. Markets completely fail in all of these four objectives, here is the alternative proposal:

Quantity Control: a global commodity agreement within the framework of the United Nations, similar to global agreement for climate protection or biodiversity, which controls the extraction quantity of critical raw materials. National states partly relinquish their sovereignty because the raw materials are not their "property" but rather the common heritage of mankind, however under the condition that the global distribution is regulated within the UNO in compliance with democratically stipulated and sovereign-determined principles, for example:

(a) For non-renewable raw materials which do not cause any relevant damage to ecosystems—global extraction is limited in such a way that global reserves are sufficient for at least a further seven generations of mankind.
(b) For ecologically problematic raw materials whose processing or recycling impairs ecosystems or the world climate—global extraction is limited to the extent that no appreciable impairment of ecosystems or the earth's ecosystem occurs (e.g. heavy metals, carbon dioxide).
(c) For (regionally) renewable and ecologically unproblematic raw materials there is no necessity for quantity control (e.g. gravel, sand, wood).
(d) If indigenous populations live nearby or in the place of discovery of the raw materials, they will be involved in the decision whether these materials are extracted at all and under which conditions the extraction takes place for example oil, gold, bauxite.
(e) In order to prevent the surplus production of agricultural raw materials, production levels will be stipulated for example coffee, cotton, milk.

Price Control: The determination of prices for mineral raw materials ensues in such a way that the raw material companies can cover all their costs including investment and research expenditure.

(f) The production price of agricultural raw materials, which serves as a livelihood of the farmers (coffee, cocoa, cotton, milk), is determined so that the farmers can live well from small scale (size limited) and ecologically sustainable production. After a transition period only ecologically produced products will be authorized on the world market, or the level of duty will vary according the Common Good Balance Sheet results of the agricultural enterprise.
(g) In order to guarantee food as a human right, basic foodstuff for example rice, corn, grain must be accessible for everybody worldwide by price capping or food subsidies but also by fair distribution of fertile farm land.
(h) To prevent the surplus production of agricultural commodities, quotas for states and regions as well as size limits could be specified.

None of the previously mentioned considerations is totally new, there were and there is for example:

- Global Commodity Agreement: in 1980 under the umbrella of UNCTAD a Common Fund for Commodities (CFC) was established to reduce price volatility for commodities and stabilize the markets. One hundred and five states are associated with this agreement with Germany being a member in the agreement for coffee, olive oil (since 1963), cocoa, sugar (since 1973), tropical wood and grains (since 1995). The fund was set up on the initiative of the poor UN members but is blocked by the industrial states because they hope for cheap commodities due to competition between producer countries.
- Quantity regulation: in the EU up to 2015 there were national quotas for milk production (production and processing quotas) in order to prevent extreme surplus production. As a result of market fundamentalism these quotas expired in 2015 with the consequence of a price collapse and acceleration of structural change towards industrial agribusiness.
- Price regulation: up until the 1950s in Germany prices for foodstuffs were regulated. In the government statement in 1949 Chancellor Adenauer spoke of "prices, which allow the production costs of efficiently operating average enterprises to be covered and at the same time, also allow the poorest to buy these products."[12]
- Land reforms: these are a common phenomenon in history and would be an important answer to large estates which are not sustainably used or lying dormant as well as to "land grabbing."

Political commodity regulation approaches are therefore reality in all aspects, however readers will nevertheless think that this proposal is completely utopian and "not politically viable" because governments and nation states are not prepared to defer their "national interests" or prefer to enact regulations in the interests of commodity corporations rather than in public interests and therefore there will never be global agreement, which would be advantageous for everybody, but would fail on short-term profit interests. To this purpose here are some considerations:

- Government awareness is not public awareness. In particular with regard to ecology and questions of distribution it can be seen that the general public often thinks and decides in a different way than its representatives in government. In Austria, Italy and Lithuania the sovereign population voted against the use of nuclear energy in a referendum thereby placing ecology ahead of profit interests (in contrast to its government). In Iceland the public determined that commodities are a public good and not private property. In the new constitutions of Bolivia and Ecuador nature is even entitled to an intrinsic value, which is tantamount to a revolution in the understanding of nature and relation to nature. The Earth Charter is an impressive initiative that aims at global sustainable

---

[12]Konrad Adenauer: Government Statement to the German Bundestag on 20 September 1949.

12.6 Commodity Markets—Global Commodity Agreement   133

human civilization based on respect for nature. In the EU, a citizen's initiative for nature rights is in preparation.[13] Worldwide trends of deep ecology, eco-philosophy, permaculture, transition town and similar approaches are on the increase. Capitalism and market economy have, apart from the standard formula rules of "supply power" and "demand power," nothing to offer concerning the topics of ecology, sustainability, and respect of nature.

- "National" or "ethnic" awareness is without a doubt still prevalent, however at the same time global awareness is emerging worldwide with more and more people recognizing the world problems and in search of global solutions. They are shifting from the politics of national interests to ecologically sustainable and distributively just "world domestic policy." The proportion of these people is growing worldwide similar to those who once wanted democracy instead of monarchy and slowly grew until they were capable of gaining a majority.
- Should the mentioned proposal not yet be capable of gaining a majority and if the states do not initially join the global agreement, this would not be a deterioration of the current situation. In the case of the climate protection agreement which has been ratified by many states, but nowhere near all states, this development is currently taking place. Would it be better if there were absolutely no international climate protection policy?
- International politics would certainly fundamentally change if governments did not satisfy interests closest to them or minority groups but rather had to trade and negotiate with a binding mandate from the public (referendum, democratic monetary system). Probably more environmental protection agreements would be made and mankind would implement the idea that natural goods are public goods as well as the idea that money is a public good.

A final glance at the Ecuadorian constitution Article 408 illustrates the fact that awareness is more developed in other places than in Europe and North America: non-renewable natural commodities in general and mineral and fossil deposits, substances which possess other characteristics than the earth, including those which are found under the sea and in coastal zones, as well as biodiversity and its genetic wealth and the radio electric spectrum are inalienable, imprescriptible and non-pledgeable property of the state. These goods can only be extracted under rigorous adherence to the principles laid down in the constitution." If one replaces the state of Ecuador by the international community, the first element of a global sustainable commodities agreement has already been written.

A draft constitution of a directly elected people's convention was also compiled in a similar spirit and was accepted by the population of Iceland with a two thirds majority, "The natural resources of Iceland, which are not private property, are a common shared and permanent property of the nation. Nobody can purchase the natural resources or rights associated with them as property or for unlimited use and they cannot be sold or bonded. Publicly owned natural resources consist of marine life, other ocean resources within the economic zone of Iceland as well as

---

[13]http://www.natures-rights.org/

water resources and water usage rights, geothermal and mining rights (...). Sustainable development and public interest should be used as a guideline for the use of natural resources."[14]

References

Admati, Anat/Hellwig, Martin (2013): *Des Bankers neue Kleider. Was bei Banken wirklich schiefläuft und was sich ändern muss*, FBV, München.
Bank for International Settlements. 2013. *Statistical release: OTC derivatives statistics at end-December 2012*, Monetary and Economic Department, Basel, May 2013.
Dohmen, Caspar (2011): *Good Bank. Das Modell der GLS Bank*, Orange Press, Freiburg.
Hirtle, Beverly. 2007. *Credit derivatives and bank credit supply*, Federal Reserve Bank of New York Staff Report no. 276, February 2007.
Office for the Comptroller of the Currency. 2013. OCC's quarterly report on bank trading and derivatives activities, 1. Quarter 2013, Washington.
Oxfam Germany (2012): *Mit Essen spielt man nicht. Die deutsche Finanzbranche und das Geschäft mit dem Hunger*, brochure, 60 pages, Berlin.
Peukert, Helge (2012): *Die große Finanzmarkt- und Staatsschuldenkrise*, 4th revised edition, Metropolis, Marburg.
Rügemer, Werner (2012): *Rating-Agenturen. Einblick in die Kapitalmacht der Gegenwart*, transcript, Bielefeld.
Schulmeister, Stephan: (2010): *Mitten in der großen Krise. Ein 'New Deal' für Europa*, Picus Verlag, Wien.
Schweitzer, Albert (2013): *Die Ehrfurcht vor dem Leben. Grundtexte auf fünf Jahrzehnten*, C.H. Beck, 10th edition, München.
Von Uexküll, Jakob (2010): *Die Finanzwelt muss der Wirtschafts dienen, nicht umgekehrt*, Süddeutsche Zeitung, 25 February 2010.
Weed/Lipke, Isabel (2003): *Derivate. Das unbekannte Wesen*, Brochure, 39 pages, Berlin.
Zeise, Lucas (2012): *Geld – der vertrackte Kern des Kapitalismus: Versuch über die politische Ökonomie des Finanzsektors*, 3rd revised edition, PapyRossa, Köln.

---

[14]A Proposal for a New Constitution for the Republic of Iceland, authored by a constitutional convention.

Chapter 13
Secure Pensions

Abstract This chapter describes the strategic privatization of the pension systems in Austria and Germany, following the bad examples of Chile and Great Britain. The privatization has been pushed through although private pensions perform worse according to all relevant criteria such as costs, stability, or solidarity. PR campaigns against the public systems have succeeded and undermined trust in these systems thereby preparing the path for progressive privatization. It is argued that the aging of the population is not necessarily a threat to the financial viability of public pension schemes, rather for private provisions. The winners and losers of a reform towards private pensions are presented and, finally, concrete measures are proposed how a public and joint pension system can be strengthened and deprived of its—still existing—weaknesses: sufficiently high minimum pensions for a decent existence, more generous consideration of phases with no employment income, improvement of pensions for women.

> *And we must recognize and say that due to the evolving age structure of our society our exemplary health care and pension systems will no longer be affordable in our lifetime, if we do not change anything. We have to have the courage to dare to try something different. In doing this we will have to bid farewell to some of those things that have become precious to us, and unfortunately expensive.*
>
> Gerhard Schröder
> (Vereinigte Dienstleistungsgewerkschaft 2003, p. 1)
>
> *Just saying that pensions are guaranteed is absurd. Everybody knows that they are not secured, even the public knows it.*
> Georg Kapsch[1]

The "senseless" role that money plays today can be clearly seen using the discussion about pensions as an example. The "end of all capital income" as proposed in this book (as previously done in the book "Change Everything") provokes a fear response instead of being considered, weighed up and appraised by many people: "And what

---

[1]President of the Federation of Austrian Industries (IV). *Der Standard*, 24 November 2013.

will I finance my pension with?" Although capital income is only of benefit to 10% of the population, since the start of pension privatization a large proportion of the population believes that without interest, dividends and capital gains they would be exposed to poverty in old age. This opinion is an absolute success for capitalistic ideology (in general and in particular of the insurance sector)—without returns on investment we are lost. We should actually all start laughing, however fear has a tight hold on us. In this chapter I would like to show that:

- the pay as you go (PAYG) pension and inter-generation contract can be financed without a problem in future,
- it is not the demographic bomb which is the problem, at least not for the PAYG pension,
- pension provision via capital markets is in all aspects a poor alternative,
- political subsidization of private provision is a bad case of cutting off one's nose to spite one's face,
- there is a whole string of possibilities to close the "pension shortfall" without capital returns and capital pension savings.

13.1 The PAYG Pension is Easily Financed

The pension trap is comparable to the single market large banks trap. The extent of deception and manipulation of the general public which the governments, in Germany (SPD–Green Party), in Austria (SPÖ–ÖVP and ÖVP–FPÖ), have managed is comparable to the ploy of announcing an efficient EU financial market and instead of this creating systemically important banks. With the pension reform secure pensions were not created, as promised, but rather an Eldorado was created with high turnover and profit for banks and insurance corporations.

The escapade against the PAYG pension system began with a pseudo-scientific alarm: the population is becoming older; soon every employee must finance a pensioner—impossible, unsustainable! So an alternative must be found—privatization and changeover to the so-called "funded schemes." With the advantage of a financial market based pension the people making pension provisions would enjoy high returns on investment (hahaha!) from liberalized financial markets and would in doing so escape the demographic trap (ROFL). The lemmings were guided into the speculation trap with fear slogans, and the "demographic bomb" narrative was planted with the demographic forecast stretching up to 50 (!) years into the future, which is about as professional as a forecast for the weather in four months' time. With repetition being the mother of manipulation, the message to be learned was obediently internalized—the PAYG pension cannot be financed and must be "supplemented" by private pension provisions, in doing so the "pension shortfall" can be "filled" by financial returns.

Is the PAYG pension indeed unaffordable? The PAYG system in the publicly-funded pension insurance is based on the inter-generational contract—the current workforce generation pays for the pensions of the retired generation via social

13.1 The PAYG Pension is Easily Financed

insurance contributions and taxes and with this payment acquires an entitlement that future generations pay for their pensions when they are at retirement age. Whether this generation contract will "hold" and is affordable is indeed dependent on demographic factors that is from the ratio of young to old, but by no means exclusively. In total there are 10 (!) factors which are decisive for better or poorer financial feasibility of the PAYG pension system: income level, productivity development, labor market participation (activity rate), unemployment, wages level, pension contribution rate, tax subsidy, state of health, retirement age and life expectancy! One of these factors alone does not particularly reveal much, it would be like certifying the end of a decathlete's career because he or she's performance in one discipline is dwindling. So it can be said that population ageing is not a fairytale, it is taking place, however in the first place for over 100 years without pensions becoming pathetically low, on the contrary, they have been ever increasing. Secondly, consideration of one from 10 factors is simply too little. In Bangladesh there are 29 employed persons for every pensioner—do you want to exchange your German or Austrian pension for one from Bangladesh? Precisely. It cannot simply be connected with the ratio between young and old people. However if these, admittedly complex issues, are not communicated by the media but rather only the alarm bells of selected experts, pension fear is generated in the population lined with the artillery of advertising propaganda of the insurance sector. Pension insecurity in Austria began with a study by the economic expert Bernd Rürup, who was later the chief economist of AWD—one of the largest German financial services companies. Rürup calculated in 1997 that in 2030 in Austria every employed person must maintain one pensioner.

Instead of the corresponding benefits cuts, the contribution rate would have to be raised from 22.3% to 31% (an average of the three pension insurances). Two acknowledged pension experts from the Austrian Institute of Economic Research WIFO took the trouble of carefully examining the long term prognosis compiled by Rürup (Guger and Mayrhuber 2001). They discovered that he had employed some highly unlikely suppositions, which had led to the horror scenario for example that the extremely low labor participation in Austria would also persist for the next 33 years at an atypically low level by European standards. Although especially undisputed population ageing results in a larger proportion of the shrinking active population being necessary for the creation of economic product. In concrete terms it would have been sufficient for the activity rate in Austria to be equal to the already achieved level in Denmark or Norway in 1997 in order for the contribution rate not to rise to 31% but instead to 25%, (while) maintaining pension benefits at an unchanged high level. The contribution rate increase from 22.3% to 25% between 2000 and 2030 would have been a lower increase than the increase between 1970 and 2000, namely from 17% to 22.3%.

However both experts from the Economic Research Institute were more or less ignored. Instead combination journalism comprising of advertising promotional messages (baby to parents: "I am not a pension provision!") and editorials resulted in the pension fear being slowly but surely built up. "50% of young people alone believe that their pension is no longer secure." It sounded like a success message.

The most absurd thing about the horror prognosis was that all calculations made at that time presumed a long term productivity and economic growth level of 1.5–2.0%, which would have meant almost a doubling of economic output and real income between 2000 and 2030. These assumptions were shared by all including Rürup and other experts in the insurance sector. This would however have meant that even if the contribution rate had risen to 31%, this would have been delivered by an 80% higher income in real terms. In 2000 a contribution rate of 22% means that from a real income of 100 euros there is a remaining disposable income of 78 euros. In 2030 a real income of 180 euros with a contribution rate of 22% results in a remaining income of 140 euros, with a contribution rate of 31% this would mean 124 euros. The complete spectrum of prognoses—from the reason minimum to the Rürupian horror scenario would have been in the region between 124 and 140 euros in 2030 instead of 78 euros in 2000, at the same level of purchasing power! Where is the mega problem, where is the bomb?

Granted that this calculation entails the increase of real income which is not guaranteed and which has not been the case in recent years. However none of the participants in the pension debate has ever questioned this assumption and despite this there is terror! With a much less favorable assumption of an annual increase in real income of for example 0.5% between 1997 and 2030, net income would rise from 100 to 118 and the complete pension question would be whether in 2030 instead of 78 euros an amount of 92 euros (22% contribution rate) or 82 euros (31%) would remain in one's pocket but the contribution rate should not increase at any price, not even to 25%. In the autumn of 2013, Ingo Kramer, President of the German Employer's Association called for all efforts to be made in order to prevent the contribution rate from rising to over 22%.[2] But why not if it makes so little difference to disposable real income? "No further burdens should be created which future pension contributors cannot shoulder." In the light of the figures which have been submitted, this is not a convincing argument. The largest of all burdens for the broad majority of the population is the notorious pay restraint in favor of a fetishistic and already too high competiveness—this connection will be explained later in Chap. 12.

Although an upward spiraling of the contribution rate would not be a catastrophe in the long term, there are several alternatives. The contribution rate screw is only one of 10 screws. It would be possible to slightly adjust each of them:

- The de facto retirement age can be increased towards 65 years. In Austria it was already at 62 in 1970. At present it is between 58 and 59 years. This is counter-productive; retirement age should increase proportionally to life expectancy.
- Health-related early retirement can be reduced by more humane working conditions and a healthier lifestyle—cue: company Common Good Balance Sheet.
- Labor market participation can be raised to Swiss or Icelandic level. This is already in process which is why the pension burden level (the ratio of pension

---

[2]*Frankfurter Allgemeine Zeitung*, 29 November 2013.

13.1 The PAYG Pension is Easily Financed

recipients to contributors) in Austria in 2012 was lower than 1996 despite an ageing population.[3]

- Migration is as little foreseeable as population growth, depending on political objectives more or fewer people can immigrate and enhance in-payments in the social security system.
- Unemployment must be decisively addressed with for example a general reduction in working hours of 10–20%.
- Net income of the workforce must increase in step with productivity and real economic growth, which has been the biggest weakness in Germany in the last 25 years.
- Relating there to the wage ratio of national income must at least remain constant and not decline.
- More effectively contribution obligation can be extended to the total national income that is from only labor income to capital income also.
- The state can widen the flow of pensions from the general tax coffers, in Austria provision is made for a statutory one-third—employee contribution, employer contribution and tax subsidy. In 2012 "federal contribution" amounted to 23.3% (7.3 billion euros from total pension costs of 35.7 billion euros), significantly under the statutory maximum of 33%.[4]

In total these are nine further measures which could support the screw of "rising contribution rate" and secure the financing of the PYAG system. A further basic condition which could reduce the drama of the financing situation, which is also as chronically disregarded as the "bomb" is conjured—the elderly are indeed increasing in numbers while young people are becoming fewer and both must be maintained by the actives. Crucial for the financing burden of the actives is not merely the old-age ratio itself but rather the sum of the old-age and youth ratio— the total ratio. And lo and behold in 2001 one hundred people of working age had to carry 43.9 elderly people and 38.1 young people—a total ratio of 82. In 2020 it will be 55 elderly people and 33 young people, in total 88 people. Within a period of 20 years there is no significant change to the total ratio! (Bingler and Bosbach 2004, p. 744) On the basis of the big picture alone, it is no longer the case of a "bomb."

By virtue of all these possibilities and their utilization, the financing situation of the PYAG system can be significantly improved and there is considerably more in it than merely maintaining the benefits level until 2030. This is also necessary, as the statutory pension still has a series of gaps:

- There is still no minimum pension which is sufficient to live life in a dignified manner,
- Childcare periods are not strongly enough taken into account,

---

[3] Statistisches Handbuch der Österreichischen Sozialversicherung 2013, Chart 3, 03.
[4] Handbuch der österreichischen Sozialversicherung 2012, 119.

- Pensions for women are lower due to lower wages and salaries—here the gender gap must be progressively closed,
- In order to create more justice between occupational groups, everybody should pay into a unitary pension or retirement fund.

To ensure that the statutory pension is poverty-resistant, we need to adjust all ten screws slightly—as the objective is not only to maintain the level of benefit and a net replacement rate of 80% of the last income for 45 working years, but rather gap closure in the spectrum of the PYAG pension and increased trust in the inter-generational contract.

13.2 What Makes Private Provision Better?

For a statutory pension supplement with a state supported private provision to make sense, the private pension would have to perform better. "Better" in terms of pension insurance means the following:

i. The private pension must be less vulnerable to demographic change than the PYAG pension system.
ii. The contributions which flow into the private provision scheme ("premiums") would have to be paid higher interest than the contributions for the PYAG pension.
iii. The costs of the private scheme would have to be less than the statutory pension scheme.
iv. Distribution would have to be more just in order to reduce the risk of old-age poverty.
v. The framework conditions which are necessary to support the private pension scheme may not debase those of the statutory scheme.

Now let us move on and take a look at this point by point; however before doing this how does a private provision scheme—the ominous "funding scheme"—function in the first place? In private pension provision the contributions do not go to the PYAG fund but rather as "premiums" to private insurances which are then invested in shares, bonds, funds, real estate, commodities and derivatives in the hope that the financial returns are so high that the saved capital grows and by "dis-saving," the sale of securities between retirement age and death, a generous pension is possible, and more generous than is possible with a PYAG system. However where do the capital returns come from and who buys the "pension bonds" from the pensioners? It is the younger, active generation! Technically speaking it is the exact same system as the PYAG system, surprise! The money always flows from the younger to the older generation. In one case directly, in the second case indirectly via the financial markets and private intermediaries—the insurance and investment management sector. In 1952 the economist Gerhard Mackenroth became famous with the "Mackenroth

13.2 What Makes Private Provision Better?

Theorem" by being the first to point out and that there is no fundamental difference between both pension methods. "Well the simple and clear principle is valid that all social security expenditure must always be covered from the national income of the current period. There is no other source, nor has there ever been another source from which social security expenditure could flow—there is no accumulation of funds, no transfer from income shares from period to period, no "saving" in the sense of the private sector—there is absolutely nothing but the current national income as a source of social security expenditure" (Mackenroth 1952). To put it in a nutshell the young finance the elderly in the PYAG system directly via their employment income (A) and in funded schemes indirectly via capital returns or the previously touched upon "private capital tax" (B). It is also valid for the pension system that money does not "work" and nothing ventured, nothing gained. The young generation must in any case work for the pensions for the elderly. Why should method B function fundamentally better than method A?

13.2.1 Are Private Pensions Less Vulnerable with Regard to Demographic Factors?

As already mentioned, the demographic bomb has been exploding for over 100 years. In 1900 in Germany for one person over 65 years there were still 12.4 people of employment age (15–65 years), in 1950 there were only 6.9 and in 1980 this figure fell to 4.3 and for 2020 there will be 3.0 and for 2050 only 2.0 are forecasted (Vereinigte Dienstleistungsgewerkschaft 2003, p. 8). Since not all people between 15 and 65 are in employment (education, unemployment, families with one breadwinner), it could in the worst case be a 1:1 ratio—for one pensioner only one contributor. How is the demographic ratio in private pension systems? As everybody looks after him or herself, there is only one ratio possible, namely a 1:1 ratio. That in itself is more than somewhat strange with the prospect that, but not even as a certain development, the ratio of payers to drawers in the PYAG system will sink to 1:1 by 2030, the necessity for a systemic change is justified. However in the "new" system which should provide a solution, the "horror scenario" 1:1 is the only possible ratio between payer and drawer! How come this should suddenly function here?

It is conceivable that demographic change will have a larger impact on the funded scheme than the PYAG system—the funded scheme lives off the fact that young people buy the saved securities from the elderly. However if there are fewer and fewer young people, who should then buy all the securities from the elderly? The more dramatic the demographic development is, the worse the securities squeeze for the elderly generation. Who do they want to sell their shares, bonds and certificates to, if there is no longer anybody to sell them to? This is where the demographic bomb detonates, without a silencer.

13.2.2 Are the Premiums in Private Pensions Paid More Interest than Social Security Contributions?

The standard horror scenario in the funded scheme should therefore function because the returns on financial markets are so high, higher than the "intrinsic" returns of the PYAG system—wage and salary increases. With the introduction of the Riester Pension in Germany and the analogous "retirement savings" (as well as "severance payment scheme") in Austria, fully unrealistic dream returns were promised, a possibility of 6% capital returns in the long term for everybody was under discussion. A prospectus for a private pension scheme from the Bank Austria portrayed various interest scenarios; the best-case scenario was 12% actuarial interest with 6% as the worst-case scenario. The money out of money alchemy was celebrated amongst the masses with the great hangover being predestined. The history of capital markets is marked by manic-depressive fluctuations, extreme instability and regular collapses of private pension insurance companies. Historical facts could however not weaken the political will to let the general public plummet into risk. The risk alias pension privatization is a commercial crusade in which governments play the PR department. Independent scientists and specialized civil society organizations such as Attac have always warned about the guaranteed collapse of such empty promises of funded schemes; we were hardly noticed by the media. I was allowed to compile opinion pieces on several occasions in the Austrian *Standard*, however apart from one expert hearing in parliament it had no effect. I mentioned that there had been a collapse series of private insurance companies in Japan, Great Britain and Switzerland, which had been intercepted by the state and bailed out (Reimon and Felber 2003, pp. 135–165). I referred to Great Britain where, according to a study from the University of Bristol, soon 50% of people are threatened by old-age poverty due to the privatization measures which were pushed through by Margaret Thatcher. People were voluntarily returning back to the state system, from which they had been hunted out of by the "Iron Lady," and doing so in their millions. I also reported about Chile where the duo comprising of the dictator Augusto Pinochet and US economist Milton Friedman fully privatized all pensions except those of the army and police. In 2000 there were only nine of the numerous funds remaining, with four of the largest being mostly in foreign hands. Only 45% of the members were still able to pay regular contributions. The funds only managed a return of 1% over the long-term average. With a normal savings account those insured would have gained more, the fund owners in contrast earned an equity capital return of 27% (Keppler 2009). Today hardly anybody in Chile can expect a pension which will ensure a decent standard of living. I also reported that private insurers change the mortality tables, decrease pension benefits or simply increase the premiums without consulting anybody and without even the faintest public outcry.

Now similar experience is being made with the Riester Pension, with company pensions and the Retirement Savings in Austria. Almost every year there are cuts, the guaranteed interest is reduced and often returns are negative. We really could have saved ourselves all of this!

13.2.3 Are Private Schemes Cheaper?

A second reason why the private schemes do not perform better than the public PYAG funds, besides instable financial markets, is due to the fact that they are horrendously expensive in comparison. In Germany and Austria 2% or even somewhat under 2% of the contributions paid into the pension system goes on administration costs. Private Insurers in Latin American devour between 13% and 26% (Whitehouse 2000), in Australia 11–35.5% (Williams 2000, p. 10), in Great Britain 20% (Disney 1999, p. 32) and on an international average 15–25% (Orszag and Stiglitz 1999). They are more inefficient by a factor of 10. Why is this? Firstly due to the fact that they make costly investments, secondly because they have high outlays for advertising—up to 40% of the total costs go into marketing. Every pension fund must convince its target group that it can earn a higher return than all the competition. Thirdly because fund managers earn quite a bit more for their shining "performance" than social insurance employees do. Fourthly because private insurers are profit oriented (see the above 27% ROI). The pension system does not distribute any profit to the social insurance agency or state, in contrast some private insurers are listed on the stock exchange, which helps to explain the "factor of 10" between the "state" and "private" systems in costs.

The promised dream returns fail to materialize pursuant to these framework conditions—instable financial markets and horrendously expensive fund management. A test carried out by the Öko Test magazine of 144 Riester Pension products revealed that returns to the age of 86 amounted to a return of 0.6%, in the case of fund-linked products the return was continuously negative.[5] The Austria Consumer Protection Association VKI calculated the actual return of a fund-linked life insurance. After 20 years of paying in a total of 24,000 euros it results in 27,698 euros—a return on investment of 1.4%, the reason for this being the high insurance (6,520) and fund costs (6,870).[6] It is not easy to find out about the exact costs—with the 33 investigated Riester products, not one of them transparently revealed the total costs. It is also not so easy—subscription fee, management fee, securities account expenses, transaction costs, administrative expense, commissions, additional services, capital guarantee costs, annuity costs ... and so it gets to the factor of 10.

13.2.4 Is the Private Pension System Distributively Fairer?

The private pension system is not only risky and expensive but also unjust, because only those who pay in receive a pension. Those who do not pay in because they are presently unemployed, pregnant, nursing or ill receive nothing, which is how simple actuarial is. People who only pay in 100 euros per month

---
[5] *Manager-Magazin*, 30 May 2011.
[6] *Der Standard*, 28 January 2011.

will not receive a sizeable pension. The pension becomes sizeable if the employer and employee both pay in 10% (in total 20%) to 15% (in total 30%) of the wages or salary, that is sufficient today and it would be sufficient until 2030. People with no income would totally collapse within the private system because they cannot acquire any form of pension entitlement. In a solidary pension insurance all challenging life situations are cushioned and could with existing political will be even better compensated for. Amongst other things a minimum pension must be determined—this is something which private pension systems do not do on principle. This is something which only exists in a real community of solidarity, in an intergenerational contract, which excludes nobody and lives the principles of solidarity and human dignity. Every percent of privatization and every step away from the PYAG system is a step towards old-age poverty for the masses.

13.2.5 The Methuselah Conspiracy

In Germany as in Austria pension privatization was pushed through with the main argument that the contribution rate should not exceed 22% by 2030, specifically to prevent a contribution rate of 26% by 2030 in Germany. Here is the trick: the—impossible—26% would have been financed by 13% from the employer and 13% from the employee. With the 22% cap the employer and employee pay a maximum of 11% each in the (reduced) state pension. However there is a further 4% for the private pension system exclusively paid for by the employee, which then makes a contribution rate of 15% and for the employer a rate of 11%, so together 26%! The result of this exercise is exactly what was supposedly not possible and this impossibility caused the start of entry into the private pension system. It is apparent from this trick that it is not about preventing high contribution rates but rather distribution to the benefit of employers at the expense of employees and to the benefit of the insurance sector, as the 4% Riester Pension is now grist to their mills. We see that the "Methuselah Conspiracy" (Schirrmacher 2004) really exists—it is devised by employer associations, banks and insurance companies and the SPD, Green Party, CDU/CSU and FDP governments and parliaments loyally cooperate. On the day of the introduction of the Riester Pension the headline in the newspaper Handelsblatt did not read "pensions are secured" but rather "a million euro deal for insurance companies." In Austria the *Standard* headline read "big business for the Vienna Exchange."

13.2.6 Do Favorable Framework Conditions for the Private Pension System Also have a Favorable Impact on the PYAG Pension System?

Although the funded scheme is clearly inferior to the inter-generational contract in all three main requirements of a pension system—security, fairness and

13.2 What Makes Private Provision Better?

efficiency—many people nevertheless argue with the "three pillar tactic" or "eggs in more baskets" hypnosis. It is advised not to put all your eggs in one basket (inter-generational contract) but rather to at least "additionally" set up the second pillar (company pension) and the third pillar (private pension). The picture appears to be reasonable, however it is incorrect—then if an existing model which is better in all aspects than a new model is only replaced in part this all in all results in deterioration.

The addition in the sense of "closure of the pension shortfall" is not only an illusion, because privatization in reality tears open a gap instead of closing it, but is also rather from the economic perspective a complete first degree misnomer. Then the favorable framework conditions for the PYAG system are: full employment, high growth in wages and salaries as well as low financial returns, which make real investment and the creation of further workplaces attractive. Favorable framework conditions for the funded scheme are in contrast: high interest, big increases in share prices and high real estate prices and rents—pensioners shoot themselves in the foot threefold:

- The higher interest is, the more extreme distribution is from the many to the few—as we have already seen in Chap. 5. Moreover because of high real interest more and more companies move from being debtors to creditors. Instead of investing they begin to speculate and as a result unemployment rises, this we have also already seen (Schulmeister 1995).
- The higher the hope of capital gains or dividends is, the more ruthlessly large corporations are pressurized and exploited. In extreme circumstances a pension candidate loses his/her workplace in the same company in favor of higher dividends for the pension fund.
- The higher the real estate prices and rents are, the higher the cost of living is and this is also a trade-off for the majority of Germans and Austrians, who do not own real estate or who have to pay a high price for it.

Good thriving conditions for the funded scheme are an extensive distribution from the small Riester Pension savers and those who cannot afford this to the owners of capital. Pension privatization was a large-scale ploy with many people falling into the trap of thinking that they had the same interests as wealthy rentiers. The fairytale which we learnt about in Chap. 6 is valid for the complete pension system. The more people bank on private pension schemes and capital income, the more insecure pensions will become and the bigger the inequality will be. Attac attempts to investigate and inform about these connections as well as the Project Bank for the Common Good which provides information about these background details with a sort of "adult education center for money." This form of monetary education should be a component of the Common Good Charter of banks. When banks are profit oriented, they are interested in covering up and fraud because this increases their profits. If they turned towards common good orientation, which would be an element of "money and credit as a public good" a secure pension for everybody would be included in their objectives and they would correspondingly make their contribution to information and clarification.

13.3 Alternatives

The consequences of the quoted arguments are obvious:

- The state should completely withdraw from the support of the private pension system and funded scheme. People are free to make use of private schemes, to save financial wealth—it is about the fact that this is not financed by the tax payer and that the negative effects of the funded scheme are not paid for by the general public. In the past in the Austrian statutory pension system, there was the possibility of insuring oneself at a higher rate on a voluntary basis, which is in my opinion still the best supplementary personal protection.
- The solidarity pension insurance and inter-generational contract should be enhanced in order to close them off from the constant population ageing of the last hundred years and its continuation as well as closing the still existing gaps in benefits: minimum pension for a decent existence, more generous consideration of phases with no employment income, improvement of pensions for women. With the ten screws, public pensions can be raised to a level where they provide a decent existence.

References

Bingler, Klaus/Bosbach, Gerd (2004): *Kein Anlass zu Furcht und Panik. Fakten und Mythen zur 'demografischen Katastrophe'*, Schriftenreihe des Verbandes Deutscher Rentenversicherungsträger, volume 59, November/December 2004, pages 725–749.

Disney, Richard. 1999. *OECD public pension programmes in crisis: An evaluation of the reform options* Washington: World Bank.

Guger, Alois/Mayrhuber, Christine (2001): *Arbeitsmarktperspektiven und Pensionsfinanzierung bis 2030*, WIFO monthly reports 9/2001.

Keppler, Toni (2009): Rechenfehler mit schweren Folgen. Chiles privates Rentensystem wird zum Sanierungsfall für den Staat, in *Welt-Sichten* 4/2009.

Mackenroth, Gerhard (1952): Die Reform der Sozialpolitik durch einen deutschen Sozialplan, in *Schriften des Vereins für Socialpolitik*, NF, Volume 4, Berlin.

Orszag, Peter R. and Stiglitz, Joseph E. 1999. *Rethinking pension reform: The Myths about social security systems*. Presentation at the conference "New Ideas about Old Age Security", IBRD, Washington, DC, 14/15 September 1999.

Reimon, Michel/Felber, Christian (2003): *Schwarzbuch Privatisierung. Wasser, Schulen, Krankenhäuser – was opfern wir dem freien Markt?*, Ueberreuter, Vienna.

Schirrmacher, Frank (2004): *Das Methusalem-Komplott*, Karl Blessing Verlag, Munich 2004.

Schulmeister, Stephan: (1995): *Zinssatz, Wachstumsrate und Staatsverschuldung*, WIFO monthly reports 3/95, pages 165–180.

Vereinigte Dienstleistungsgewerkschaft E.V. (2003): *Mythos Demografie*, Brochure, 28 pages, Berlin.

Whitehouse, Edward. 2000. *Administrative charges for funded pensions: An international comparison and assessment*. Social Protection Discussion Paper No. 0016, Social Protection Unit, The Human Development Network, IBRD.

Williams, John B. 2000. *Social security privatization: Lessons from the United Kingdom*. Center for Retirement Research at Boston College, Working Paper, 10.

Chapter 14
Global Tax Cooperation

Abstract This chapter proposes a broad range of strategies and measures for global tax cooperation in order to finance public goods and services in a sufficient and just manner. Public property, including taxes, should not be protected less than private property. For this purpose, all incomes should be reported to the fiscal authorities compulsorily and automatically. Financial assets should be included in a global register similar to real estate assets. Cross-border movement of capital should only be free in the case of full cooperation in tax policy between countries. This would end the existence of tax havens—inside and outside the US and the EU. Finally, a set of measures is proposed regarding how corporations can be properly taxed: They have to publicly report where they carry out which kind of operation and pay what amount of taxes. Then, they are taxed globally according to their real activities. If tax rates differ from country to country, the imputation method in bilateral tax cooperation treaties could remedy tax competition and avoidance.

> *The first three decades after WWII were the decades of the most concentrated movement of capital restrictions in the history of international capitalism to date. They were at the same time an era of particularly strong growth, high employment, and considerable increase in real income and social progress.*
> Jörg Huffschmid (1999, p. 109)

14.1 Systemic Tax Evasion

When it comes to the subject of taxes, it appears that we are approximately half way between feudalism and democracy or vice versa. While in particular private property of the wealthy is protected with the united efforts of public and private security forces, with the state showing exceptional commitment in this area, the finance ministers and private tax consultants work effectively together in the same manner in order to maintain the tax payments of these same wealthy individuals, whose property is highly protected by the state, at as low a level as possible.

The tip of the iceberg is prominent—Cristiano Ronaldo, Weseley Snipes, Lindsay Lohan, Ozzy Osbourne, Pamela Anderson, Christina Ricci, Freddy Quinn, Uli Hoeneß, Boris Becker, Karl-Heinz Grasser, Julius Meinl or Herbert Stepic. A share of the wealthiest private individuals manages to shift multimillion and multibillion sums to tax havens with the assistance of lawyers, chartered accountants and tax advisors and notaries. Legions of escape agents aid and abet in tax evasion. On the other hand transnational corporations shift their profits to low tax countries and tax havens while paying little to no taxes where they actually operate in real economic terms and make use of state benefits. This is thanks to their friends in parliaments who have enabled the free movement of capital to tax havens, ineffective double taxation agreements and privatized the "clearing" of trans-border movement of capital.

Starbucks, Amazon, Apple, Google, Ikea, Accenture are all spectacular cases of tax evasion or fraud. 386 large corporations from the OECD lower their tax payments annually by 106 billion US dollars according to a Credit Suisse study.[1] Google even saved 44 billion pounds in tax payments with the assistance of the tax oasis Ireland (52 billion euros—the EU bailout for Ireland amounted to 85 billion euros) and Apple paid a tax rate of 2%.[2] The Deutsche Bank has according to its annual report 440 subsidiaries in the super tax haven Delaware and on the Cayman Islands—more than at its Frankfurt headquarters.[3] Starbucks reported a profit of zero in Switzerland in the years 2008, 2009 and 2010, with tax payments being at the same level.[4] The profits of US companies in Bermuda amount to 646% of economic output of the small country, on the Cayman Islands 547% and on the British Virgin Island 355% of GDP (Gravelle 2013, p. 13). Immense wealth is bunkered in the tax havens of the world. Conservative estimates of the Tax Justice Network believe that private financial assets of between 21 and 32 trillion US dollars are skipping tax "offshore" (Henry 2012, p. 5).

Some wealthy private individuals and multinational corporations have a problem with fairness. When it comes to taking they are at the forefront (state infrastructure from education and health to streets and airports to law and security), when it comes to giving they chicken out (tax payments). They are not prepared to adhere to democratic game rules; they deride the rule of law and liberal fundamental principles. They more resemble a "band of robbers" than honorable businessmen und responsible citizens. Poor people do not have this choice—they have no assets which they can shift, they do no earn company profits which they could declare at alternative locations, they have no significant capital income which they could hide from the tax authorities. They earn low to medium incomes from which taxes and social insurance are automatically deducted and if they

---

[1] *Neue Zürcher Zeitung*, 22 October 2013.
[2] Figures stem from Senators John McCain und Carl Levin, cited in *Financial Times*, 15 October 2013.
[3] Research by Attac Deutschland: www.attac.de/?id=9546
[4] *Handelszeitung*, 16 July 2013.

14.1 Systemic Tax Evasion

spend the small amount which they have, VAT lashes out with full force. Wealthy individuals and multinational corporations in contrast can park and propagate their wealth and profits "off shore" in the long term and can choose from the worldwide locations where they declare their profits. In addition they can rake in capital income using special legal constructs in such a manner that the relevant tax authority is left out in the cold. Tax evasion and tax fraud trigger a vicious circle in a democratic community:

- It is unfair and disparate if a part of the population evades its tax obligations.
- It is particularly unfair when those who break the rules are those who could most easily adhere to them.
- If the constitutional state unilaterally fails in tax enforcement, trust in the authority, in the legislative process and justice is weakened.
- The tax morale of everybody declines, if one group can turn it to their advantage.
- The tax burden is shifted to honest individuals and those who have less chance of evading tax—away from capital income and company profits to employment income and private consumption.
- State income declines, public benefits must be cut or cancelled.
- Therefore equal opportunities in turn decline and with them the possibility for people from lower classes of earning wealth by themselves and joining the privileged classes. The worse the public health system, education system, public security and social facilities are the fewer chances the poorer class who is reliant on these benefits has, because unlike the wealthy they cannot privately afford these.

Measures to prevent tax evasion and tax fraud should therefore enjoy the same level of political attention as property protection. In the case of the latter, the state is on standby and strictly ensures that the rules of the game are adhered to. In contrast to tax enforcement which protects the property of the general public it appears that there is an international culture of laxness, leniency, amnesty and constitutional apathy—at least in the case of the big fish.

In the process the state ought to have an intrinsic interest in just taxation and effective tax enforcement—if a share of the taxpayers refuses its contribution or minimizes it, the state does not have the means at its disposal which are due to it, public services cannot be provided and public property cannot be established. Tax enforcement deficits represent expropriation of the general public. Indicative for pre-democracies is that the same individuals who insist on stringent protection of property (and advocate a strong state in this respect) see no necessity for action regarding expropriation of the general public due to tax fraud but in contrast advocate a weak state and laws which allow the continuance of this expropriation— free movement of capital to tax havens, "liberating" tax agreements, generous corporate tax schemes, bank secrecy ....

A responsible democracy takes tax enforcement as seriously as protection of property and pays attention to the rights and obligations of citizens without distinction.

The more one-sided the attention of the state with regard to property protection is, the more "feudal" or neo-feudal it is and the more balanced the sovereign commitment is the more democratic a community is. Even the General Declaration of Human and Citizens Rights of 1789 did not prominently stipulate in Article 13 by chance that a "general levy for all citizens, according to their possibilities must be equally distributed." This was as a result of the fact that before the bourgeois revolution the first and second levels of society—the nobility and clergy—were exempt from tax liability, while ordinary people had to bear the complete tax burden although they represented the weakest group and had the least "chance" of all groups in society with regard to making tax payments. Both central fundamental principles of taxation law in democratic states have arisen from this historical inequality:

Universality: all citizens are subject to the same tax obligations.

Ability to pay: the larger the economic "wealth" then the larger the ability is to make tax payments and the more the personal contribution is—people who have more can give more—not only absolutely (an equal piece from a bigger cake) but progressively. The larger the income and wealth cake is, the larger the piece of cake is which can be relinquished to the general public. The wealthiest still have more than everybody else.

As in the case of property protection, there are certain prerequisites for tax enforcement. Details regarding ownership structure must be clarified so that it can be protected by the state for example land and property registry entries, entries in the company's register or declaration of creditor claims. A similar prerequisite catalogue for tax enforcement includes transparency of income and assets to the relevant tax office. This transparency for a section of earnings has been enforced in most democratic states—tax offices are not only automatically notified about wages and salaries but also the social security agency and appropriated taxed, however this is not the case with capital income. In some countries this is only partly or not at all registered with financial authorities and in addition it is taxed many times lower than employment income. The most famous example is again Warren Buffet, who calculated that he only pays 17.4% tax on his multi-million income, whereas his employees pay on average 36%.[5] In Germany the top taxation rate for employment income is 47.5%,[6] capital gains tax is 25%.

In some particularly feudal countries such as Austria and Luxembourg, capital income is subject to banking secrecy and therefore remains anonymous. This contradiction is sensational with a fully-automatic notification to tax offices in the case of employment income in order to ensure successful tax enforcement and legal data protection in the case of capital income in order to maximally obstruct tax enforcement! The international Attac movement addressed this topic at the turn of the century which has resulted in some slow movement in this matter in recent years with tax competition, tax havens and banking secrecy starting to go

---

[5] *New York Times*, 14 August 2011.
[6] Including "wealth tax (Reichensteuer)" and solidarity supplement.

on the defensive. The EU, OECD and USA are proceeding with initial measures. Tax equality and tax justice are however not yet prevalent and despite the increasing number of scandals in recent years these have still not led to a fundamental change in the situation. Automatic notification to financial authorities of all income and assets is still a task which remains to be dealt with in democratic constitutional states. Globalization is no hindrance and a solution could comprise of several steps:

14.2 Step 1: Automatic Registration of All Domestic Income

As we have seen a section of income is already automatically registered with the financial authorities. The equal treatment of employment income, which represents the main source of income for 90% of the population and capital income which to a significant extent perhaps benefits 10% of the population, commands the same automatic declaration to the tax authority—all capital income ranging from interest, dividends to fund gains to capital and betting gains. Equal treatment would naturally also be possible in the opposite direction: "banking secrecy" which is actually capital income secrecy—also misleading here—will be extended to employment income. Those advocating interest, dividend and capital gains secrecy must also be logically in favor of wages and salaries secrecy that is the same "data protection" for all private forms of income. Or if the term "banking secrecy" refers to institutions and is not valid for the form of income, "company secrecy" equally protects employment income of private individuals from the inquisitive eyes of financial authorities, as is the case with bank capital income.

Equal treatment in *this* direction would however be a backward step from transparency for taxation policy. In the concrete conflict of objectives tax enforcement versus data protection, tax obligation trumps data protection because the advantage of a universal and fair tax system prevails over the disadvantages that father state is informed about its citizens' incomes. Or on the other hand the advantage of data protection—all income is secret—is lower than the disadvantage that hardly any tax is enforced therefore resulting in fewer schools being built and fewer public services being financed.[7] Part of the game rules of a new monetary system is that father state makes the public good money available to citizens who then in turn disclose their income and assets, which the state can then effectively and fairly tax. In a modern political system all incomes are equally disclosed. If income and assets can assume the virtual form of book money, these must then also be registered in the same way as the purchase of property which is registered in the land registry and on the basis of which the state can demand tax payments. In the era of new electronic forms of income and assets the ability of tax

---

[7] I developed a more exact argumentation as a reaction to my unthoughtful nomination for the "Big Brother Award": Felber (2010).

enforcement practice must grow with this in order to comply with the same principles as in the past—individuals with higher income and/or assets can absolutely *and* relatively contribute more state financing. A prerequisite for this is that the tax authority is notified about all income and not just a fraction of it.

If all tax-relevant data converges at the tax authority, complete income can be subject to a uniform rate of income tax. Tax separation and tax advantage of capital income (without performance) vis-à-vis employment (performance) income would come to an end. Social security obligations could also be extended to complete personal income instead of only recording wages, salaries and income from self-employment activities. That would not be a tiny screw in the pension system but rather a big one.

14.3 Step 2: Multilateral Agreement on Information Exchange

After "domestic" (the democratic sovereign is currently primary sovereign within nation states) equal treatment of all income has been achieved with automatic registration and notification, the same principle can be employed for income earned by national citizens abroad to prevent tax evasion. The good news: to this purpose there is already an initial step towards a multilateral agreement within the EU with some non-member states (EU Interest Directive) as well as bilateral agreements with the USA ("FATCA") and, since 2017, an agreement of automatic exchange of tax relevant data within the OECD. This could be extended progressively to a global tax agreement, which is exactly what started to happen between the final editing of the original version of this book in German and the more current English version, 53 nations committed to start with automatic information exchange in 2017, another 47 nations will do so in 2018.[8] This means that the zone of beginners is already sufficient in order to persuade other states to participate and in case they are uncooperative they could be obliged to do so. This would be according to the completely legitimate motto—we cooperate in the form of free movement of capital, if you cooperate in questions of tax policy, if you do not cooperate, we will not do so either. In the case of non-cooperation the tax havens would suffer, they would be cut off from international financial markets and would therefore shift over to cooperation immediately, if for example the EU or OECD addressed the issue seriously. This is currently the core problem—the industrial nations (the countries where tax evaders are located) do not mean business. One reason is that they belong to the peer group of tax havens. The USA—with its super tax havens Nevada, South Dakota, Wyoming and, first and foremost Delaware, will *not* participate in the OECD agreement. On the other hand, tax havens and aggressive tax competition on the part of

---

[8] http://www.oecd.org/tax/automatic-exchange/commitment-and-monitoring-process/

some (national) states are *not* the main problem. Tax havens and tax competitors can only exist as long they are tolerated by the countries where minimizers, evaders and criminals are located. The crucial lever is the free movement of capital. If the flight countries hold back tax-relevant data and do not cooperate, then there is neither anything in the Bible, Koran nor in any constitution in the world (exception: EU Lisbon Treaty, which is however not a constitution) which states that this must be free. Even the IMF provides for movement of capital controls, "Members may exercise controls of capital transfers as are necessary to regulate international capital movements."[9]

14.4 Trust and Cooperation

Free movement of capital is a vote of confidence from one state to another. This should first be granted if the partner has earned this trust by cooperating in matters of tax enforcement and financial market regulation. Should this not be the case, then granting free movement of capital should be patiently waited for.

This is extremely sensible—when do you give a person the key to your apartment or your laser card: on the day you meet them because you are a "liberal" person? Or only when the person has earned your trust and you are sure that "opening up" is not going to be abused. This is clear, so why should it be any different between states?

Perhaps another comparison will help—"liberal globalization" is readily described as the "free movement of people, goods, services and capital." This is however threefold misleading and obscure:

1. The unilateral enforcement of economic freedom—free movement of capital, free movement of goods and services—with simultaneous non-enforcement of binding human rights, labor norms, health standards, social welfare systems, tax rates and environmental laws is not "liberal" and does not ensure equal rights and freedom for all but rather a radical preferential treatment of the biggest, most powerful and most ruthless market agents—illiberal predemocracy.
2. Movement of people is, contrary to what is claimed, not free. People are discriminated in three classes by the EU and its member states: first class persons enjoy the same complete freedom of travel as capital does, second class persons must overcome many bureaucratic requirements before being allowed entry to the EU on a temporary basis and just as they have begun to get comfortable and have made friends they have to leave—without mercy. Persons from "undeserving" countries are not allowed to enter at all and the fortress Europe is increasingly hermetically sealing itself off from globalization

---

[9]International Monetary Fund, Articles of Agreement, Article VI, Section 3.

losers (who are the result of unfair economic EU policies). The budget of Frontex, which was solely established for the purpose of preventing the free movement of people, has multiplied in recent years. In comparison with people all foreign capital enjoys unlimited entry—regardless of quality and origin.
3. Free movement of capital and its supervision are then again another kettle of fish, as a comparison—even if movement of people is free, this does not mean that there are no checks at the border, registration, declaration and authorization obligations, spot checks and possible sanctions—rules of the game. The same is in the case of movement of goods—basic freedom of movement in no way means that there are no custom controls, immigration authority, identity card requirement and other game rules. In 2016, the USA and China both had 60,000 custom officers, each (World Customs Organisation 2016). Only in the case of capital, free movement of capital suddenly means that the state regulation, supervision, tax authorities, registration system disappears and stops existing? This is the outrageous real situation, it is neither liberal nor democratic nor constitutional and in no sense reasonable.

Free movement of capital is not an end in itself and in no case should it be the end of all regulations. Progressive nations should in future submit multilateral tax cooperation agreements to non-member states for signature and refusal to sign or enforce these agreements should be met by limitation to movement of capital. This was seen in the example of the USA-Switzerland (Foreign Account Tax Compliance Act—FATCA) which will hopefully become a global model—and also be applied to the USA itself!

14.5 From the previous EU Interest Directive to the Sound Capital Income Directive

Meaning business however also means a second issue and not just only being prepared to impose sanctions when the movement of capital partner does not corporate. It also primarily means setting a good example. The EU interest directive can be considered as an unperturbed "Swizz cheese" with regard to the number of loopholes it possesses. In the beginning of the directive, only interest income was taxed but neither dividends nor capital gains and only natural persons and no corporate bodies. Austria and Luxembourg did not participate at all in the automatic exchange and negotiated special treatment in the form of tax at source in order to protect their bank secrecy, namely their wealthy class.

In conclusion there is therefore a long list of unfinished assignments which prove that those parliaments who have taken action so far do not really mean business. They are completely occupied with defending the wealthy class against access by the tax authorities or undermining this access, which is a further reason for allowing the sovereign to decide on the rules of the game, and not the representatives of the A class.

A serious capital income directive includes *all* kinds of capital income of *all* natural and legal persons, without exceptions. To make it possible, fiscal authorities have to be informed about the wealth that exists.

14.6 World Financial Registry

One decisive prerequisite for the execution of international tax justice is transparency about financial assets. To date there is no international registry where owners or beneficiaries of financial assets appear by name, which would be the prerequisite for the assignment of assets and income to persons liable to tax. Here, an analogy between immobile (real estate) assets and mobile (financial) assets helps: a national—registry of real estate assets is a matter of course of a democratic society. These registries fulfill two objectives: (a) the protection of the right to property and (b) the basis for tax duties and execution. The same would help for financial assets. Gabrial Zucman (2014), a former student of Tomas Piketty, proposes a "world financial registry" which could be defined as a condition for the free movement of capital. Only those countries who cooperate and inform about all taxable assets held in accounts and legal persons in their country by foreigners, will enjoy free(er) movement of capital. Those who refuse to cooperate, will suffer restrictions of the movement of capital. As already said, free movement of capital is not a natural law, but a freedom which is given in exchange for responsible behavior, in this case: full cooperation in tax policies.

14.7 Technical Implementation

What does "limiting movement of capital" mean? In order to understand this, it is worth taking a glance at the usual technical processing of movement of capital which is currently in place, since some people are of the impression that tax evasion takes place in fully packed cases with cash and is personally smuggled or smuggled by traffickers through rugged countryside and transported with motorboats—which is not the case. Some people think that the local bank transfers millions with a mouse click to a tax haven, which is superficially applicable. Behind the scenes there are so-called "clearing banks," via which the majority of international movement of capital is processed, for costs reasons. It is simply cheaper, if thousands of transfers are channeled at the same time via the data highway. These clearing banks provide the service of transferring beloved money from "onshore" to "offshore" locations and of course not free of charge, each transaction involves a fee. If you like, these clearing banks are private customs authorities for border crossing of international capital. Would we privatize the customs authority for movement of goods—including processing profits? I think that it is clear that this is a sovereign function which should be carried out directly by the state, by the central bank for example. Today a share of clearing is carried out by the central banks (e. g. the "Target system" of the European Central Bank), so it would only have to be "consolidated." Alternative to this the public domain could specifically commission the private clearing banks, including the limitation of the movement of capital; however this would be the privatization of customs clearance. There are at least two possibilities for limiting the movement of capital: tax haven movement of capital is taxed at such a high rate that the "flight" becomes unattractive—or the banks, located in declared tax havens, are denied participation in movement of capital and they receive no accounts at clearing banks.

The first model variant has the advantage of the possible differentiation depending on the graveness of the fiscal fencing. A possible classification instrument is the "Financial Secrecy Index (FSI)" of the international Tax Justice Network.[10] It would for example be possible to tax movement of capital to tax havens in gradual stages with 3–30%, depending on the result of the index. As the fences operate with various "enticements," this proposal would appear to me to be the better one. In addition it is procedurally as well as educationally geared, and in my opinion this proposal would appear to be better. After the end of banking secrecy for interest income, reporting obligation could be extended to other forms of income, to legal entities, to the trust register and other gaps. Even within the EU such an "incentive mechanism" would make sense—Austria and Luxembourg would keep their freedom to continue making use of the tax at source instead of automatic reporting of capital income, it would just cost a little more. Every country would have the chance of tax free movement of capital in this "collective learning process." The only difference to today would be that this status would be no longer free of charge and unconditionally granted, but rather it would be the highest level of reward after homework has been done in the subject of tax cooperation.

The EU Lisbon Treaty already currently provides the legal basis for the clearing process via the European Central Bank system. The ECB protocol states, "The ECB and the national central banks can make institutions available and the ECB can issue decrees in order to guarantee efficient and reliable clearing and payment systems with the EU and *in transactions with non-member countries.*"[11]

14.8 Globally Just Corporation Tax— "Entire Group Taxation"

After the fair and liberal taxation of individuals the next liberal gap closure, in terms of equal rights and obligations of all, is a globally coordinated corporate taxation. In this case, again, liberal argumentation must actually be sufficient. From the point in

---

[10] www.financialsecrecyindex.com

[11] Protocol No 4 "on the statute of the European system of central banks and of the European central bank," of the treaty on European Union and of the Treaty on the functioning of the European Union.

14.8 Globally Just Corporation Tax—"Entire Group Taxation"

time when a common trade zone comes into effect via a political agreement, and a level playing field which is frequently striven for is politically established, the same rules of the game must be valid for everybody on this field. Who would be interested in the football world championship, if every team had their own rules? Far-fetched? The use of metaphor by "free trade fans" is debunking—they continuously talk about a "level playing field" for "global players." However while fervent negotiation endeavors are taking place at the WTO about level customs duties and the dismantling of "trade barriers," harmonization of labor, social, health and environmental or even tax standards are taboo themes. A "level playing field" would however mean equal tax rules (and all other standards) for everybody, so that entrepreneurial productivity and creativity can completely concentrate on the development of the best products and services and not be distracted by comparison of taxation rates and distorted and misguided by tax-motivated location decisions.

The current tax system is characterized by fourfold inefficiency:

- Companies spend enormous amounts of money on lawyers, fiduciaries and tax advisors to minimize their tax payments by tricks such as internal transfer prices, credits from subsidiaries to headquarters, license fees to subsidiaries or holdings in tax havens and by setting up non-transparent meshes of companies. This money could be employed for better things.
- Lawyers, fiduciaries and tax advisors are ethically comprised by assisting the most powerful members of global society not to pay their fair and just tax contribution, systemically a step backwards behind the bourgeois revolution.
- Tax offices must go to great efforts to track down companies, which would not be necessary if there were uniform consolidated corporation balance sheets and the tax rate were measured on the basis of real company activity in the respective country.
- Tax evading companies therefore one-sidedly make use of state benefits and public infrastructure without paying an appropriate amount of tax for these.

The result is a multi-billion tax deficit in every country because it has been decided not to tax corporations appropriately, transparently and uniformly.

This not being enough—as a result of the shift of profits to tax havens, all non-tax havens end up in tax competition and all reduce their profit tax rate towards complete tax exemption. In Germany during the Kohl era corporate tax rate was still at 60%, today it is the half of this.[12] In the OECD between 1995 and 2009 corporate tax rates sank from 37.7% to 26,3%.[13]

It would be logical and liberal if the most important existing trade areas—EU and WTO—were also to create uniform tax regulations, a uniform basis of assessment as well as a minimum tax rate, then tax competition would be a thing of the past. There are preliminary stages to uniform corporate taxation which could be practised single-handedly by one country, at least by the EU.

---

[12]Corporate tax and commercial tax.
[13]KPMG: corporate and indirect tax rate survey 2007 and 2009.

14.8.1 Country of Residence Principle

This principle states—no matter where an international company operates, the earned profits are taxed the same as in the home state of the company—through subsequent taxation of the difference. The usual double-taxation treaty between states could be organized according to two methods: 1. According to the *exemption method*: a German corporation has established a subsidiary in Ireland, in Switzerland or in Singapore. Profits are only taxed abroad, also if the tax rate is lower than in the homeland. 2. According to the *imputation method*: profits are taxed normally abroad, however if the tax rate there is lower than in the national territory, the difference in the homeland is "subsequently taxed." The first option is the most usual and naturally contains an incentive to establish a subsidiary in a tax haven or in a low tax country. In the second case the incentive to establish a subsidiary in a low tax country for tax reasons and the shift of profits there would be eliminated.

Austria has gained another task here. Since 2005 thanks to the almost in the meantime notorious "group taxation," Austrian companies can also offset their foreign losses "at home" against their profit that is reduce their domestic profit. This is however not valid for profits earned abroad, these are not added onto to their domestic profits. The argumentation is always the same with these tax tricks: it is never concerned with values (justice) but rather with the threat of disadvantages (competition). The competition cudgel has been used against better labor conditions, social security, environmental and climate protection, transparency for consumers, limiting inequality, more democracy and basic rights. Unfortunately an international competition system does not allow for all things to be nice, true and good is what we learn, in contrast unfair behavior creates advantages. This ethically anti-constitutional argumentation[14] which is in the interest of global players does not have to be adopted by a sovereign, it can decide in favor of justice, fairness, equality and democracy. An Austrian corporation's loss in Eastern Europe is offset against its profit in the same country and the latter is taxed accordingly. The difference between the profit tax rates in the home state is subject to subsequent taxation in Austria. In this manner the competition basis for subsidiaries, investments and profits of multinational corporations with tax rates is removed.

14.8.2 Unitary Taxation or Overall Group Tax

Corporates could react to the domicile principle by shifting their legal domicile and indeed Philip Morris did this by moving to Switzerland and Accenture moved to Bermuda. A more far-reaching alternative is necessary here and it is in the form

---

[14]Most of the constitutions of democratic states "justice" as a constitutional value; Competition or competitiveness are according to my knowledge not considered a value in any constitution.

14.8 Globally Just Corporation Tax—"Entire Group Taxation"

of "unitary taxation," "global proportional tax" or "overall group tax."[15] With this taxation approach the corporation is obliged to compile a global consolidated balance sheet, subsequently the share of each country in the global added value (on the basis of factors such as capital expenditure, employees and turnover) is calculated and this calculated share of the global consolidated profit is subject to the valid tax rate of the respective country. With this not only would headquarters relocation to a tax haven be futile because in the case of Accenture for example the bulk of its business is carried out in the USA and not on Bermuda. It would also not matter where the corporation shifted its profits to with the aid of various tricks such as internal transfer prices, lending from one part of the company to another, excessive license fees (as is the case with Ikea) etc. Then what counts is only the real business activity. Tax havens would be pointless, as an entry in the companies register neither creates turnover nor employment.

Unitary taxation is not utopian and was already applied in 1925 in the USA in several federal states to combat US domestic tax competition. California for example wanted to prevent film companies from shifting their profits to Nevada. However the massive pressure from corporations and the EU fear of double taxation resulted in many states diverging from the path of global proportional tax. For a long time the OECD blocked every investigation with regard to the impact of a unitary tax and a UNO initiative became dormant again.

If however sovereigns decide and not with the governments who are connected to the wealthy class, unitary taxation could be introduced swiftly. In times of globalization unitary corporation taxation is a logical principle. The Tax Justice Network explains, "The uniform access is based on the perspective that a corporation's income is earned by the corporation as a whole, it does not attempt to identify or quantify how much of it was earned from which part of the corporation." In contrast "the current international tax system" considers "trans-national corporations as a loose collection of companies or units, which are separated from each other in different countries" (Picciotto 2012, P. 10 und 1). Official policy is unfortunately marching in the opposite direction and according to the tax expert of the Vienna based WIFO, Margit Schratzenstaller, "The EU commission appears to be diverging even more from 'unitary taxation' as the centerpiece of an effective way of combatting profit shifting."[16]

With a unilateral implementation of unitary taxation the "real location competition" would not yet be over—companies could relocate their real activities to countries with low tax rates which is why the Global Tax Justice Network, a pioneer in this area, proposes the combination of both alternatives, namely global proportional tax and the domicile principle. Then all loopholes would be closed and global tax competition within the discipline of "company profits" would come to an end.

The proposed global tax authority—see Chap. 7—could begin with the implementation of overall group taxation and lay down uniform rules for a globally consolidated corporation tax balance sheet broken down according to country.

---

[15] www.attac.de/kampagnen/konzernbesteuerung/unitary-taxation/gesamtkonzernshysteuer

[16] Opinion in *Der Standard*, 25 October 2013.

14.9 A Go-It-Alone by the EU is Possible!

The European Union could lead the way and connect three approaches:

1. After pushing through a common tax basis for transnational companies, which has been worked out by the commission and advocated in a resolution, the second equally necessary step is the determination of a common corporation tax rate in the EU, at least a high minimum tax rate in order to pacify tax competition in the single market.
2. The principle of unitary taxation will be implemented by all companies active in the EU—manufacturing, sales or investment companies. Ikea could shift the same large share of its profits to tax havens; the "assessment basis" would be the turnover, employment and capital commitment in every individual EU member state.
3. All double taxation agreements will be rewritten to the imputation method. If EU companies pay tax at lower rates abroad, the difference will be subject to subsequent taxation in the EU, in order to discourage the shifting of production locations for tax purposes.

If the political will were present, it would already be possible to establish tax justice today and I can well imagine that is not something which governments in the coming years want and I can even better imagine that if sovereigns could decide for themselves that they would vote for a just tax system in the EU and worldwide.

References

Felber, Christian (2010): *Attac an BBA: Erfordern die Bürgerrechte ein Lohngeheimnis?*, Rechtfertigung zur Nominierung für den Big Brother Award 2010, 2 pages, in the internet: www.christian-felber.at/schaetze/BBA_Attac_Felber.pdf

Gravelle, Jane G. 2013. *Tax havens: International tax avoidance and evasion*. Congressional Research Service, January 2013.

Henry, James S. 2012. *The price of offshore revisited*, Studie des Tax Justice Network, July 2012.

Huffschmid, Jörg (1999): *Politische Ökonomie der Finanzmärkte*, VSA-Verlag, Hamburg.

Picciotto, Sol. 2012. *Towards unitary taxation of transnational corporations*. Tax Justice Network, Study, 19 pages.

World Customs Organisation (2016): *Annual Report 2015 – 2016*, Brussels, 13th July 2016.

Zucman, Gabriel. 2014. Taxing across borders: Tracking personal wealth and corporate profits towards unitary taxation of transnational corporations. *Journal of Economic Perspectives* 28(4): 121–48.

Chapter 15
Income and Ownership Caps— "Negative Feedback"

Abstract This chapter proposes diverse solutions to the current global number 1 problem of excessive and growing inequality. After describing the current state of inequality in income, property, inheritance, and size of companies, interdisciplinary arguments for the limitation of inequality are presented. On this basis, concrete measures towards the limitation of inequality in income, private property, inheritances and the size of companies are proposed. According to different surveys and public proposals, the highest incomes could be capped at 10-fold or 20-fold the lowest incomes. Private property could be limited to for example 30 million US dollars, inheritances to one million US dollars for personal wealth and 20 million US dollars for participation in companies. Finally, a size limit for corporations could be set at a maximum turnover of ten, 25 or 50 billion US dollars. The concrete limits should be defined and decided on, like all other fundamental questions, within the framework of sovereign conventions.

> *The fair distribution of income and resources is one of the fundamental prerequisites for trust and the belief in the community. With this, social justice is also the basis of trust in money and a prerequisite for a crisis-proof economy, which also people who are well-off ought to be interested in.*
> Christina von Braun (2012, p. 165)

15.1 Excessive Inequality

One of the largest current problems is undoubtedly extreme inequality and the associated power concentration in the economy and politics. Inequality has a large chain of further problems connected to it—poverty and marginalization, loss of equal opportunities, loss of political participation possibilities, lobbyism and misregulation, environmental destruction and climate change, financial instability .... It is becoming evident for more and more people that capitalism in its current manifestation has become the biggest enemy of democracy. The renowned political scientist Colin Crouch writes, "The concentration of economic power is the actual cause of the dilemma which modern societies are confronted with (…) political procedures and governments are increasingly developing in a backward direction, which was typical of pre-democratic times" (Crouch 2008, p. 142 und 13). The former IMF chief economist Simon Johnson writes, "All finance crises in recent times were triggered by an economic elite class gaining too much power" (Johnson 2010). Robert Reich, employment minister under Bill Clinton makes it clearer, "Super-capitalism has captured politics and engulfed democracy" (Reich 2008, p. 214). Colin Crouch speaks of "post-democracy" and looking into the future I speak of "pre-democracy." To begin with let us take a look at the power concentration in the current economy:

- According to Oxfam International, the richest eight billionaires own the same amount of wealth as the poorest half of the world (Oxfam International 2017, p. 2).[1]
- Income inequality in the USA has risen to an extent which some consider to be virtually unbelievable—a person working for the statutory minimum wage of 7.25 US dollars[2] with an average full-time working week of 40 hours, working 48 weeks per year earns 13,920 US dollars. The highest known yearly income was earned in 2010 by the hedge fund manager John Paulson and at an incredible 5 billion US dollars[3] was the 359,000 times this!
- The gap in property distribution is not only increasing in the USA and Brazil but also in Germany—while in this country 50% of the population own no (!) net assets (their share of total assets is 0.0%), 40% of the population own together 38.9% and the richest 10% a proud 61.1% of total assets (Deutsches Institut Für wirtschaftsforschung 2009, p. 59). In Austria, according to the latest calculations of the University of Linz, a mere 1% of the population reaches even 37% of the total assets which amounts to 469 billion euros, which is exactly double the state debt of 234 billion or 17 times as much as 50% of the population owns—only 27.5 billion or 2.2% of the total assets (Eckerstorfer et al 2013, pp. 28–29). The richest households in Germany (the Aldi family) have 33.8 billion euros, 40 billion in Austria (the Porsche Piëch family) and 42 billion euros in Spain (Amancio Ortega).
- The larger the fortune the faster inequality grows—Valluga AG writes that the fortune of "ordinary" millionaires grows by 8% annually. In contrast the annual growth of the Forbes 400 in the period from 1993 to 2009 amounted to about 10% on average (Valluga AG 2010, p. 13). The first million is in contrast to the last by far the most difficult and is for most people unattainable.
- At the end of the 1990s the 500 worldwide largest companies employed 0.05% of the world population but controlled 70% of world trade, 80% of foreign investments and 25% of world production (Laszlo 1988, p. 70). The joint

---

[1]The calculations use wealth of the richest individuals from Forbes Billionaires listing and wealth of the bottom 50% from Credit Suisse Global Wealth Databook 2016.
[2]http://usgovinfo.about.com/od/moneymatters/a/Federal-Minimum-Wage.htm
[3]*The Wall Street Journal*, 28 January 2011.

turnover of the Fortune 500 companies accounted for 72% of economic output in the USA in 2000; in 2011 it was 78%.[4] Forty percent of the corporate value of 43,000 transnational corporations is currently held by only 147 companies, based on the results of an investigation carried out by the ETH Zürich—"The top owners in the core can therefore be considered as a 'super unit' in the global corporation network" (Vitali et al 2011). The creative destruction (Schumpeter) quite obviously does not manage to compete with oligopolization and the re-feudalization of the markets, not even with the assistance of anti-cartel laws and state merger controls.

While there is a string of theorists and economists who explicitly advocate inequality, I am not aware of any prominent plea for *infinite* inequality. In contrast there is a long ancestral line of thinkers who advocate the limitation of inequality—for various reasons. The most important arguments will be dealt with here.

15.1.1 Liberal Argument

The liberal archetypal principle says that all people enjoy the same freedom and therefore a person's freedom must be limited at the point where his/her freedom would restrict another person's freedom. This fundamental principle is confirmed by several liberal thinkers; Milton Friedman writes that "freedom must be restricted in order to safeguard another person's freedom" (Friedman 2006, p. 49). Friedrich A. von Hayek played from the same score, "In order to be free from dictatorial influences, power must also be restricted" (Hayek 2004, p. 25). He concluded, "The task of a freedom policy must therefore be to reduce compulsion or its detrimental effects" (Hayek 2005, p. 14ff). The former Austrian Minister for Finance Karl-Heinz Grasser secured a Readers Digest issue of Hayek's "The Road to Serfdom." In the preface of the small book he wrote, "Power is the opposite of freedom." Obviously everybody agrees that too much power is illiberal. It is striking that "liberal" thinkers do not also hold this true for the concentration of *economic* power—for the concentration of private property, inheritances and corporations. My argument is that the over-concentration of power is detrimental everywhere regardless of whether it is political, economic or sexual power. Here as well as there, the principle of separation of power applies—in a liberal democracy *every* concentration of power should be prevented no matter whether it is the restriction of legislative terms, the distribution of power between legislative, executive and judiciary power in order to prevent cartels and monopolies on markets or to restrict inequality of income and wealth.

The differentiated thought is that it is not about the *abolition* of freedom of ownership but rather the *securing* of it for everybody by way of restriction of

---

[4]http://money.cnn.com/magazines/fortune/fortune500/world-economies-interactive

excess. In the case of almost all other types of freedom so much dialectic is expected of adult individuals:

- We should not touch other people without their consent—this is neither illiberal nor a tenderness ban.
- We should not drive so fast on streets, as some people would like to—this is neither illiberal nor a ban of motorized private transport.
- We are not allowed to build houses as high as we would like to and also not everywhere—this is also neither illiberal nor does it represent a general ban on building.
- We are permitted to run for certain political offices only once or only a few times—this is also neither illiberal nor a challenge of the political offices themselves, on the contrary.

All forms of freedom are restricted in order to safeguard the same freedom and rights of others. Only ironically in the case of income and wealth those masquerading as liberal advocates of the boundless concentration of power try to argue that a restriction of these forms of freedom are directed "against freedom" or even represent "communism." The Styrian Chamber of Commerce states in a brochure that it is dedicated to the common good economy for example, "With regard to the restriction of ownership rights, the borders of a liberal democratic legal system are exceeded (…) this corresponds to a communist system" (Styrian Chamber of Commerce 2013, p. 1 und 23). The mix up of "communist" and liberal is certainly remarkable. My argument: the freedom of income and ownership must be equally restricted as in the case of all other forms of freedom in order

- to prevent an over-concentration of power,
- to avert an excess of inequality,
- to secure the same economic and political participation chances for all to guarantee the maximum amount of freedom for all.

Donald Trump and the Bush dynasty in the USA, Berlusconi in Italy or Frank Stronach in Austria very clearly show which idea billionaires come up with—they buy football clubs, TV channels and in Frank Stronach's case a whole parliament club. If political decision-makers become a saleable commodity, democracy and equal freedom for everybody becomes a thing of the past. Trump was elected after the publishing of this book and is unexpectedly clear evidence of the argument developed here.

The "public good money" should obstruct this. Every individual should be permitted to acquire and own as much to be able to afford a comfortable life, however nobody should attain so much power that his or her political influence annuls the equal participation chances of others. Liberal means "maximum freedom for all (on the basis of equal rights and chances)." Illiberal is the "maximum freedom for a few (as the result of unequal chances and rights)." Stronach even confirms this, "The world was and is dominated by the golden rule: he who has gold makes the rules. I do not want to be dominated by anybody but I also do not want to have the possibility of dominating somebody. The question is how can we sever the chains of domination constructively."[5] By not allowing anybody to own so much gold that he can make the rules.

15.1.2 System Theoretical Argument

The insight that "positive feedback" can lead to the collapse of living systems is thanks to system theory. On the other hand "negative feedback" ensures sustained stability and the survival of a system or organism. The specifically means that in complex living systems there are developments such as warming, growth or increase of concentration or particular substances or populations. If these tendencies are not offset by cooling, sweating, chemical counter-reactions, propagation of natural enemies or beneficials, this leads to overheating, hyperacidity, over populations and finally to the tilting and collapse of an ecosystem.

Capitalism is a positive feedback system—the wealthier, larger or more powerful a person or company is, the easier it is to become wealthier, larger and more powerful. This leads to an over-concentration and excessive inequality and endangers system stability. Exactly the opposite would have to be the case for economic systems to remain stable in the long-term and for the "appropriation resistance" to progressively increase—the richer, larger and more powerful somebody is, the more difficult it should be to become richer, larger and more powerful, to an absolute limit of growth. Then this economic system would be in negative feedback and stable: at the start of working life there are strong incentives and assistance for people to be able to acquire modest wealth, however the larger this becomes the more the system starts to thwart this up to the point where there is no further headway on a material level. From which point this is the case should be democratically decided. A possible ceiling would be the threshold to "ultra-high net worth individual"—this rating is conferred by money managers starting from 30 million US dollars private assets. The balance sheet total of banks could be capped—prior to which the stipulated equity capital progressively increases. Industrial companies could be back-coupled whereby they are progressively democratized and socialized as of a certain size. If the company proprietors are primarily concerned with innovation and meaningful products, they will cope with progressively democratic structures. If on the other hand they are primarily concerned with power, this would be a strong incentive to remain small. The decision to "grow and share power" or "remain small and maintain power" would remain the decision of the entrepreneurs. Today a large company can simply devour another smaller company; this is legal and from time to time leads to an even bigger success for the cannibal. Last but not least some global players become so powerful that controlling and regulating them is no longer successful. The corporations in contrast tame democracy. Some politicians call this "market-conformed

---

[5]Sommergespräch, *Der Standard*, 7 September 2013.

democracy."[6] Democracy which is in line with market requirements should however not exist—a state system which orientates itself towards the market is an economic and financial dictatorship.

15.1.3 Performance Justice and Equal Opportunities

"Performance must be worth it again" is a common opinion of the party chairmen of the SPD and CDU.[7] The "performance-oriented society" is invoked in many places and is found in the content of numerous party programs. However in order for performance to indeed be worth it, the first million must be the easiest. Today the first million for 99% of the people in Germany and Austria is unattainable regardless of what and how much they actually do and perform. Yet the second million is much easier to earn and in the case of the hundredth million the person in question can probably no longer say what performance led to this million. People who own a 1000 million and earn an 8% assets pension annually have to spend 220,000 euros daily in order not to become *richer*—what a nice meritocracy!

According to the data from Credit Suisse, 38% of all billionaires in the OECD have inherited large assets (Credit Suisse 2012, p. 31). Profit earnings or capital income which they make on this initial capital, which was a free gift to them, again constitute a basic income without performance. While some slave away for the minimum wage or less, others do absolutely nothing and "let their money work for them," which in concrete terms means that others who actually perform *work for them*. These are striking contraindications of a real "performance-oriented society" or meritocracy. However those who advocate a performance-oriented society and in particular "performers" appear not to have noticed any of this or do not want to know about it. Those who advocate a truly equal opportunities performance society must ensure that:

- everybody is in the start position with the same assets,
- personal commitment and effort are exclusively evaluated in performance appraisal,
- small companies have the same chances on the market as large companies,
- new companies have the same chances as existing companies,
- children without wealthy parents and whose parents who have poor connections have the same chances as children from good and influential families,
- disadvantages through no fault of one's own—physical and mental weakness, traumata, illnesses, poor aptitude do not lead to income disadvantages.

---

[6]Federal Chancellor Angela Merkel at a press conference on 1 September 2009. Source: www.bundesregierung.de/Content/DE/Mitschrift/Pressekonferenzen/2011/09/2011-09-01-merkel-coelho.html. Retrieved on 2 November 2013.

[7]CDU chairman Helmut Kohl 1982. SPD party chairman Kurt Beck, *Die Welt*, 19 August 2006.

Equal opportunities and performance justice mean that people who make the same effort under the same conditions obtain the same income and wealth. That is never entirely achievable but unequal opportunities and performance injustice can be minimized by removing the largest obstacles in the way.

15.1.4 The Financial Stability Argument

As seen in Chap. 6 there is a growing surplus of wealth which is not only an expression of unfair distribution and larger inequality but also the material from which bubbles are created. At a certain point of wealth the wealthy have no alternative but to channel their fortune into the global financial casino where it enhances the creation of bubbles. If unequal distribution remains, debts grow parallel to the assets until the bubbles burst and assets are destroyed. If the wealthy want to avoid a painful destruction of their wealth, they should be interested in negative feedback and if democratic society is interested in systemic financial stability, it should in addition to other measures ensure that trillion surpluses of private wealth do not occur which then become real estate bubbles, commodity bubbles, state debt bubbles, share bubbles or derivative bubbles on the "free financial markets." A much larger loss of wealth can be incurred during a crisis than as a result of taxes. As a result Ulrike Herrmann writes, "It might appear paradoxical but for the wealthy the best money investment would be if they paid more taxes" (Herrmann 2013a, P. 234). In the event of a crisis-related destruction of wealth, it is simply gone but if it flows into taxes instead it results in schools, hospitals, transport, social and public security as well as chances for everybody to also acquire a fortune tomorrow and lead a good life.

15.1.5 The Health Argument

A further argument against boundless inequality is the fact that societies are torn apart and become less happy. It is empirically measurable that all quality of live and social indicators regress if inequality is too large. It is not inequality itself which has a detrimental impact but rather *exorbitant* inequality. The British epidemiologists Richard Wilkinson and Kate Pickett have collated a myriad of studies which confirm the connection between inequality and social indicators and have presented an impressive overview—exorbitant inequality leads to an increase in insecurity, fear, violence, crime, prison populations, drug abuse, teenage pregnancies, less favorable treatment of women and a decrease in life expectancy. These results in detail are as equally astounding as they are explicit—regarding the topic of fear in the second half of the twentieth century in the USA alone 269 studies were evaluated with a continuous upward trend (including depression illnesses). In the late 1980s fears in children were higher than those in psychiatric patients in the 1950s. In Great Britain in the 1990s people in their mid-twenties suffered from anxiety twice as often as people of the same age in 1958 (Wilkinson and Pickett 2012, p. 50). The German fear index doubled between 1991 and 2010.[8] Inversely trust amongst people is declining to the degree that the pay disparity in their country is increasing (…) in 1960 the trust rate in the USA was still at 60%, in 2004 it was less than 40% (Wilkinson and Pickett 2012, p. 68 und 71). Wilkinson and Pickett (2009) summarize, "If the prevailing income differences in the USA declined to a degree, as it is verified with regard to equality in the leading industrial nations Japan, Norway, Sweden and Finland, then the share of Americans who believe they can trust others would increase by 75% (….) The rates of people suffering from psychological disorders or overweight could each go down by two thirds, the number of teenage pregnancies could be halved, the number of prison inmates could sink by 40%, people would live longer and in doing so work the equivalent of two months less annually" (Wilkinson and Pickett 2012, p. 300).

15.1.6 The Happiness Argument

It is quite surprising: I am not aware of any religion, philosophy or school of thought which endorses or recommends boundless material wealth, on the contrary—restraint, moderation and equilibrium are the target everywhere and sometimes also frugality, modesty and humbleness. In contrast selfishness, greed, avarice, stinginess and materialism are clearly negatively connoted and even ostracized as "deadly sins." Capitalism defies the essence of all religions, it is a substitute religion. The best are not those who are moderate, help others and find happiness in missions other than money but rather those who have the most and continue to boundlessly propagate their wealth.

"Money brings happiness" is only applicable under two conditions: (a) if it is not the only happiness factor and (b) if basic needs can be covered by it. In other words up to a certain point money is essential today to cover basic needs but beyond this there is no scientific evidence that more money brings more happiness. On the contrary, the available research results indicate no or even a negative connection between "even more money" and happiness. The happiness researcher Richard Layard writes, "In the USA real income and with it the standard of living has doubled but people are in no way more satisfied than in the fifties."

Neither the number of unhappy people has declined nor has the share of happy people increased (Layard 2009, p. 43). Also amongst countries the figures speak for themselves, "If we contrast the western industrialized countries, we notice that the rich ones are not happier than the poor ones" (Layard 2009, p. 46). The highest threshold I am familiar with above which the correlation between more money and more happiness ceases is that of 290,000 US dollars annual income (Nickerson et al 2003),

---

[8]R+V Angstindex: www.ruv.de/de/presse/download/pdf/aengste-der-deutschen-2010/20100909-grafik-aengste-der-deutschen-2010.pdf

which on the basis of dollars would be approximately 20-fold the current minimum wage.

In brief: excessive inequality is illiberal and destroys equal freedom and opportunities for everybody, it undermines democracy and systemic stability, and it is hostile to performance, unhealthy and tears society apart. Excessive wealth also does not bring happiness …. The first argument, the liberal one, would actually be sufficient, however I have argued here in somewhat more detail because there is vehement and highly emotional opposition towards the proposal of limiting inequality and concentration of power. The former chief editor of the Austrian *Presse* Michael Fleischhacker dubbed me in several editorials due the thoughts submitted here as a "sacred heart Marxist Attac propagandist," "anti-liberal dispossession euphoriast" and "neo-communist common good pseudo-economist."[9] Those wanting to distract from a debate yielding insights at best start throwing heavy punches, however in a democracy it should not be the loudest who assert themselves but rather those with the best ideas. How could the convention be asked these questions sensibly?

15.2 Limiting Income Inequality

There are two levels in the limitation of income equality: the internal inequality (business level) and the economic maximum difference between the statutory or collective wage agreements minimum wage and the highest permissible income.

The limitation of internal inequality has long been the subject of discussion, John Pierpont "J.P." Morgan of all people introduced a model at the end of the nineteenth century whereby the top-earners of the company were not permitted to earn more than 20-fold of the lowest wage (Von Braun 2012, p. 269). Not being aware of this proposal, I repeated it in 2006 in the "Justice Formula 2010" (Felber 2006, p. 276ff). In January 2013 the founder of the World Economic Forum Klaus Schwab caused people to sit up and take notice by making the same proposal in Davos,[10] and in doing so captured the zeitgeist. At the same meeting George Soros also warned about ever-growing inequality. There is already something going on: in 2011 the first pioneer companies of the Economy for the Common Good movement created their Common Good Balance Sheets and accounted for income inequality. Likewise in January 2013, the Aargau cantonal parliament legally restricted maximum income in public banks to 10-fold of minimum income. Although a nationwide Swiss public initiative initially failed with the proposal 1:12 the topic is certainly still not over. I see three reasons for this initial failure: firstly, there was only one proposal to vote

---

[9]Hinter den Potemkinschen Kulissen der Sozialmechanik, in *Die Presse*, 13 August 2011; Den großen Wurf gibt es nicht, in *Die Presse*, 22 October 2011.

[10]*Frankfurter Allgemeine Zeitung*, 20 January 2013. In the *FAZ*-Interview Management salaries which are too high are no longer socially acceptable: Schwab literally said, Whether the ratio is now supposed to be 1–20 or 1–40 is of secondary importance. If it is however 1–100 and higher then it is no longer socially acceptable. I have by the way not lost any of my entrepreneur friends as a result, they understand my motives.

upon, secondly, it was made by the Young Socialists—some who did not want to be associated with "socialism" voted against although they supported the proposal; thirdly, not few voted against because factor 12 was too high! What they did not intend and what was not transparent is that by rejecting factor 12, the winner was factor 900—although it was not an option! It is just the current state of the art .... The biggest advantage of an economic convention is that several proposals are made and the individual proposals are not aligned to individual persons or groups.

A second aspect is the maximum difference between minimum wage and maximum income. In Switzerland there is an initiative advocating a minimum wage of 4,000 Swiss francs monthly, which is a lot measured on 1,300 US dollars which is the statutory minimum wage in the USA (on the basis of a 40-hour week). In the USA the question could be whether the current minimum wage of 7.25 dollars should be raised to 10 dollars and for those who think that this appears to be a large jump—the minimum wage in the USA was already 11 US dollars, however in 1968. This was naturally not nominally as it was 1.60 US dollars at that time but in purchasing-power comparison ("in constant 2013 dollars") this corresponds to a value of 11 US dollars today. However today the minimum wage of 7.25 US dollars constitutes a real value loss of a third! Taking a third away from the poorest is a brutal form of dispossession, but it is never called dispossession or "financial repression," these victim attributes are reserved for the moneyed aristocracy who defends its privileges with exclusive rhetorical and journalistic weapons. The fact that minimum wage recipients earn a third less than in 1968 is important for the "running gag" that a "junk job" is no longer sufficient for a dignified livelihood so that more and more people must have several jobs and therefore work longer hours than 20 years previously and bottle up this growing frustration with "junk food"—obesity in the richest countries is present to the same extent as malnutrition in the poorest countries.

This is however not as a result of abundance but rather a lack of purchasing power! The point being that the minimum wage should not only be sufficient for a humane life but it should be periodically valorized to offset the loss of purchasing power against inflation.

Then when the minimum wage is (a) determined, (b) sufficient for a human life and (c) periodically valorized, the economic maximum income can be expediently determined with a specific multiple of the minimum wage. The easiest possibility is the resolution of the Aargau cantonal parliament (factor 10), the proposal by Klaus Schwab (factor 20) in addition to a factor completion with the factors 7, 10, 15 and 30 or maybe 50 are voted on along with the "zero option" the current legal position (no limit). Then, I am fully convinced, that the "winner" will not be factor 900.

15.3 Capping of Private Property

The discussion with regard to a capping of private property is tricky, since some argue that the right to private property is a fundamental right and therefore sacrosanct and not subject to limitations. However there are other interpretations of this fundamental

15.3 Capping of Private Property

right: does it really mean that the one millionth euro and the one billionth euro are as protected as the first? Or does it mean that those belongings which a person needs to lead a human life are protected as a non-negotiable fundamental right?

As long as the fundamental rights do not conflict the case is clear: I have an unrestricted right to physical inviolability, you have the same unrestricted right to inviolability of your body. If I respect your right, my right is not reduced in any way and the rights of both parties are fully maintained. It is a different situation with right to property: if this is unrestricted and the latter, namely the 200 billionth dollar of one party, is still protected by fundamental rights, even if he already owns the whole world—then it is clear that nobody else can at all exercise his basic right to private property and with it the intended self-determined dignified life. The logical consequence of this is that the right to private property must be somehow or other restricted.

In the author's opinion this boundary should be considerably above the threshold which is necessary for a humane life but beneath the threshold whereby the size of private property of one party:

- restricts the same economic freedom and chances of others,
- endangers the democratic participation and rights of co-determination of others,
- endangers social cohesion and freedom as a result of the extent of inequality.

The measure to ensure this could take the form of a progressive wealth tax, which could be implemented at the threshold above which an individual can be regarded as wealthy for example possessing a home worth 500,000 euros in addition to financial wealth of 250,000 euros. As of 750,000 euros a tax rate of 0.5% could be used which progressively increases initially slowly but then more rapidly—up to 100%. The "cap" could for example be set at 10, 20, 30, 50 or 100 million euros—the maximum should be a decision of direct democracy. With this a person can still afford all kinds of luxury but just no football club, TV channel and above all no political party with a parliamentary club. Frank Stronach spent an impressive 10.7 million euros, more than all the other parties which have in part existed for 130 years and are exclusively represented in parliament by vote.[11] If the ceiling for private property were at 10 million euros, this would not be possible for him and if this was the boundary for access to the club of ultra-high net worth individuals, it would also not be possible. An individual with 30 million would hardly spend 10 million at one go. If the example on the other hand sets a precedent, in a few years every country will have its billionaire in the government.

The use of private property exclusively for one's own advantage is currently already anti-constitutional in Germany. In Article 14 of the Basic Law it is stated: "Property entails responsibility in addition its use should also serve the common good." It could actually not be more unambiguous; however no exclusive law ensures the protection of the principle—neither in Germany nor anywhere else. The financing of a personal party from private assets which is even called after its

---

[11]Focus Research/APA, 19 October 2013.

founder—does this serve the common good? Who asked John Paulson about what he does with the 5 billion US dollars he earned in 2010 for managing a hedge fund? Who checks the common-good performance of the Porsche und Piëch family who earned an impressive 301 million euros on dividends in 2013 or the Mercks who earned 295 million on interest on capital?[12]

Where is the constitutional instance which examines the common good obligation of people who inherit billions, as strictly as the German constitutional state checks whether somebody has his identity documents with him or whether somebody is growing marijuana at home, adhering to parking rules or has sprayed a public wall with graffiti?

The constitution is no isolated case—in Article 128 of the Spanish constitution it is stated that, "All assets of a country in their various forms and no matter who they belong to are subordinate to public interest." The Spanish constitution also does not forbid private property by any means; it merely subjects it to conditions. In the same spirit Pope Paul VI in the social encyclical "Populorum progressio" of 1967 formulated as follows, "Private property is therefore not an unconditional or unrestricted right. Right to property should never be used to the detriment of the common good."[13] The evidence for limiting private property and making it subject to conditions are endless, and I am not aware of any explicit and prominent advocacy for boundless inequality or unconditional private property—apart from the German CEO of Goldman Sachs.[14] Some wealthy individuals could live with a capping of wealth, and according to Ivan Glasenberg CEO of Glencore, "In the final analysis it does not make a difference whether assets amount to one billion or six."[15] Vis-à-vis the current state it would indeed be a mark of progress if nobody was permitted to own more than a billion. Ivan Glasenberg could introduce this proposal in a democratic money convention.

15.4 Inheritance

"Inheritance tax also serves the purpose of preventing the accumulation of immense wealth in the hands of a few individual persons." Rosa Luxemburg's diary? The Communist Manifesto? No, Article 123 of the currently valid Bavarian Constitution. Constitutions are with regard to inheritance law partly more explicit than is the case with property. The spirit from which this formulation flowed is however not communist (in the Free State of Bavaria!) but rather liberal—the constitution saves society from the over-concentration of property and power to protect freedom and democracy. Along with progressive wealth tax, progressive inheritance tax is a further effective lever. Actually it is sufficiently effective—with a limitation on

---

[12]*Frankfurter Allgemeine Zeitung online*, 10 August 2013.
[13]Populorum Progressio, Recital, pp. 23–24.
[14]Alexander Dibelius, see citation at start of the book.
[15]*SonntagsZeitung*, 5 May 2013.

15.4 Inheritance

(a) maximum income and (b) inheritance law, there would be no necessity to limit private assets because these would not reach an excessive magnitude.

Inheritance taxes can be splendidly argued along the performance principle: should one's own performance decide whether somebody attains a large fortune or the property of one's parents? Is it economically more advantageous that children of wealthy parents inherit large companies or for the most talented children to take over responsibility? Even billionaires like Warren Buffet are suffering from heartburn with regard to the current line of succession in the business world; he refers to them as "the wealth aristocracy instead of the meritocracy." In the world of sport that would be as if "the 2020 Olympic team consisted of the eldest sons of the Olympic champions from 2000."[16]

The fact that the USA has another approach to inheritance tax demonstrates the gradual increase of the inheritance tax top rate in the New Deal after the Great Depression from 20% to 45%, then to 60 and later to 70 and finally to 77%! (Schachermayer 2011). In the UK, it went to 80 per cent after a powerful remark made by Winston Churchill. He called inheritance tax "a certain corrective against the development of a race of idle rich."[17]

There are two fundamental approaches to inheritance tax:

- The *feudal* approach: Only birthright decides who inherits and how much.
- The *liberal* approach: Only one's own performance decides how much wealth is attained in life—for this it would be necessary to have the same starting out position for everybody, amongst other things equal starting-out capital.

While the second approach is probably closer to the values of contemporary society—performance, equal opportunities, justice—the first approach is the law which is currently valid. The first approach does not provide for any form of inheritance law restriction, the second abolishes it resolutely. Is there a third alternative? A middle ground would be that small assets, also farms and family companies could be passed on inheritance wise, while large assets are taxed and revert to the community. Schumpeter's "creative destruction" would also affect capital concentration acquired during one's lifetime; this would disintegrate with the death of the individual—as in nature. However the established values would survive, only the over-concentrated title of ownership would decompose. With inheritance assets which are above the limit either state expenditure could be financed for example feeding it into a "generation fund" to assist with pension financing or it could top up starting-out capital of those who were "unlucky" at birth and inherited nothing—in the form of a "negative inheritance tax." Gil Ducommun calls the giving of a share of the wealth of departing generations to the subsequent generation "democratic dowry" (Felber 2012a, p. 91ff. und Ducommun 2005, p. 131ff). Even with this, completely equal opportunities could not be created but at least flagrant and illiberal unequal opportunities could be significantly diminished.

---

[16]*New York Times*, 14 February 2001.

[17]"The case for death duties. How to improve an unpopular tax," *The Economist*, 25 October 2007.

References

Credit Suisse Researche Institute. 2012. *Global wealth report 2012*, Zürich.
Crouch, Colin (2008): *Postdemokratie*, suhrkamp, Frankfurt a. M.
Deutsches Institut für Wirtschaftsforschung (2009): Wochenbericht des DIW Berlin, 4/2009.
Ducommun, Gil (2005): *Nach dem Kapitalismus. Wirtschaftsordnung einer integralen Gesellschaft*, Publisher Via Nova, Petersberg.
Eckerstorfer, Paul/Halak, Johannes/Kapeller, Jakob/SchÜtz, Bernhard/Springholz, Florian/ Wildauer, Rafael (2013): *Vermögen in Österreich. Bericht zum Forschungsprojekt 'Reichtum im Wandel'*, Johannes Kepler University of Linz, July 2013.
Felber, Christian (2006): *50 Vorschläge für eine gerechtere Welt. Gegen Konzernmacht und Kapitalismus*, Deuticke, Vienna.
Felber, Christian (2012): *Die Gemeinwohl-Ökonomie. Eine demokratische Alternative wächst*, 2nd revised new edition, Deuticke, Vienna.
Friedman, Milton (2006): *Kapitalismus und Freiheit*, Piper Taschenbuch, 3rd edition, München/ Zürich.
Hayek, Friedrich August (2004): *Der Weg zur Knechtschaft*, Deutsche Readers Digest edition, Friedrich August v. Hayek Institut, Vienna.
Hayek, Friedrich August (2005): *Die Verfassung der Freiheit*, Mohr Siebeck, 4th edition, Tübingen.
Herrmann, Ulrike (2013): *Der Sieg des Kapitals. Wie der Reichtum in die Welt kam: Die Geschichte von Wachstum, Geld und Krisen*, Westend Verlag, Frankfurt a. M.
Johnson, Simon (2010): *Wir müssen die Macht der Wall Street brechen*, Interview, Süddeutsche Zeitung, 18 May 2010.
Laszlo, Erwin (1988): *Das dritte Jahrtausend. Zukunftsvisionen*, Suhrkamp, Frankfurt.
Layard, Richard (2009): *Die glückliche Gesellschaft. Was wir aus der Glücksforschung lernen können*, Campus, Frankfurt a. M.
Nickerson, Carol/Schwarz, Norbert/Kahnemann, Daniel (2003): Zeroing in on the Dark Side of the American Dream. A Closer Look at the Negative Consequences of the Goal for Financial Success, in *Psychological Science*, Vol. 14, No. 6, November 2003, 531–536.
Oxfam International. 2017. *An economy for the 99%*. Oxfam Briefing Paper, Oxford, January 2017.
Reich, Robert (2008): *Superkapitalismus. Wie die Wirtschaft unsere Demokratie untergräbt*, Campus, Frankfurt a. M.
Schachermayer, Walter (2011): *Der Rechenfehler der Schuldenbremser*, Kommentare der anderen, Der Standard, 17 December 2011.
Styrian Chamber of Commerce (2013): *Wachstum und Wirtschaftssysteme. Bruttoinlandsprodukt, Gemeinwohlökonomie & Co*, Standpunkte der Wirtschaftskammer No. 01/2013, Graz.
Valluga AG (2010): *D.A.CH.-Vermögensreport 2010*, Vaduz.
Vitali, Stefania, Glattfelder, James B., And Battiston, Stefano. 2011. The network of global corporate control. Scientific study, ETH Zürich, 28 July 2011.
Von Braun, Christina (2012): *Der Preis des Geldes. Eine Kulturgeschichte*, Aufbau Verlag, Berlin.
Wilkinson, Richard/Pickett, Kate (2009): *Gleichheit ist Glück. Warum gerechte Gesellschaften für alle besser sind*, Tolkemitt Verlag, Berlin.

Chapter 16
Currencies—Time for a Bretton Woods II

Abstract This chapter proposes a cooperative international monetary system. A first proposal for such a system was submitted by John Maynard Keynes at the Bretton Woods conference in 1944. Keynes foresaw a complementary currency for international economic exchange, called Bancor, operated by an International Clearing Union. Furthermore, sanctions both for trade surplus and deficit countries would have dis-incentivized and remedied trade imbalances. His proposal was rejected by the US. Instead, the dollar hegemony was established. Consequently the Bretton Woods system collapsed in the 1970s due to its inherent construction failure. Macroeconomic instability, but also the debt crisis in low-income countries characterized the following decades. As a result of the financial crisis in 2008, the Keynes proposal has been rediscovered. UNCTAD senior economist Heiner Flassbeck presented an alternative model based on real effective exchange rates (REER) which deems the adjustment of exchange rates to real purchasing power in both countries as sufficient. A synthesis of both approaches, Keynes and Flassbeck, is proposed.

> *Lord Keynes was right ... and the world will bitterly regret that it did not accept his proposals.*
> Geoffrey Crowther (Cited in Monbiot 2003, p. 178).
>
> *The dollar reserve system will probably expire, if it is not doing so already.*
> United Nations (2009, p. 115)

16.1 Failure of Bretton Woods I

The current international monetary system is, "consistent" with the complete monetary and financial system, a source of massive speculation, systemic instability and inefficiency. The public good "monetary stability" does not currently exist. In contrast to other areas of the monetary system there was however an attempt at a political system, which was for a short time successful: the Bretton Woods system from 1944 to 1973. Towards the end of WWII 44 contracting member states signed the agreement at the Bretton Woods conference in the US federal state New Hampshire on monetary cooperation and implemented it. The US dollar was declared as the reserve currency and backed by gold,[1] the exchange rates of other participating states were fixed to the dollar and capital controls were agreed on to ensure macro-financial stability. Two global institutions, the "Bretton Woods Twins"—the World Bank and International Monetary Fund, institutionally bolstered the agreement. Despite its successful conclusion, the conference did not take place in the spirit of real cooperation, there were two recommendations on the table one from Great Britain and one from the USA. The USA boycotted the in every aspect superior recommendation made by the Briton John Maynard Keynes to push through its own project with "dollar hegemony," which was systemically more unfavorable. This design flaw led to the predictable collapse of the Bretton Woods system at the beginning of the 1970s, after it had rendered good services for a quarter of a century as well as providing relative stability.

The mis-constructed model which the US Secretary of State Henry Dexter White had forced through consisted of the US dollar being, along with its role as national currency in the USA, designated as the world reserve currency with which all important commodities and global debts are quoted, which is the case down to the present day. This entailed a double massive advantage for the USA because it (a) is the only country in the world which can purchase commodities in its own currency—all other states must first purchase dollars before they can buy oil and other commodities and (b) no country can borrow abroad in its own currency as much as the USA. The USA still enjoys these privileges, as it is only the Bretton Woods system which has collapsed, the US dollar is still 70 years after the historical conference the undisputed number one global reserve currency, with a share of over 60–65%, followed by the euro with 20–25%.

The conflict of objectives of the dollar hegemony was that the USA could either keep an eye on financial and monetary stability and for this put aside its national interests or else consequently pursue its own interests but at the cost of systemic stability and ultimately the complete Bretton Woods system. The USA decided on the second option and in order to finance the Vietnam War the Federal Reserve cranked up the banknote press at the end of the 1960s, which resulted initially in the gold backing disappearing in 1971. At the same time the external value of the currency declined as more and more greenbacks came into circulation but not more pounds, d-marks or francs. In 1973 the USA therefore decontrolled the dollar exchange rate which sealed the end of the Bretton Woods system. Since then the exchange rates have been generated according to demand and supply on the foreign exchange markets, which immediately led to the onset of speculation and with this began a sustained era of currency instability.

Keynes had—possibly based on Silvio Gesell's ideas[2]—submitted a better alternative. Instead of overburdening a national currency with the additional role

---

[1]The gold reserves stored in the famous Fort Knox—to the present day.
[2]Gesell writes about an "international value association". BETZ (1998), 39 surmises that Keynes was inspired by this.

of a worldwide or commodity reserve currency and with this creating an unfair advantage for this country, he proposed that a global "complementary currency" should be created for international trade, in addition to national currencies. An international clearing union should issue and account this reserve currency called "Bancor." Keynes proposed that it was to consist of a basket of member currencies. The exchange rates of the national currencies of Bancor should be politically determined and periodically adjusted to real economic trends. In doing so the Keynes model would have achieved something which the euro is not capable of doing, namely reconciling the two core objectives of stability and flexibility—the euro only provides stability in the form of a unified currency but not for flexibility with adjustable exchange rates, which in the current misconstruction of the single currency endangers the stability and even its continued existence. Keynes theorem would have provided a joint solution for the currency and trade issues. This lucid aspect of his proposal is little known, as the complete idea in the first place. Keynes had observed that trade disparities were a repetitive source of crises and even wars. The background—the sum of all trade balances in the world is zero. Every current account surplus of a country is another state's deficit, every world export champion requires a world import champion. If a country sells another more than it buys from it, the deficit country is in debt to the surplus country and is sooner or later insolvent. This is exactly the same as the situation between two individuals—if one person continuously sells more than it buys from the other, the second person is soon or later heavily indebted, insolvent and bankrupt—to the detrimental effect of both parties.

An export surplus is perfectly fine as a one-off occurrence but strategically striving for this on the long-term is an undermining of the stability of the world economy as well as being the coercive bankruptcy of at least one trading partner. Keynes therefore allowed for a further mechanism in order to maintain equilibrium in the trade balances: the more states deviate from equilibrium in the balance of trade, the more they should be penalized for this and would have to pay back a part of their Bancor account surplus. This would have been a massive incentive, to consent to the revaluation and devaluation of their currency in order to avoid payment of fines. The complete system would therefore have returned to its balance. Keynes was not only driven by macroeconomic considerations, he had above all one main concern as a result of the effects of WWII and previous monetary disputes—global peace. He retained this in 1943, not without pathos, as he presented his 1930s revised proposal in Bretton Woods "In the post-war world a greater willingness towards supranational agreements must be demanded. If the proposed agreement can be described as measures of financial disarmament, they are however mild in comparison with military disarmament measures, which must presumably be accepted by the world (...) the plan makes a start on the way to a new order of future economic ties in the world, amongst nations and to a 'profit of peace'" (Keynes 1943, p. 16).

In contrast to the failed euro and the EU, the plan which Keynes contemplated would actually be a—global!—peace project. The euro project remains way behind Keynes because it has simply suppressed the trade issue as well as the issue of tax cooperation and the joint regulation of the financial system, which all fell by the wayside with the introduction of the euro in 1999—thanks to a "new consciousness" which was proclaimed by Mario Monti. These omissions carried out by the euro governments were however not made in the interest of their populations, on the contrary by combining the euro with tax competition and deregulation of the financial markets they made decisions which no sovereign would probably have made in a democratic vote. For good measure in doing so they dug the grave for the euro at its birth. The euro with the "business-as-usual" policy will collapse due to its design defects in the same way the Bretton Woods system predictably collapsed as a result of its core design defect (Felber 2012).

16.2 Shortcomings of the Current Monetary Order

Since the gold reserve of the dollar was abandoned and the dollar exchange rate was deregulated in 1973, the exchange rates have been determined as a result of supply and demand on the foreign exchange markets. However the market is also here, as with the commodities, a conceivably bad instance for determining currency exchange rates—price determination for currencies on markets comes with a series of severe disadvantages:

- Instability: since the collapse of fixed exchange rate system of Bretton Woods the deutsch mark-dollar rate and later the euro-dollar rates has resembled a rollercoaster, with the same applying for other currencies, from Southeast Asian countries to Turkey and Iceland.
- Irrationality: the US dollar did not always increase in comparison with the d-mark and euro when the US economy grew rapidly; now and then it was the reverse or it went massively overboard (Schulmeister 2007, p. 82). Many other currencies struggled with exchange rate movements which had nothing to do with the development of the real economy.
- Inefficiency: instability costs. All real economy participants—exporters, importers, investors—must ensure themselves against exchange rate fluctuations and do this with derivatives which in turn cause the emergence of new speculation possibilities. In economic text books derivatives are usually "justified" with two examples: with fluctuating commodity prices and fluctuating exchange rates. The possibility that the price of commodities and foreign exchange rates could also be stable occurs just about as often as non-violent communication in military basic training. Expensive hedging transactions with foreign exchange derivatives were first necessitated because currencies were traded on the markets.
- Invitation to speculation: the possibility that foreign exchange rates fluctuate invites financial betting on rate changes. Ruthless parties try to specifically influence rates and to destabilize in order to make profits. Today in major banks there are foreign exchange departments which speculate with the smallest rate changes in order to make cheap profits. If a foreign exchange trader buys US dollars for the value of 10 million euros, an exchange rate shift of a thousandth (0.1%) is

16.2 Shortcomings of the Current Monetary Order

sufficient to attain a profit of 10,000 euros when re-exchanged. If this happens three times per hour, this results in hourly earnings of 30,000 euros and the more the exchange rates fluctuate the larger the profit chances are. The foreign exchange speculation industry is genuinely interested in instability and uses various tools: computer programs ("arbitrage speculation"), media rumors and concentrated attacks on currencies ("speculative attacks") via illegal agreements. The most notorious but not only example is the collective attack on the British pound "led by" the financial investor George Soros in 1992. The attack was "successful" in the sense that the Bank of England stopped defending it by buying pounds and devalued the pound. Soros raked in a profit of one billion US dollars. What was his "performance?" What "philanthropy?" Foreign exchange speculation is merely concerned with money out of money transactions and should not be permissible. The separation of money transaction from the real economy and from life creates "criminal energy." The manager of the foreign exchange trading department of Citigroup London was suspended after the finance authorities started investigations into a series of major banks for foreign exchange rate manipulation. At the time of printing of this book according to the media reports the latest scandal could "assume larger dimensions than the Libor scandal."[3]

- Macroeconomic imbalance I (Exchange rate and debts): if the currency of a country which has a high level of external debt falls sharply or is driven down by speculation the external debt becomes more expensive in the domestic currency leading to a danger of sovereign default (not every country can borrow abroad in its own currency and refinance its debts like the USA), as was for example the case in Argentina in 2000 or Iceland in 2010. The complete Eurozone could be the next on the list. The systemic risk is in my opinion already so high that even Eurobonds are considered to be "junk bonds" by a number of financial investors that is "from the financial markets" this could therefore finally shout death to the euro (Felber 2012, p. 48ff).[4]

- Macroeconomic imbalance II (interest and exchange rates): if there is no global central bank which distributes debt in a neutral currency then just about all countries must borrow in the reserve currency and in doing so at times incur deadly risk. Particularly as the US dollar is the world reserve currency, the Federal Reserve caused a lethal interest shock by raising the key interest rate by about 20% at the end of the 1970s and start of 1980s for the in US dollars indebted developing countries, whose loans had been cheap shortly before the interest increase. Many of these countries have to date still not managed to exit this debt hole which they have been in since the 1980s and have paid a high price for it including several lives.

- Macroeconomic imbalance III (trade balances): monetary and trade policy are inseparable, whether a country has a balanced trade balance or one which deviates also depends on the exchange rate amongst other things. If this is forced up or

---

[3]*Süddeutsche Zeitung*, 5 December 2013.
[4]The EU lost the AAA at the end of 2013.

down as a result of speculation, there is a massive impact on the balance of trade. The free market allows dumping and unfair trading which leads to imbalance in the trade system, as well as currency speculation and betting on sovereign default which in total makes the "macroeconomic equilibrium" often enshrined in constitutions impossible to adhere to.[5] Without speculation trade balance is also endangered which the example of the USA (import world champion) and China (export vice world champion) demonstrates or the combination of Germany (surplus) and Euro-Mediterranean countries (deficits).

- Macroeconomic imbalance IV (foreign-exchange reserves): not only trade surpluses lead to a piling up of foreign-exchange reserves. Even deficit countries must arm themselves against speculative attacks with foreign-exchange reserves as "ammunition" in order to be able to support their own currency by acquisition (and sales of foreign exchange) in the event of attack. The more liberal the financial markets are the larger the risk of attack is and the larger the need for ammunition. In 2012 global foreign-exchange reserves amounted to 15.2% of global economic output, 15 years previously it was only 5.6% (United Nations 2009, p. 112).[6] As the US dollar is the number one reserve currency (two thirds of all foreign-exchange reserves), it thus not only results in a futile wasteland of valuable resources but also to cheap financing of the USA by poor countries. In total the poor countries lent the rich countries 3.7 trillion US dollars in 2007 at extremely low-price conditions. The "surcharge" which the poor countries pay when they borrow money from rich countries is larger than the total development aid payments they receive (United Nations 2009, p. 113).

In total the current currency system is just as much multi-dysfunctional as the whole monetary system, it is "unstable, not compatible with global full employment and enhances inequality," according to the UN report issued by the Stiglitz commission (United Nations 2009, p. 109).

16.3 Pledge for a Bretton Woods II

A public discussion regarding an alternative monetary system as set out by Keynes hardly took place before the crisis. Although the debate whether the US dollar will retain its role as global reserve currency or whether it will be replaced by the euro or yuan or whether there will be a "tri-polar constellation" has been smoldering underground for some time. However the brilliant idea proposed by Keynes which not only poses the question with regard to the global reserve currency but also proposes a just global solution for the international community had, up to the onset of the 2008 crisis, almost completely fallen into oblivion.[7]

---

[5]For example in the Basic Law, Art. 104b and 109.

[6]www.statista.com

[7]An exception is Monbiot (2003), 172ff. He in turn became aware of Keynes proposal from the book "Goodbye America! Globalisation, Debt and the Dollar Empire" by Michael Rowbotham (2000).

I published this initially in 2006 and had to listen to claims from prominent economists during public discussions that these were "planned economy" visions.[8] However the crisis created a rapid renaissance for the idea and in March 2009 the Governor of the Chinese Central Bank Zhou Xiaochuan, on the occasion of the G20 summit in London, wrote in a letter to the international public: "The creation of an international clearing unit according to the Keynes proposal is an audacious initiative which demands unusual political vision and courage (…) unfortunately this proposal was not accepted" (Xiaochuan 2009, p. 2). In September the commission of experts chaired by Joseph Stiglitz released a report to the UN General Assembly concerning how the global financial markets could be restored. The 140-page catalogue of measures dedicated more than 12 pages to Keynes' proposal and it is acknowledged as "an idea whose time has come." A "global reserve currency" issued by a "global reserve bank" within the framework of a "global reserve union" is recommended to the international community. The global trade currency could be "composed of a basket of all currencies of all member states" (United Nations 2009, p. 109ff). With it they also tie in with the special drawing rights of the IMF which had already been created in the 1960s and are a currency basket composed of the US dollar, pound, d-mark and yen. These "special drawing rights" (SDR) have represented a global complementary currency for 45 years but up to now it has not attained any great importance. Up to the onset of the crisis the value of all issued drawing rights amounted to less than 35 billion US dollars which is 0.2% of world trade volume (22 trillion US dollars). In 2009 the G20 decided also on a further SDR tranche of 250 billion US dollars in the course of stepping up the IMF's funding.[9] It is heading in the right direction. Stephan Schulmeister proposes as the "first step" the "fixing of bandwidths" for the exchange rates between the dollar, euro, renminbi and yen. In the long term "a real global currency" could materialize "which could serve as a benchmark for global economic stocks and flows composing of a bundle of the most important national currencies. The rest of the countries could then in principle stabilize their currencies in a fixed, but in emergency cases adjustable rate to 'Globo', or also have the rate determined on the free market; however they would hardly do this as it would not be in their interest." Schulmeister researched the issue, "Taking a look at economic history shows that periods of prosperity were always periods of fixed exchange rates" (Schulmeister 2010, p. 85).[10] I am now waiting for the IMF to become involved in the discussion—my personal tip is "The Bancor Plan revisited."

---

[8] So for instance the doyen of macroeconomics Erwin Streissler, also lecturing in Oxford, during the Ö1 live discussion "Im Zeit-Raum: Götterdämmerung auf den Geldmärkten. Wie kann der Finanzkapitalismus gebändigt werden?" on 4 December 2008 in Vienna.

[9] This decision was controversial. The former Chief Economist of the ECB, Jürgen Stark was of the opinion: "That is pure money creation. That is helicopter money for the world". *Handelsblatt*, 7 April 2009.

[10] *Salzburger Nachrichten*, 14 September 2013.

16.4 Global Monetary Cooperation

The following is Keynes's proposal in more detail which I have slightly modified:

- The UNO member states whose sovereign advocate this option determine a UN agreement on a global monetary cooperation—the Terra Union.
- This establishes a global "Clearing Union" (Keynes), "global reserve bank" (Stiglitz Commission) or a Terra bank which clears world trade and other cross-border flows of capital between its member states in the "Terra" unit. Every member state has an account at the clearing bank. It resembles the clearing banks which exist today and which process cross-border capital movement.
- The member state currencies are freely convertible into Terra, with a fixed exchange rate in purchasing power parity to one another. My suggestion as to how this could proceed looks like this: a consumption basket composing of 25–50 every day goods and services would have a constant value of 100 Terra in international trade and this would be a stable reference value for all participating currencies. If the same market basket costs a real 50 pounds in Great Britain, the exchange rate to Terra would be 1:2. If the cost for this market in Germany were 100 marks then the exchange d-mark and Terra exchange rate would be 1:1. In Austria with a market basket price of 200 schillings, one receives 2 schillings for 1 Terra—and the value ratios of all currencies (exchange rates) to one another would be accordingly.
- If the various developments of macroeconomic indicators (productivity, wages, inflation ….) lead to the balance of trade of a member state not being even, its exchange rate is adjusted in order to restore the balance. A surplus country such as China or Germany would have to revalue its currency, whereas a deficit country such as the USA or Greece would have to devaluate. If the "deviators" refuse to revalue or devalue, they must pay a fine and it becomes higher the more and longer the deviation is—an effective incentive to adjust the exchange rate after all.
- All-important commodities are quoted in Terra—the end of the dollar hegemony I.
- The World Bank grants interest-free development loans in Terra—the end of the dollar hegemony II.

One of the compelling advantages of Keynes's proposal is: it would not only provide stability (fixed exchange rates—speculation is hardly possible, insurance against exchange rate fluctuation is unnecessary) but also flexibility. If an economy develops differently than the reference basket for example due to slower productivity progress or higher inflation, the exchange rate of their currency would be adjusted to the real conditions and the total system would remain balanced.

16.5 Adjustment of Exchange Rates according to Purchasing Power Parity

A "light" alternative to the global reserve union has been suggested by the Keynesian and UNCTAD chief economist Heiner Flassbeck. He advocates a "system of real effective exchange rates" (REER). The UNCTAD is of the opinion

16.5 Adjustment of Exchange Rates according to Purchasing Power Parity

that it would be sufficient to adjust exchange rates regularly to real purchasing power parity for trade balances to return to equilibrium (UNCTAD 2011, p. 171ff).

For this purpose, the following is a (real) example: in Greece and Germany productivity increases by 2% in a year. In a working hour 102 industrial goods are manufactured instead of 100. Greece increases wages by 2% parallel to increased productivity—unit labor costs remain constant (more units per hour are manufactured but at the same earnings per hours). Germany reacts differently: wages remain the same. With that unit labor costs decline by 2%—102 units are manufactured for the same basic price/wages as 100 in the previous year. As a result Germany's products become cheaper in relation to Greece's products and Germany's competitiveness increases by 2%, however not because productivity and consequently performance have risen faster in Germany but rather because of unequal distribution. In the euro system Greece has no chance to neutralize the aggressive wages policy in Germany owing to the devaluation of the national currency by 2%. As a result Greece loses against Germany in inner-European trade competition. In the first 10 years after the introduction of the euro (and the loss of the possibility of exchange rate adjustment) the price and competition advantage of Germany against the Mediterranean countries was in total about 25% (Flassbeck 2010, p. 87). The "solution" pushed through by the Troika is not the—fair—"real" revaluation of Germany by raising wages there by 25% (which would secure pensions) but is the brutal devaluation of Mediterranean countries, where real wages dramatically decline—those being fair are punished. (In addition pensions in Germany are endangered). Declining real wages and purchasing power for imports in Greece have the same effect as increasing real wages and purchasing power in Germany—Greece's current account deficit clattered from 15% in 2009 to almost zero in 2016.[11]

The alternative proposal made by UNCTAD would be as follows: the central banks of two trading partners with their own currencies would initially determine an exchange rate, which reflects real purchasing power parity. If for example a party can buy an equal amount with a pound in Great Britain as somebody with 2 US dollars in the USA, this would result in a "purchasing power parity" exchange rate of 1:2 or 2 US dollar for every pound. If this ratio for example changes so that the pound loses purchasing power and with a pound in Great Britain, it is only possible to buy as much as with 1.95 US dollars then the central bank in both countries—if necessary—would adjust the nominal exchange rate to the real rate of 1.95 US dollars to the pound, by concentrated buying-in of dollars.

This proposal could be attempted by a group of countries, as written by UN authors and also UNCTAD, "Rule-based exchange rate management can be practiced as a unilateral exchange rate strategy, or with significantly larger leeway for central bank intervention, via bilateral agreements or as a core element of a regional cooperation. The largest benefit for international financial stability would however result if these rules were practiced multilaterally as part of a global financial regulation" (UNCTAD 2011, p. 178). It would be worth a try. However if it

---

[11] https://tradingeconomics.com/greece/government-budget

did not work the "second course": the sanctions for deviators whose trade balances are not in equilibrium as proposed by Keynes could be switched on.

A possible compromise variant between the UNO-Keynes-Stiglitz model (ultimate target: balanced trade balances) and the UNCTAD-Flassbeck model (ultimate target: purchasing power parity) could be that Terra, as described above, is introduced which however aims at exchange rate adjustments for maintain purchasing power parity and not the equilibrium of trade balances (which from Flassbeck's perspective would adjust itself as a result). For example: if the constant Terra product basket costs 55 pounds in Great Britain one day, the pound exchange rate decreases automatically to 0.55 pounds to 1 Terra. England would not lose competitiveness due to the adjustment vis-à-vis a trade partner whose price level remains unchanged. The system would also remain stable and flexible in this version and in addition penalties for deviations could be switched on for trade balance deviations.

The immediate advantage of the UNCTAD proposal is that no new organization, no global complementary currency and no sanction measures are necessary—therefore the "light" label. Its clear disadvantage in contrast would be that it would "only" solve the currency and trade problem and neither the commodity currency nor the debt currency would be addressed. Should that continue to be the US dollar? The captivating aspect of Keynes's proposal is that it would solve (a) the currency problem, (b) the trade issue, (c) the commodity currency and (d) international debt management in one, which is why I prefer this proposal.

For some readers the difference between both alternatives might appear too technical, too detailed and even irrelevant. However what progress it would be for international relations, for the shaping of the global economy by autonomous sovereigns if we, instead of being helplessly trapped in the unfair and unstable dollar hegemony, could enjoy the luxury of deciding between a Bretton Woods II with a focus on purchasing power parity and a Bretton Woods II with a focus on balanced trade balances! What a benefit for democracy this would be! Within a short time countless people would know about and be heatedly discussing both proposals knowing that they themselves could make a decision with global consequences, should their governments continue to be inactive!

16.6 Epilogues

16.6.1 Planned Economy in Peking und Zürich

Switzerland and China are both examples of a "planned economy" in the sense of political stipulation of the exchange rate which shows that it is possible.

In China the exchange rate is politically determined and that is final. However it is unilateral and therefore follows the same self-interest as in the USA with dollar hegemony—the past, or in jargon: neo-mercantilism.

Switzerland "capped" the franc exchange rate which is becoming more popular as a result of instability in the Eurozone and the growing mountain of debt in the

USA and Japan, which however drives the rate to dizzy heights and ruins Swiss exports. Therefore the central bank intervenes by selling enormous amounts of francs and purchasing foreign currency to cap the rate. The stock of foreign currency exploded from 45 billion Swiss francs in 2008 to almost 700 billion francs by the end of 2016. The stocks of foreign currency constitute 93% of the balance sheet total of the Swiss National Bank (Swiss National Bank 2017, p. 158). The Swiss National Bank even purchases Australian dollars: "I never thought that I would see something like this. An anti-inflationary conservative institution such as the SNB keeps our currency as a reserve" commented the Australian central banker Glenn Stevens.[12] This results in the fact that the balance sheet total of the Swiss National Bank has inflated faster than that of the Fed, the Bank of England or ECB—by 650%. It would be more effective to simply fix the exchange rate but this is evidently an ideological taboo. Before politically determining the exchange rate, it is preferable to pump the markets with multi-million amounts to power down market forces. Incidentally, the strategy of the Swiss National Bank failed: At the end of 2015 it had to yield to the enormous market pressure and relinquish its strategy. As a consequence, Switzerland had to pay twice: for the loss of its national bank (23.3 billion francs in 2015) and for the skyrocketing franc that painfully hit its economy, slowed down growth and destroyed a large number of jobs.

16.6.2 End of the Dollar Hegemony?

What would happen today if the USA lost the role of global reserve currency without implementation of the institutional proposals which have been presented here? Specifically, what would happen if the most important commodities were suddenly noted in euro or in another currency?

- The demand for the US dollar would collapse and with it exchange rates. Oil and all other commodities would become prohibitively expensive for the resource giant; the economy would fall into a recession which in turn would create an explosion of public debt. Rating agencies would sound the death knell for the USA; the country would be bankrupt within a short period of time, which is why the USA is prepared to wage war to avoid this scenario.
- For those who are of the opinion that this short chain appears too simple one should become aware of the fact that the USA due to its political economic monopoly position is the only country in the world where the IMF does not intervene, although it exhibits an imposing "twin deficit"—in its state budget and trade balance. In the case of all other IMF members the alarm sirens would have been howling long ago and the "financial firefighters" from Washington would have been on the scene with sirens blaring and would have prescribed hard structure adjustment programs for the "crisis country" so that it can further service its

---

[12]*Business Week*, 24 August 2012.

foreign debt. The IMF operates a double standard but it is also not a democratic or even egalitarian international organization but rather a shareholder company of majority owners of the most powerful industrial nations. The only country which possesses veto power in turn is the USA—we have come full circle.
- The prospect of war for the USA is perhaps an acceptable scenario, losing the key reserve currency role to the euro or renminbi is certainly not. Evading this worst possible of all narcissistic insults, could provide an impetus for a "pragmatic" faction in the USA which could work towards a neutral monetary system in order to avoid replacement of the US dollar by the euro or another global reserve currency.

What would happen if the proposal made by Keynes were implemented?

- Commodities including oil would be quoted in Terra, which as a result would rapidly decrease the demand for the US dollar. This would however, in contrast to a system of free exchange rates, have less dramatic effects because the exchange rates would be politically determined according to purchasing power parity—the US dollar would remain roughly stable.
- On the other hand the USA could have problems with foreign debt, as it would no longer be necessary as a reserve currency. This role would be taken over by the Terra and the USA would at least no longer be able to dispose of any further debts abroad. Due to the miserable macroeconomic key performance indicators its rating would rapidly deteriorate and its bonds would incline towards junk status. The USA would have to borrow domestically (Japan model) instead of worldwide. This can go well but can also go wrong. In case of an emergency wealth taxes could be steeply increased, which could protect every industrial nation against sovereign default without difficulty.
- There is on the other hand one thing which is certain: the trade imbalance between the USA and China would not have been able to occur within a Bretton Woods II system, as both states would have been forced to adjust their exchange rates—USA, the deficit country to devaluation and China as surplus country to valorization—or alternatively to pay fines. Therefore no large trade imbalances could have emerged.

16.6.3 Local and regional complementary currencies

As long as the global monetary system and the monetary and financial system remain as unstable as they are currently, in my opinion local and regional complementary currencies are a very good thing, as they cushion a lot of disadvantages created by financial dictatorship. The values of regionalism, resilience, sustainability and democracy are good reasons for these initiatives.

The awareness about the monetary system which is created by the "Chiemgauer," the "Sterntaler," the "Voralberg Talente" and other local complementary currencies is extremely valuable. It would even be obvious that the first "democratic monetary conventions" occur in a community which is already working with regional money or another complementary currency. In Chap. 1, I suggested supporting these experiments by posing the question to the monetary conventions whether regional and local political authorities should receive the right to issue an "official" complementary currency. This could be furnished on a voluntary basis without an obligation to accept it as legal tender or also with an obligation to accept it as a valid regionally-limited legal tender—the sovereign decides. There is an abundance of specialist literature on regional currencies which is why I conclude with a reference to the works of Bernard Lietaer (Lietaer 2002), Margrit Kennedy (Kennedy 2006), Tobias Plettenbacher and Charles Eisenstein (Plettenbacher 2008 und Eisenstein 2013) as well as the successful Langenegger Talente,[13] the Chiemgauer[14] and the Sterntaler.[15]

References

Betz, Thomas (1998): *Was der Euro soll und was eine internationale Währung wirklich sollte*, Zeitschrift für Sozialökonomie, edition 117, pages 35–43.
Eisenstein, Charles (2013): *Ökonomie der Verbundenheit. Wie das Geld die Welt an den Abgrund führte – und sie dennoch retten kann*, Scorpio Verlag, München.
Felber, Christian (2012): *Retten wir den Euro*, Deuticke, Vienna.
Flassbeck, Heiner (2010): *Die Marktwirtschaft des 21. Jahrhunderts*, Westend, Frankfurt a. M.
Kennedy, Margrit (2006): *Geld ohne Inflation und Zinsen. Ein Tauschmittel, das jedem dient*, Aktualisierte Neuausgabe, Goldmann Taschenbuch, München.
Keynes, John Maynard (1943): *Vorschläge für eine International Clearing Union / Union für den internationalen Zahlungsverkehr*, Collected Writings Vol. 25 – Activities 1940–1944, Cambridge 1980, pages 168–195; translation by Werner Onken.
Lietaer, Bernard (2002): *Das Geld der Zukunft. Über die zerstörerische Wirkung unseres Geldsystems und Alternativen hierzu*, Riemann, 2nd edition and special edition, München.
Monbiot, George (2003): *United People. Manifest für eine neue Weltordnung*, Riemann, München.
Plettenbacher, Tobias (2008): *Neues Geld. Neue Welt. Die drohende Wirtschaftskrise – Ursachen und Auswege*, 2nd edition, planetverlag, Salzburg.
Schulmeister, Stephan: (2007): *Finanzspekulation, Arbeitslosigkeit und Staatsverschuldung*, Intervention 1/2007, pages 73–97.
Schulmeister, Stephan: (2010): *Mitten in der großen Krise. Ein 'New Deal' für Europa*, Picus Verlag, Wien.
Swiss National Bank. 2017. *Annual report 2016*.
UNCTAD. 2011. *Trade and development report 2011*, New York und Geneva.
United Nations. 2009. *Report of the commission of experts of the President of the United Nations general assembly on reforms of the international monetary and financial system*. 140 pages, New York, 21 September 2009.
Xiaochuan, Zhou. 2009. *Reform the international monetary system*. Essay on G20-Gipfel in London, 23 March 2009.

---

[13] www.allmenda.com/langenegger-talente

[14] www.chiemgauer.info

[15] www.regiostar.com/

**Part III:
Kick Off**

Chapter 17
The Path to the first Convention

Abstract This final chapter describes how a democratic process of implementation can be started anywhere at the local level, that is in municipalities, districts, or regions. A "sovereign money municipality" could for instance be the next step after becoming a clean energy city, a fair trade city, or a climate protection city. The chapter describes how a democratic assembly can be constituted, how the questions at stake could be elaborated and, very importantly, how decisions could be efficiently made via "systemic consensus" whereby the resistance against all options is measured and the winner is the proposal which generates the least resistance. A possible set of questions—including several alternatives for each—is provided as an appendix to this last chapter. Once many municipalities or regions have implemented a democratic monetary convention, they could send delegates to a national or even international convention that would prepare the monetary part of a constitution or the EU Lisbon Treaty—directly decided upon by the sovereign citizens.

> *"You never change things by fighting the existing reality. To change something, build a new model that makes the existing model obsolete."*
>
> Buckminster Fuller

Now you have ploughed through the main part of the book. For some it was probably not the easiest of subjects and others are surprised that the monetary system is understandable after all, at least along general lines. I have tried to focus on the fundamental questions, the fundamental building blocks of the monetary system. Perhaps one or other aspect or issue has been short-changed or has not been dealt with at all, which is not such a bad thing as the question catalogue presented here does not represent a catechism but rather a starter. It should and will be further developed in as many smaller and larger conventions as possible.

Some will perhaps be already itching to plan a private mini monetary convention for the next meet-up with friends, families, club or neighbors, which would be the first step to implementation and an active alternative to resignation and a feeling of helplessness. Others are probably sitting lamed and are asking themselves how such a task of the century could ever be implemented. Lao Tse once said "The longest journey also begins with the first step." A first milestone in the long journey to real democracy is holding the first "municipal monetary convention" in a pioneer municipality which can be talked about and copied by other municipalities. The more successful the process is in the first municipality, the further the premier experiment will radiate.

17.1 Bottom-Up-Strategy

Everybody can strive for their own commune of residence to become a pioneer municipality, which is still a large project but one with a much higher prospect of success than directly target a federal convention. Even better than a pioneer municipality would be an association of pioneer municipalities for example in a region (administrative district, federal state, canton, comunidad autónoma, …). It would then immediately have the character of a regional development project and a regional new departure to a democratic economic system. The process could be continued up to a global level. The widespread and common feeling of helplessness that municipalities must bear the brunt of globalization but have not been involved in being able to shape it would be opposed with a strong democratic signal.

I observe a continually growing awareness for the difficulties of the monetary system also with provincial governments and presume that some of them will soon support pioneer municipalities. The avant-garde would from the start therefore gain a large amount of recognition and greater political weight. A possible option would be the backing and documentation of the pioneer process within the framework of a research project. The Economy for the Common Good movement is currently developing an "Economy for the Common Good" chair with the UNESCO, which will also include research and practice projects alongside teaching—this chair could realize this back-up and documentation function. A third variant would be that the municipalities which have already realized regional money projects make a start, given that they have a higher level of expertise with regard to monetary issues and have developed practical alternatives. The "misery" of the current monetary system is so great that comprehensive help from many sides is expected as soon as the first seed of a democratically new system has sprouted.

From the perspective of municipal policy and development, a municipal monetary convention can smoothly tie in with existing municipal development initiatives for example local agenda 21, municipal climate alliance, fair trade alliance or the common good alliance. The latter is a part of the Economy for the Common good movement which has been rapidly growing on the international stage since 2010.

Common Good municipalities are characterized by a diversity of projects:

- They compile the Common Good Balance Sheet in their own enterprises.
- They invite all companies in the private sectors to compile the Common Good Balance Sheet.
- They annually honor exemplary businesses.
- They make use of common good criteria in public procurement.
- They tie up business development with common good criteria or rather with the compilation of the Common Good Balance Sheet.

- They establish local "hubs" (breeding ground and birth places for new companies) where Common Good enterprises are established.
- They promote the establishment of a regional common good exchange or participate in it.
- They advise local banks with regard to compiling a Common Good Balance Sheet or commitment to a Common Good Charter.
- They involve citizens in the development of the "municipal quality of life index" and the "municipal economic convention."

The "municipal economic convention" is the close model for a "democratic monetary convention" at municipal level. So it would be "organic" that a selection of the first common good municipalities become "sovereign money municipalities," as the "spirit" and the possible process is already known and even already embedded there.

The first common good municipalities developed in 2013 in Spain—Miranda de Azán (Salamanca), Carcaboso (Extremadura) and Orendain (Basque Country)—as well as in northern Italy (the South Tirol municipalities Schlanders, Laas, Mals and Latsch), two and a half years after the start of the Economy for the Common Good movement. These were composed of several strategic sub-threads; the three pioneer groups are enterprises, municipalities and universities. The municipalities cover the political-democratic strategy thread which should lead to the first democratic economic constitution, containing an alternative economic system (Felber 2012).

According to surveys, 80–90% of the representatively surveyed population in Germany and Austria would like a new economic system (Bertelsmann Foundation 2010, p. 1 und 2012, p. 7). My personal impression is that this result would be heading towards 100% with regard to the monetary system and the willingness and motivation for municipal monetary conventions is even higher than for democratic economic conventions.

17.2 The Process of a Democratic Monetary Convention

The Economy for the Common Good movement has already developed a 20 page guide for a democratic *economic* convention which can be downloaded free of charge from the website.[1] This can easily be adapted for a municipal monetary convention—the potential content question catalogue is available at the end of this book with 47 questions in total. The framework guide deals amongst other things with the following issues:

i. Who initiates a convention?
ii. How is a convention put together?
iii. How is the convention implemented?
iv. How is decision making carried out?

---

[1] www.ecogood.org/en (search for "municipalities").

17.2.1 Who Initiates a Convention?

The impulse could come from the sovereign as well as its parliamentary and government representatives. There are sharp minds everywhere who want to change the current disorder. Best practice has proved to be that enthusiastic citizens and members of the local council pull together and politically "play together." In order to prevent the initiative from being instrumentalized by a party or particular group, one should pay attention to a representative minimum range of supporters.

17.2.2 Who is in the Convention?

There are several possibilities for the composition of the conventions and the same model must not be employed everywhere. In the practice of citizen participation various models were developed for example all citizens could be invited to participate in a series of meetings during the period of a year or 10–20 citizens are randomly selected who do the rough content service—a tried-and-tested procedure in the USA and Vorarlberg called "citizens council."[2] There are various possibilities and it is perhaps best that various ways are taken in the various municipalities. The guide can include the various variants whereby selectable options emerge for following pioneer municipalities.

17.2.3 How is the Convention Implemented?

The stations of such a convention could be as follows:
- Meeting 1: kick-off, getting to know each other, clarification concerning the project, presentation of the "questions to the convention."
- Meeting 2: agreement on questions, splitting into reporting groups, which research the content of the issues and compile a pro and contra argument list.
- Meeting 3: "Raw reports," initial mood and division into (e.g. 12) working groups which do detailed research over a longer period of time and work out the final questions.
- Meeting 4: detailed reports with question/issue formulation, final clarification and modification of the questions.

---

[2]Regulation of the federal state of Vorarlberg for convening and implementing citizens' councils: www.vorarlberg.at/pdf/buergerratrichtlinie.pdf

- Meeting 5: voting
- Meeting 6: public disclosure of results and election of delegates for the next level as well as invitation to all neighboring municipalities to also organize a convention.

17.2.4 How does communication and decision making take place?

There are two "human high-tech" methods crucial for success: heedful communication and democratic decision making. In public political discussion "fouls" such as interrupting (instead of allowing to speak to the end), judging (instead of arguing), criticizing (instead of offering praise), speaking too long (inefficient and boring) and stressing with mimics and gestures (instead or relaxed and attentive listening) are unfortunately bad habits which are widespread.

Experience has shown that agreeing to attempt to practise all elementary principles of heedful communication and accepting penalties as a result of breaking rules (invitation, warning, allocation of expression, ruled out of order) creates quite a different talking and discussion atmosphere which inspires and does not exhaust. From heedful dialog methods such as non-violent communication, "dialog" or "council," universal basic principles of successful communication crystalize for example speaking from the heart, listening with the heart, not commenting, being economic with words and being silent from time to time.

A discussion or working group which works according to these principles enables depth, it is fun (instead of frustrating) and as a rule brings forth productive results. In my experience heedful and respectful communication is generally the most challenging in political work, while at the same time being the most fundamental part of it. If we do not respect each other during discussions, then the results cannot be good and community and democracy cannot be achieved.

The same applies to differences in content, they are not the problem. This cannot be the problem at all, because every person is unique and different from everybody else. The problem is that we cannot cope with different opinions and out of habit cannot accept them, judge and combat, which is why political discussion and democratic decisions are so endlessly arduous and unattractive. People never all want the same; people only more or less want the same. The art is in a decision making procedure which sensitively sieves out common ground, during which joint respect is maintained as the primary principle! The traditional democratic voting process "for" or "against" is very simple and democratically inefficient because a number of alternatives which would perhaps be acceptable are not included in the voting process. The best example is Factor 12 in Switzerland. Due to the fact that it could only be voted with "yes" or "no" to a single and unalterable proposal, the current "zero option," Factor 900 won. If there had been a broad spectrum of proposals available to vote on, another factor would have won for sure and not 900.

The following is a graph which has been compiled and created from experience which I have gained during talks and lectures.

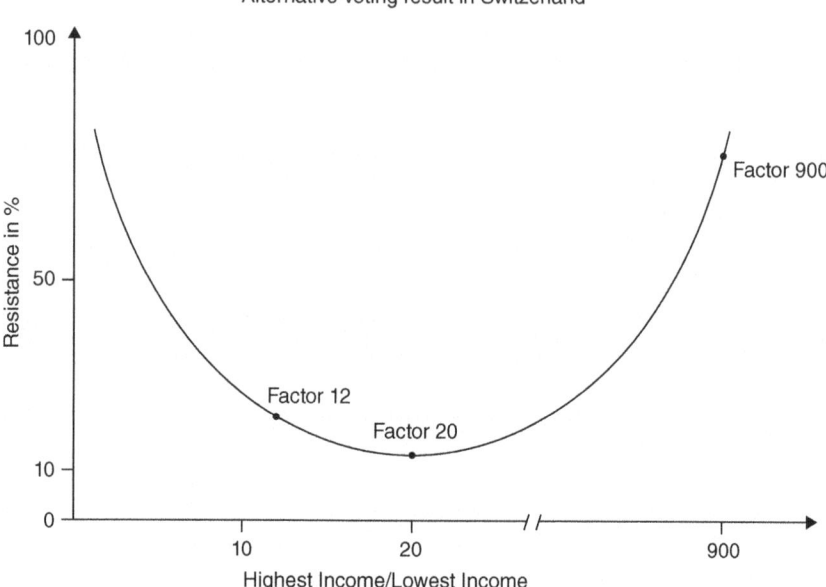

Alternative voting result in Switzerland

The graph illustrates the resistance against various proposals to limit inequality. The resistance against a very minor inequality is very high, according to the author's assessment it is lowest round about factor 10 to 20 and after this point it increases again. Above factor 1000 it would, according to the author's experience, again tend towards 100%

I have played the game "democratic economic convention" with about 50,000 participants at talks and lectures in Europe and Latin America concerning the question about maximum income inequality. Between 4 and 7 proposals are almost always made, which is evidently sufficient in order to cover all the main needs and not seldom the extreme "full equality" and "boundless inequality" are amongst the proposals. If they are included they are as a rule represented with great passion, more than the proposals in between, from time to time also aggressively in the sense that it is said or suggested that the acceptance of every other proposal would represent a total loss of freedom/equality. Even when there are no extreme proposals included the voting result using "systemic consensus" (SC principle) is almost always a "trough"—the lowest and highest proposals receive relatively high resistance and somewhere in the middle area—often however not exactly in the middle—resistance attains the minimum and then rapidly increases again. In 95% of all cases, factor 10 wins by the way. The highest ever measured winner factor was factor 30 (in a private school for boys), the lowest measured value was factor 3 (in Andalusian and Austrian mountain valleys above 1,000 m above sea level).

The SC principle has many advantages:

- The "map of opinions" of the whole population becomes visible and with it the partly striking differences to public (publicized) opinion.
- Those who put forward their proposals with the most passion (most aggression) are often the smallest minority.

- The process encourages the submission of even better proposals than those which have already been submitted, it enhances empathy and democratic creativity.
- The process encourages the development of one's own opinion and the ability to listen to one's inner voice.
- The process also increases tolerance because several proposals are always cited whereby diversity becomes evident and understanding for other positions grows.
- People get away from yes-no alternatives.
- A common good culture slowly develops: only proposals are submitted which are presumed to create the least amount of pain in the population, because polarizing proposals, which rapidly becomes clear in practice, have no longer any chance of acceptance.

The best experience for me (apart from the first in the list) in the Economy for the Common Good and the Project Bank for the Common Good is the unfamiliar and work-facilitating calmness by which decisions are met in contrast to how they were met "in the past." There is often not just one good option but several good options, which cannot uncommonly be combined to an optimal proposal and if this is not the case—instead of using a lot of energy to push or force through an option, the sovereign proceeds to voting (on a rich base of alternatives). In the ideal case it is quite relaxed and emotionally as well as procedure-wise efficient. Do not let anybody say that "democracy" is inefficient—crude decision methods can be very much inefficient, but luckily there are also alternatives here.

17.3 Evolution of Contents

Some readers will perceive that the proposals in the contents section are not their optimal solutions and therefore intuitively or instinctively reject the complete procedure. This would however be a hasty reflex, not only because there is no perfect solution and every regulation evokes a certain extent of dissatisfaction, but above all because the alternatives are the currently valid laws and game rules. These evoke a by far greater amount of dissatisfaction in many more people than the "best possible" solution which can only be found with a preferably democratic procedure. Game rules which satisfy everybody completely are an illusion. The target is to find game rules with create the least possible amount of dissatisfaction and are accepted and supported by as many people as possible and can be further enhanced in future review sessions.

The first possibility for reworking the 47 questions proposed here is in the working groups in the municipal conventions. It is proposed in the guide that after the kick-off working groups for the individual subject areas (in this book there are 12, it could also be 10, 15 or 20) are formed and deal with these intensively. In the process a modification or extension of the problem can emerge, this is part of the democratic essence. A voting round in the plenary assembly regarding the proposals of the working groups is also possible where the exact issues are determined, here the working groups do not decide but everybody together. Refining democratic decision-making processes is social high-tech which cannot receive enough attention. No co-determination regarding question formulation can lead to a large amount of democratic frustration. Top-down referendums (as e.g. the Brexit) are an example of this, these contain questions which the government has preset, which many people consider impudent. The "competence responsibility" is part of the democratic essence—the sovereign must be able to decide itself about which questions it would like to vote on.

Participants of the municipal convention can be delegated to higher instance conventions via a voting procedure with a specific mandate—the respective issues and preliminary results gathered on the basis of consensus. The higher instance conventions can again modify the issues, possibly weighted according to the preliminary results. In this way a final question catalog emerges after a pathway through several "levels of maturity." The final decision is however met by the complete sovereign, which could become the most exciting day of democracy since its beginning.

17.4 International Cooperation

As soon as the first pioneer municipality has managed it, this message will spread like wildfire and motivate other municipalities to hold "their" monetary convention. My personal vision is for the conventions to spread as the bread associations of Friedrich Wilhelm Raiffeisen and later the Raiffeisen banks. The objective is that, in every municipality at least, there is a discussion whether a community monetary convention should be organized. It is not necessary for everybody to take action, a "critical mass" would be sufficient. However if you want to do something for the future and be prepared for critical questions coming from your children, you can do this by ensuring that a convention takes place in your community.

The cooperation between several municipalities makes everything easier and it will be more energetic if the municipalities internationally go the course together. There are already candidates for Common Good municipalities from Spain and Italy to Austria and Germany. In 2016, the city of Seville announced its intention to help weave a European wide network of ECG municipalities. This movement could grow and the movement of "democratic monetary municipalities" could fuse with the Economy for the Common Good movement and create synergies.

17.5 From Monetary Convention to Constitutional Convention

Even if the vision of this book—a democratic monetary system in a constitution, ideally in several nation states and embedded in the EU treaty and as a result an emerging initiative for a global monetary cooperation, a world financial authority or a global tax authority—is realized, it would not be the end of the story but the start of an even deeper democratic movement. Besides monetary and economic conventions, education, public service, common goods, media and finally democratic conventions could be initiated. As already described in a real democracy the constitution must be written by sovereign citizens and their representatives must adhere to these democratic game rules. The most obvious is often the most difficult to see: the fact that democracies are in such a sorry state is due to the fact that the sovereigns are so powerless. They have no effective rights of determination and rights of influence. With constitutional conventions which are also initiated from the bottom, dignified and self-confident sovereigns could emerge for the first time. Since the first wave of enlightenment was just a gentle springtime greeting of collective freedom, I would very much still like to experience the realization of this vision.

References

Bertelsmann Foundation (2010): *Bürger wollen kein Wachstum um jeden Preis*, Umfrage-Studie, July 2010.

Bertelsmann Foundation (2012): *Kein Wachstum um jeden Preis*, Umfrage-Studie, Kurzbericht, July 2012.

Felber, Christian (2012): *Die Gemeinwohl-Ökonomie. Eine demokratische Alternative wächst*, 2nd revised new edition, Deuticke, Vienna.

Chapter 18
Questionnaire for the Monetary Convention

18.1 Creation of Money

Question 1a: Who is permitted to create cash (= legal tender)?

Zero Option:
The state central bank exclusively.   RP: ___ out of 10
Alternatives:
Commercial banks too?   RP: ___ out of 10
Companies too?   RP: ___ out of 10
Private individuals too?   RP: ___ out of 10
Regional authorities too?   RP: ___ out of 10

Question 1b: Who is permitted to create book money (= legal tender)?

Zero Option:
Private commercial banks exclusively (as a means of payment).   RP: ___ out of 10
Alternative 1:
The state central bank exclusively.   RP: ___ out of 10
Alternative 2:
Companies too?   RP: ___ out of 10
Private individuals too?   RP: ___ out of 10
Regional authorities too?   RP: ___ out of 10

Question 2: Who should be permitted to issue complementary currencies, which are valid as legal tender and therefore have to be accepted by all exchange partners?

Companies?   RP: ___ out of 10
Private individuals, clubs?   RP: ___ out of 10
Regional authorities?   RP: ___ out of 10

18.2 Sovereign Money Reform

Question 3: Should a sovereign money reform be undertaken?

Zero Option:
The current money creation practice carried out by both the central bank and commercial banks remains in place, current accounts remain part of bank balance sheets, money creation profits flow mainly to commercial banks.   RP: ___ out of 10

Alternative:
The public money creation monopoly will be extended to book money. The money in circulation will come exclusively from the central bank, current accounts will be excluded from bank balance sheets and become the property of bank customers, and profits earned by money creation entirely benefit the general public.   RP: ___ out of 10

18.3 Central Bank

Question 4: Who should the central bank belong to?

As the zero option is different depending on the various states, 3 alternatives are available, which contain all zero options.

Alternative 1:
The central bank should be in the possession of private commercial banks.   RP: ___ out of 10

Alternative 2:
The central bank should be in mixed—private commercial banks and state—possession.   RP: ___ out of 10

Alternative 3:
The central bank should be public.   RP: ___ out o 10

Question 5: How should the decision-making bodies of the central bank be put together?

Zero Option:
Primarily or exclusively bankers.   RP: ___ out of 10

Alternative:
All community groups should be represented by delegates.   RP: ___ out of 10

Question 6: Which objectives should the central bank pursue?

Alternative 1:
Price stability and full employment are equal objectives, no state financing.   RP: ___ out of 10

Alternative 2:
Price stability has priority over full employment, no state financing.   RP: ___ out of 10

Alternative 3:
Price stability and full employment are equal objectives, as well as limited state financing.   RP: ___ out of 10

18.5 Banking System

Question 7: Should the money creating central bank be constituted as an independent fourth state power – the "Monetative"?

Zero Option:
No, the current model of an independent ECB is sufficient. RP: ___ out of 10

Alternative 1:
The central bank should be bound by the instructions of the European Parliament. RP: ___ out of 10

Alternative 2:
For the purposes of a further power differentiation a "monetary authority", independent from the government and parliament, should be established and its objectives determined by direct democracy. RP: ___ out of 10

18.4 Sovereign Debt

Question 8: Should states be permitted to incur interest free debts from their own central bank on a limited and conditional basis?

Zero Option:
No, state financing via the central bank should remain forbidden; states must borrow on markets or from private banks and pay the interest charged by the markets. RP: ___ out of 10

Alternatives:
Yes, limited to 25% of economic output. RP: ___ out of 10
Yes, limited to 50% of economic output. RP: ___ out of 10
Yes, limited to 75% of economic output. RP: ___ out of 10
Bound by the authorization of a committee in the future. RP: ___ out of 10
At the discretion of the parliament. RP: ___ out of 10

Question 9: What should happen if the level of debt is exceeded?

Zero Option:
The governments must borrow the amount, which exceeds the debt limit, on the markets. RP: ___ out of 10

Alternative 1:
Automatic purely revenue-related stabilizers come into effect (higher inheritance tax and large assets tax). RP: ___ out of 10

Alternative 2:
Automatic purely expenditure-related stabilizers come into effect (a "mowing" of all state expenditure). RP: ___ out of 10

Alternative 3:
Automatic stabilizers come into effect – 50% expenditure-related ("mowing effect") and 50% revenue-related (wealth tax). RP: ___ out of 10

18.5 Banking System

Question 10: Must loans always serve the common good and should there be an ethical credit check along with the financial credit check?

Zero Option:
No, this is unnecessary bureaucracy. RP: ___ out of 10

Alternative:
Yes, it would be wise and constitutional. RP: ___ out of 10

Question 11: Should it be permitted to grant financial loans?

Zero Option:
Yes, every borrower should be able to decide what to do with the loan.   RP: ___ out of 10
Alternative:
No, money-out of-money transactions should be declined in principle and   RP: ___ out of 10
not be enhanced by borrowing.

Question 12: Should banks be obliged to grant regional loans?

Zero Option:
No, globalization makes financial markets more efficient and is in   RP: ___ out of 10
accordance with economic freedom.
Alternative:
Yes, this would be wise because there is a surplus of financial assets in   RP: ___ out of 10
more and more countries. Banks should be obliged to grant loans in the
same region where the savings deposits come from.

18.6 Commercial Banks

Question 13: Should there be a size limit for banks in order to prevent economically and politically "too big to fail" institutes?

Zero Option:
No, "Global players" without size limit are permissible.   RP: ___ out of 10
Alternative:
Yes, they should not exceed a pre-determined upper limit. The EU   RP: ___ out of 10
Financial Market Authority monitors this upper limit and initiates
measures, in the case of exceedance of this upper limit, to divide or
restrain this institution.

Question 13a: If yes, what value should this upper limit have?

At 30 billion euro balance sheet total?   RP: ___ out of 10
At 50 billion euro balance sheet total?   RP: ___ out of 10
At 75 billion euro balance sheet total?   RP: ___ out of 10
At 100 billion euro balance sheet total?   RP: ___ out of 10

Question 14: When handling systemically important banks further costs will probably be incurred. Who should carry these costs?

Zero Option (Plan of the EU Banking Union):
Owners, creditors, national tax payers and EU tax payers.   RP: ___ out of 10
Alternative:
Only the owners and creditors with reserve liability for owners.   RP: ___ out of 10

Question 14a: If tax payers: Should an EU-wide wealth tax, which is at least cost-covering, be instigated in order to handle banks which are too big to fail?

Zero Option:
No, the tax policy used to date is sufficient.   RP: ___ out of 10
Alternative:
Yes.   RP: ___ out of 10

Question 15: Should state assistance such as (a) access to the central bank, (b) deposit protection, (c) business with the state and (d) emergency support measures in exceptional situations only be granted to banks who commit to fulfill the Common Good Charter?

Zero Option:
No.   RP: ___ out of 10
Alternative:
Yes.   RP: ___ out of 10

Question 15a: If yes: should this criteria catalogue include?

Common Good orientation in the articles of incorporation and the Common Good Balance Sheet?	RP: ___ out of 10
Conservative business model (only loans and savings deposits)?	RP: ___ out of 10
No profit payout to owners?	RP: ___ out of 10
Exit from the interest system: no interest on savings, loan fees instead of interest on loans?	RP: ___ out of 10
Common good appraisal of all loan projects?	RP: ___ out of 10
Common good orientation of profit allocation?	RP: ___ out of 10

18.7 Financial Supervision

Question 16: Should an effective and powerful EU financial supervisory authority be established, which …

… divides up banks with a balance sheet total over 30 billion euro?	RP: ___ out of 10
… keeps foreign banks with a larger balance sheet total away from the EU internal market?	RP: ___ out of 10
… shuts down shadow banking activities?	RP: ___ out of 10
… stipulates that banks have a minimum equity capital of 20–30% of their balance sheet total?	RP: ___ out of 10
… reforms accounting rules according to the lowest value principle?	RP: ___ out of 10
… audits new financial products on the basis of ethics and permits or forbids them according to the results?	RP: ___ out of 10
… prevents the access of non-authorized financial products to the EU internal market?	RP: ___ out of 10

Question 17: Should all types of funds be regulated in such a way so that they …

… are not permitted to raise loans?	RP: ___ out of 10
are not permitted make hostile takeovers?	RP: ___ out of 10
… must automatically inform the tax authorities by year end about all revenue earned by shareholders and are subject to income tax?	RP: ___ out of 10
… are permitted to pay out bonuses, maximum 50% of the yearly salary?	RP: ___ out of 10
… tie the bonuses to common good performance?	RP: ___ out of 10

Question 18: Should the creation of international financial markets further progress, be revoked or be accompanied by regulations?

Zero Option:
Global financial markets should be further liberalized for e.g. via the, currently under discussion, Transatlantic Free Trade Agreement TTIP. Supervision of these markets is the responsibility of national states and their authorities.   RP: ___ out of 10

Alternative 1:
The liberalization which has taken place to date is a mistake. The WTO   RP: ___ out of 10
Financial Services Agreement and similar agreements should be revoked
and negotiations regarding TTIP cancelled. Markets for financial services
companies from non-EU states should be closed.
Alternative 2:
Before any further liberalization (WTO, TTIP), institutions within the   RP: ___ out of 10
framework of the UN should be established to supervise and regulate the
existing markets, whose policies should match the UN goals: human
rights, sustainable development, health, labor standards, system stability,
environmental and climate protection…

If 2: Question 18a: Should a Global Economic Council within the UNO be established, which…

… ensures and watches out for coherence in international trade, currency,   RP: ___ out of 10
tax and financial policy and indicates and informs about economic, social
and ecological risks at an early stage?
… receives a mandate to control IMF and World Bank?   RP: ___ out of 10
… formally integrates the WTO into the UN system and subjects it to its   RP: ___ out of 10
objectives and rules?

If 2: Question 18b: Should a global financial supervisory authority be established, which…

… pursues the same objectives as the EU supervisory authority on a   RP: ___ out of 10
global level?
… undertakes the coordination of equity capital regulations of the Basel   RP: ___ out of 10
Committee, the development of the accounting regulations (IFSR) and the
regulation of the global financial system of the G20 and the Financial
Stability Board?

If 2: Question 18c: Should a global tax agreement be enacted and a global tax authority be established, which …

… can independently take action against money laundering and tax   RP: ___ out of 10
detrimental practices such as banking secrecy and initiate a globally
uniform corporate taxation?

18.8 Derivatives

Question 19: Should derivative transactions, which have been authorized by the EU Financial Supervisory Authority, take place on supervised exchanges and be subject to a high amount of equity capital to be determined by the financial supervisory authority?

Zero Option:
No, that is too restrictive for economic freedom.   RP: ___ out of 10
Alternative:
Yes, that would make the derivatives universe more transparent, more   RP: ___ out of 10
straightforward and more secure.

18.8 Derivatives

Question 20: Should derivative transactions outside supervised exchanges....
Zero option:
... remain allowed?   RP: ___ out of 10
Alternative 1:
... be forbidden?   RP: ___ out of 10
Alternative 2:
... be released from legal protection?   RP: ___ out of 10

Question 21: Should private ratings be removed from all public and official regulations, laws and institutions?
Zero Option:
No.   RP: ___ out of 10
Alternative:
Yes.   RP: ___ out of 10

Question 22a: In the case of shares should there be...
Zero Option:
... no minimum holding period?   RP: ___ out of 10
Alternative 1:
... a minimum holding period of one year?   RP: ___ out of 10
Alternative 2:
... a minimum holding period of three years?   RP: ___ out of 10

Question 22b: Should stock voting rights...
Zero Option:
... not be tied to any minimum holding period?   RP: ___ out of 10
Alternative 1:
... be tied to a minimum holding period of 5 years?   RP: ___ out of 10
Alternative 2:
... be tied to a minimum holding period of 10 years?   RP: ___ out of 10

Question 23: Should trading with shares (on capitalistic stock markets) be phased out and after a transition period only be given back, and no longer traded?
Zero Option:
No, companies are a commodity like any other commodity and should be   RP: ___ out of 10
able to be bought and sold on markets.
Alternative:
Yes, the relationship between owner and company is closer and is up-   RP: ___ out of 10
valued, if the company share is only handed back and cannot be sold on
to third parties.

Question 24: Should financial dividends be phased out so that capital, as an economic resource, is invested according to other criteria (purpose, use, ethics, co-determination), as opposed to the criterion of financial return?
Zero Option:
No, capitalistic stock markets should remain in place. Common good   RP: ___ out of 10
stock exchange should be formed exclusively on a voluntary basis.

Alternative:
The maximum permissible dividend should progressively dwindle in the direction of zero during a transition period.   RP: ___ out of 10

Question 25: Should it be allowed to sell loans, to bundle and securitize them and trade with the resulting derivatives?
Zero Option:
Yes.   RP: ___ out of 10
Alternative:
No, banks should keep mortgage loans which they have granted in their own books.   RP: ___ out of 10

Question 26: Should credit default swaps (CDS) be permissible?
Zero Option:
Yes.   RP: ___ out of 10
Alternative:
No, this is an unnecessary and risky inflation of the financial system.   RP: ___ von 10

Question 27: Should governments and parliaments, within the framework of the UN, support a global commodity agreement, which regulates the promotion, pricing, distribution and return of sensitive and non-renewable ecological resources, whose conception is submitted to national sovereigns (with alternatives) to be voted on?
Zero Option:
No, the market should regulate the extraction, pricing and distribution of commodities.   RP: ___ out of 10
Alternative:
Yes, commodities are too strategic and sensitive to leave them to market mechanisms.   RP: ___ out of 10

18.9 Pensions

Question 28: Should politics push forward with the restructuring of the pension system in the direction of capital coverage, maintain it at the current level or revoke it once more and strengthen the apportionment procedure by operating all ten "regulatory/financing screws"?
Zero Option:
Privatizing the pension system is the correct way and this should be continued.   RP: ___ out of 10
Alternative 1:
The current mix is optimal and requires neither a further restructuring nor dismantling.   RP: ___ out of 10
Alternative 2:
State support for private pension provision should be revoked and instead the apportionment procedure and inter-generation contract should be enhanced by a diverse range of measures.   RP: ___ out of 10

If 2: Question 28a:

There should be a minimum pension for everybody.	RP: ___ out of 10
Parental-leave periods should be taken into account more generously.	RP: ___ out of 10
The total global income should be taken into consideration for the financing of the statutory pension.	RP: ___ out of 10
The state subsidy for pension can amount to up to a third of the pension benefit.	RP: ___ out of 10
Pensions for women should be brought up to the level of pensions for men.	RP: ___ out of 10
There should be one single public pension fund for everybody.	RP: ___ out of 10

18.10 Tax Justice

Question 29: Should employment income and capital income be treated equally when declared to the tax authority and should this be automatically declared?

Zero Option:

No, I am in favor of the continuation of the difference in treatment with employment income being automatically declared and capital income not.	RP: ___ out of 10

Alternative 1:

It should be the reverse: automatic declaration of capital income and privacy protection for employment income.	RP: ___ out of 10

Alternative 2:

I am in favor of equal treatment with privacy protection being extended to employment income.	RP: ___ out of 10

Alternative 3:

I am in favor of equal treatment with automatic declaration being extended to capital income.	RP: ___ out of 10

Question 30: Should my country participate in a multi-lateral tax cooperation agreement in the OECD or even UNO?

Zero Option:

I consider the current arrangement to be adequate.	RP: ___ out of 10

Alternative:

I am in favor of the participation.	RP: ___ out of 10

Question 31: Should the multi-lateral agreement be extended to all types of capital income and to legal entities, including name registers of trusts, foundations and other types of financial assets?

Zero Option:

The exceptions are justified and there should be no further development.	RP: ___ out of 10

Alternative:

All loopholes should be closed so that capital income can be comprehensively and effectively recorded and included in the information exchange system.	RP: ___ out of 10

Question 32: Should tax evasion and tax fraud in third countries, which do not participate in this agreement, be responded to with capital movement sanctions?

Zero Option:
Capital movement should remain absolutely free. RP: ___ out of 10
Alternative:
Capital movement in uncooperative third countries should remain RP: ___ out of 10
restricted until cooperation is forthcoming.

Question 33: Should the handling of the international movement of capital become a public task of central banks or of separate public clearing banks, as part of the "public good" money?

Zero Option:
No, clearing in international movement of capital should be an RP: ___ out of 10
unregulated private service.
Alternative 1:
Yes, this is an essential component of the construct of the "public good" RP: ___ out of 10
money.
Alternative 2:
It is sufficient to regulate and monitor private clearing banks so that they RP: ___ out of 10
enforce the specific restriction of capital movement (similar private
customs authorities).

Question 34: Should [Austria] [Germany] [my country] participate in an international agreement and corridor to align the tax base for company taxation?

Zero Option:
No, I am in favor of tax competition. RP: ___ out of 10
Alternative:
Yes. I am in favor of tax cooperation. RP: ___ out of 10

If yes: Question 34a: Where should the corridor be?

Alternative 1:
Between 40% and 50%. RP: ___ out of 10
Alternative 2:
Between 35% and 45%. RP: ___ out of 10
Alternative 3:
Between 30% and 40%. RP: ___ out of 10
Alternative 4:
Between 25% and 35%. RP: ___ out of 10

Question 35: Should [Austria] [Germany] [my country] convert all double taxation agreements to the imputation method?

Zero Option:
No, the government should continue to decide this at its own discretion. RP: ___ out of 10
Alternative 1:
No, all double taxation agreements should be devised using the RP: ___ out of 10
exemption method: domestic companies should only pay the respective
applicable tax rate overseas, even if this is lower than in the home
country.

18.11 Restriction of Inequality

Alternative 2:
Yes, I am in favor of a uniform taxation of domestic companies, irrespective of where they operate and generate profits.   RP: ___ out of 10

Question 36: Should [Austria] [Germany] [my country] introduce the unitary taxation principle?

Zero Option:
No, I am in favor of tax competition.   RP: ___ out of 10
Alternative:
Yes, I am in favor of the fair pro rate taxation of real economic activity.   RP: ___ out of 10

Question 37: Should [Austria] [Germany] [my country] promote the establishment of a global tax authority, which initiates the unitary taxation principle and develops rules for a globally consolidated corporation tax balance sheet?

Zero Option:
Against.   RP: ___ out of 10
Alternative:
In favor of.   RP: ___ out of 10

18.11 Restriction of Inequality

Question 38: Should there be a statutory minimum wage?

Zero Option:
No, the price of human labor should develop freely on markets.   RP: ___ out of 10
Alternative:
Yes, markets do not ensure a humane minimum income.   RP: ___ von 10

If yes: Question 38a:

8 euro/USD gross per hour.   RP: ___ out of 10
9 euro/USD gross per hour.   RP: ___ out of 10
10 euro/USD gross per hour.   RP: ___ out of 10
11 euro/USD gross per hour.   RP: ___ out of 10
12 euro/USD gross per hour.   RP: ___ out of 10

Question 39: Should this be appreciated with annual inflation?

Zero Option:
No.   RP: ___ out of 10
Alternative:
Yes, so that those people who with the lowest income at least do not lose purchasing power.   RP: ___ out of 10

Question 40: Should the maximum income be limited by a maximum multiple of the statutory or collectively agreed statutory minimum wage?

Zero Option:
No.   RP: ___ out of 10
Alternative:
Yes.   RP: ___ out of 10

If yes: Question 40a:
... 10 times?   RP: ___ out of 10
... 20 times?   RP: ___ out of 10
... 50 times?   RP: ___ out of 10
... 100 times?   RP: ___ out 10
... 900 times (Switzerland), 1,000 times (Austria), 5,000 times (Germany), 360,000 times (USA) – as is presently the case?   RP: ___ out of 10

Question 41: Should wealth tax apply and progressively increase from a threshold value, which is sufficient for a certain level of prosperity?

Zero Option (Germany, Austria):
I am against every form of wealth tax.   RP: ___ out of 10
Alternative 1:
Yes, from 500,000 euro.   RP: ___ out of 10
Alternative 2:
Yes, from one million euro.   RP: ___ out of 10
Alternative 3:
Yes, from three million euro.   RP: ___ out of 10

Question 42: Should there be an upper limit for private property?

Zero Option:
No, private property should be unlimited.   RP: ___ von 10
Alternative 1:
Yes, it should be limited to 10 million euro?   RP: ___ out of 10
Alternative 2:
Yes, it should be limited to 20 million euro?   RP: ___ out of 10
Alternative 3:
Yes, it should be limited to 50 million euro?   RP: ___ out of 10
Alternative 4:
Yes, it should be limited to 100 million euro?   RP: ___ out of 10
Alternative 5:
Yes, it should be limited to a billion euro?   RP: ___ out of 10

Question 43: Should inheritance law...

Zero Option:
... be unrestricted (Germany) or rather remain so (Austria)?   RP: ___ out of 10
Alternative 1:
... be abolished?   RP: ___ out of 10
Alternative 2:
... be capped?   WP: ___ out of 10

In the event of capping: Question 43a: Should the statutory right of inheritance per child be restricted, in the case of private assets, to

Alternative 1:
... 500,000 euro?   RP: ___ out of 10
Alternative 2:
... one million euro?   RP: ___ out of 10
Alternative 3:
... two million euro?   RP: ___ out of 10

Alternative 4:
... three million euro?   RP: ___ out of 10
Alternative 5:
... five million euro?   RP: ___ out of 10

In the case of a restriction: Question 43b: Should the statutory right of inheritance per child, in the case of corporate assets (family-run businesses or agricultural businesses), be restricted to....

Alternative 1:
... five million euro?   RP: ___ out of 10
Alternative 2:
... ten million euro?   RP: ___ out of 10
Alternative 3:
... twenty million euro?   RP: ___ out of 10

18.12 International Monetary Order

Question 44: How should international monetary relations be organized in future?

Zero Option:
I am in favor of deregulated currency markets, where the exchange rates   RP: ___ out of 10
freely develop in accordance with demand and supply and fluctuate
accordingly.
Alternative 1:
My country / the Eurozone should strive for cooperative exchange rate   RP: ___ out of 10
management with as many countries as possible with the objective of
constant purchasing-power parity and thereby constant competitive
conditions (REER Model UNCTAD).
Alternative 2:
I vote in favor of a global currency cooperation with a global reserve   RP: ___ out of 10
currency (UNO model). The government of my country should pursue
such a cooperation and the establishment of a "beginner's group" within
the UNO.

If 2: Question 44a:

Alternative 1:
Should a Bretton Woods II with a global reserve union, global reserve   RP: ___ out of 10
bank and global reserve currency "Terra" be set up with a focus on
balanced trade balances (Keynes-Stiglitz-UNO model)?
Alternative 2:
Should a Bretton Woods II with a global reserve union, global reserve   RP: ___ out of 10
bank and global reserve currency "Terra" be set up with a focus on
purchasing-power parity (Keynes-Flassbeck-Felber compromise model)?

Question 45: Which currency should commodities be quoted in in the future?

Zero Option:
In US dollars.   RP: ___ out of 10
Alternative 1:
In euros.   RP: ___ out of 10
Alternative 2:
In Yuan.   RP: ___ out of 10
Alternative 3:
In Terra 4:   RP: ___ out of 10

Question 46: What should happen with the International Monetary Fund IMF?

Zero Option:
It should remain a shareholder company that is not accountable to the UNO, with voting rights according to capital contribution.   RP: ___ out of 10
Alternative:
It should be completely integrated into the UN system and become the world reserve bank. All countries and people should be democratically represented. My government should pursue this.   RP: ___ out of 10

Question 47: What should happen with the World Bank?

Zero Option:
It should remain as it is.   RP: ___ out of 10
Alternative:
It should be fully integrated into the UN system and democratized based on the IMF model. It should only grant interest-free loans, on the basis of the Sustainable Development Goals and other agreements and objectives of the UN.   RP: ___ out of 10

This questionnaire can be downloaded free of charge at http://www.changeeverything.info/resources/ and at http://www.christian-felber.at/buecher/geldbuch.php

Index

A
Accenture, 148, 158, 159
Ackermann, Josef, 105
Adenauer, Konrad, 132
Admati, Anat, 6, 103, 111, 112, 113, 123, 128
AIFM Directive (Alternative Investment Fund Managers Directive), 107, 114
Aldi family, 162
Alternative Bank, 94
Alternative Investment Fund Managers Directive (AIFM Directive), 107, 114
Amaranth Hedge Funds, 120
Amazon, 148
Anderson, Pamela, 148
Anti-cyclical, 48
Anti-cyclical fiscal policy, 66
APC (average propensity to consume), 92
Apple, 148
Arbitrage speculation, 179
Asmussen, Jörg, 56
Asset price inflation, 3
ATM, 119
Attac, 94, 109, 142, 145, 150
Austerity program, 69
Austria Consumer Protection Association, 143
Austrian Central Bank, 55
Austrian Financial Market Authority, 107
Austrian Institute of Economic Research (WIFO), 137, 159
Austrian Trade Union Federation, 55
Automatic stabilizer, 67
Average propensity to consume, 92
AWD, 137

B
BaFin, 123
Balance sheet, 3, 17, 24, 42, 43, 46, 47, 50, 62, 63, 68, 80, 81, 87, 107, 111, 112, 157, 165, 185
Banca d'Italia, 56
Banca Etica, 94
Bancor, 177
Bank collapse, 46, 81, 99
Bank for International Settlement (BIS), 44, 45, 78, 95, 120
Banking secrecy, 5, 150, 151, 156
Bank note, 31, 42, 54
Bank of America, 106
Bank of England, 54, 59, 60, 62, 179, 189
Bank of German States, 55
Barings Bank, 78, 120
Basel Committee, 15–16, 18, 24, 27, 116
Basel II, 15, 16, 74, 111
Basel III, 13, 15, 16, 18, 74, 111, 112
Basel rules, 44, 73
BAWAG, 55, 120
BCG (Boston Consulting Group), 45, 95, 96
Bear Sterns, 120
Becker, Boris, 148
Berlusconi, Silvio, 164
Bidder consortium, 61
Big four, 62
Binswanger, Hans Christoph, v, 37
Birchler, Urs Zürich, 89
BIS (Bank for International Settlement), 44, 45, 78, 95, 120
Blackwater, 127
Book money, 3, 31, 32, 37, 38, 39, 42, 43, 45, 46, 47, 49, 51, 56, 151

© Springer International Publishing AG 2017
C. Felber, *Money – The New Rules of the Game*, DOI 10.1007/978-3-319-67352-3

Boston Consulting Group, 45, 95, 96
Bottom line, 125
Braun, Christina von, v, 2, 161, 169
Brecht, Berthold, 83
Bretton Woods, 84, 175, 177, 178
Bretton Woods II, 175–187
Bretton Woods System, 110, 117, 175, 176, 178
Bretton Woods Twins, 176
Breuer, Rolf-E., viii, 6
Brodbeck, Karl Heinz, ix
Buckminster, Fuller, 191
Buffet, Warren, 77, 85, 120, 150, 173

C

Capital controls, 110, 153, 176
Capital requirement, 111
Capital Requirement Directive (CRD), 111
Capital socialism, 97
Cash account, 46, 47, 89
Cash money, 100
Casino derivatives, 75
CDO (collateralized debt obligation), 3, 109, 128
CDR (Capital Requirement Directive), 111
CDS (credit default swap), 77, 127, 128
Central bank, 30, 31, 37, 38, 41, 42, 43, 45, 46, 47, 48, 49, 50, 53, 54–63, 66, 68, 69, 71, 89, 91, 97, 128–129, 155, 183, 184
Central Raiffeisen Bank, 81
CETA (Comprehensive Economic and Trade Agreement), 116
CFC (Common Fund for Commodities), 132
Chicago Plan, 14, 50
Chiemgauer, 186, 187
Chinese Central Bank, 181
Churchill, Winston, 173
Citigroup, 17, 106
Citizens council, 194
Clinton, Bill, 162
Collateralized debt obligation, 3, 109, 128
Commercial bank, 38, 43, 46
Commerzbank, 80, 105
Commodity price inflation, 38
Common Fund for Commodities (CFC), 132
Common good, 2, 5, 7, 16, 17, 30, 32, 54, 72, 73, 75, 76, 85, 94, 124, 172
Common good appraisal, 75, 76, 93
Common Good Balance Sheet, 24, 76, 90, 95, 115, 125, 126, 131, 138, 169, 192, 193
Common Good Charter, 89, 94, 95, 145, 193
Common good exchange, 94, 124–127, 193
Common good municipality, 27, 192, 193, 198
Common good-oriented, 16, 83–86, 95, 125

Communist Manifesto, 172
Community Reinvestment Act, 81
Comprehensive Economic and Trade Agreement (CETA), 116
Constitutional convention, 23, 198, 199
Cooperative bank, 79, 84, 94, 95, 113
Core capital ratio, 111
Council of the European Union, 57
Creditanstalt, 84, 85
Credit default swap, 77, 127, 128
Credit demand, 79
Credit-financed financial investment, 77, 79
Credit-financed real investment, 77
Credit steering, 74, 76
Credit Suisse, 95, 113, 148, 166
Creutz, Helmut, vi, 4, 92
Cross-border movement of capital, 147
Crouch, Colin, 161, 162
Crowther, Geoffrey, 175
Currency exchange management, 63
Currency instability, 176
Current account, 43, 46, 90, 98
Current account balance, 3, 29, 42, 46

D

Debt cap, 67, 96
Debt-free, 46, 48
Deflation, 53, 63
Democratic dowry, 173
Democratic economic convention, 193, 196
Democratic monetary convention, 21–28, 75, 110, 186, 193–197
Demographic bomb, 136, 141
Derivatives, 3, 62, 87, 90, 109, 119–134, 140, 178, 206
Der Standard, 22
Destroika, 13, 69
Deutsche Bank, 6, 88, 105, 111, 122, 127, 148
Deutsche Mark, 55
Dibelius, Alexander, viii, 172
Dijsselbloem, Jeroen, 104
Dohmen, Caspar, 73, 125, 126
Dollar hegemony, 176, 182, 184, 185–186
Dollar reserve system, 175
Double taxation agreement, 148, 160
Draghi, Mario, 54, 56, 57
Ducommun, Gil, 173

E

EBA (European Banking Authority), 103
ECB (European Central Bank), 31, 41, 42, 51, 53, 54, 55, 56, 57, 59, 60, 62, 63, 68, 104, 105, 123, 128, 156, 185

Index

ECG (Economy for the Common Good), 23, 25, 27, 169, 192, 193, 197, 198
Economic Coordination Council, 103
Economic freedom, 73, 75, 108, 117, 153, 171
Economic system, 57, 88, 165, 193
Economy for the Common Good, 25, 192, 197
EFSF (European Financial Stability Facility), 18
EIOPA (European Insurance and Occupational Pensions Authority), 103
Eisenstein, Charles, 187
Electronic money, 38
Entire group taxation, 156–159
Equity capital ratio, 111, 112, 113, 114
ESF (European Stability Fund), 18
ESM (European Stability Mechanism), 18, 104
ESMA (European Securities and Markets Authority), 18, 103
ESRB (European Systemic Risk Board), 103
Ethical creditworthiness appraisal, 74–76
Ethical loan appraisal, 73
Ethically reduced value, 76
Ethical risk assessment, 71
ETH Zürich, 163
EU Constitutional Treaty, 59
EU financial supervisory authority, 86, 87, 105, 109, 113
Eurobonds, 88, 179
European Banking Authority (EBA), 103
European Central Bank (ECB), 31, 41, 42, 51, 53, 54, 55, 56, 57, 59, 60, 62, 63, 68, 104, 105, 123, 128, 156, 185
European Central Bank Charter, 58
European Financial Stability Facility (EFSF), 18
European Insurance and Occupational Pensions Authority (EIOPA), 103
European Securities and Markets Authority (ESMA), 18, 103
European Stability Fund (ESF), 18
European Stability Mechanism (ESM), 18, 104
European Systemic Risk Board (ESRB), 103
Eurozone, 44, 48, 49, 62, 67, 68, 96, 100, 112, 179, 184
Exchange value, 72, 75, 93
Exemption method, 158
Ex nihilo, 48, 71
Expenditure-oriented debt cap, 67
ExxonMobil, 127

F

Fahrenschon, Georg, 88
FATCA (Foreign Account Tax Compliance Act), 152, 154
Fed, Federal Reserve, 54, 59, 176, 179
Federal Bank of Germany, 51
Federation of Austrian Industries (IV), 135
Felber, Christian, 15, 80, 116, 142, 169, 173, 178, 179, 193
Finance Watch, 16, 90
Financial alchemy, 78
Financial capitalism, 90, 121, 124
Financial casino, 3, 79, 80, 90, 120, 121, 127, 128, 129, 167
Financial creditworthiness, 73, 77, 93
Financial creditworthiness appraisal, 74, 75, 76, 93
Financial derivatives, 85, 120, 129
Financial firefighters, 185
Financial inflation, 38, 44, 48, 62
Financial investment, 62, 73, 77, 79, 90
Financial repression, 97, 98, 170
Financial risk assessment, 71
Financial Secrecy Index (FSI), 156
Financial Services Authority (FSA), 17
Financial speculation, 77, 78, 79
Financial Stability Board (FSB), 3, 11–13, 106, 107
Financial toxic waste, 86, 89, 127, 128
Financial weapons of mass destruction, 85, 108, 110, 120
Fisher, Irving, vii, 29, 50
Fitschen, Jürgen, 88, 89
Flassbeck, Heiner, 182, 183, 184
Fleischhacker, Michael, 169
Forbes, 97, 162
Foreign Account Tax Compliance Act (FATCA), 152, 154
Frankfurt Stock Exchange, 84
Free market, 17, 77, 85, 87, 89, 130, 180, 181
Freie Gemeinschaftsbank, 94
Friedman, Milton, 50, 142, 163
FSA (Financial Services Authority), 17
FSB (Financial Stability Board), 3, 11–13, 106, 107
FSI (Financial Secrecy Index), 156

G

GABV (Global Alliance for Banking on Values), 94, 126
GATS (General Agreement on Trade in Services), 15, 106, 115
GDP (Gross Domestic Product), 44, 45, 48, 50, 62, 66, 68, 78, 79, 80, 81, 93, 95, 96, 98, 120, 148
GECC (Global Economic Coordination Council), 116, 117

General Agreement on Tariffs and Trade (GATT), 85
General Agreement on Trade in Services (GATS), 15, 115
General Declaration of Human and Citizens Rights, 150
German Bundesbank, 60
German Commercial Code, 111
German fear index, 168
German Federation of Trade Unions, 90
German Reichsbank, 55, 61
Gesell, Silvio, 176
Glasenberg, Ivan, 172
Glass Steagall Act, 84
Global Alliance for Banking on Values (GABV), 94, 126
Global Commodity Agreement, 129–134
Global Economic Coordination Council (GECC), 116, 117
Global Financial Authority, 116, 117
Global foreign exchange cooperation, 129
Global player, 86, 157, 158, 165
Global reserve bank, 117, 181, 182
Global reserve currency, 18, 117, 176, 180, 181, 185, 186
Global Wealth Report, 95
Globo, 181
GLS Bank, 73
Gold, 2, 41, 42, 125, 130, 131, 164, 174, 176, 178
Goldman Sachs, 5, 7, 17, 122, 172
Goldsmith, 2
Google, 148
Government bond, 3, 16, 48, 57, 60, 61, 63, 69, 77, 87, 112, 121, 122, 127, 128–129
Grasser, Karl-Heinz, 148, 163
Great Depression, 173
Greenspan, Alan, 53, 119
Greenspeak, 54
Gross Domestic Product (GDP), 44, 45, 48, 50, 62, 66, 68, 78, 79, 80, 81, 93, 95, 96, 98, 120, 148

H
Hamburger Sparkasse, 87
Hayek, Friedrich A. von, 17, 163
Hedge fund, 5, 17, 74, 77, 78, 107, 109, 113, 114, 119, 122, 124, 172
Hellwig, Martin, 6, 103, 111, 112, 113, 123, 128
Herrmann, Ulrike, 1, 128, 167
HFT (high-frequency trading), 121
High-frequency trading (HFT), 121
Hoeneß, Uli, 148

Homo oeconomicus, 126
Huber, Joseph, vi, 3, 5, 32, 40, 41, 42, 44, 49, 50, 64, 73, 100, 111
Huffschmid, Jörg, 110, 147
Hundred percent banking, 50
Hundred Percent Money, 50, 51

I
IARS, 116
Icelandic Financial Supervisory Authority, 81
ICU (International Clearing Union), 177
IIF (Institute for International Finance), 105
Ikea, 148, 159, 160
IMF (International Monetary Fund), 12, 13–14, 176
Imputation method, 158, 160
Inflation, 3, 38, 39, 44, 47, 57, 58, 62, 63, 68, 97, 98, 111, 182
Institutional investor, 77, 97, 124
Interest-free, 46, 48, 62, 182
Interest-free loans, 62, 65, 66, 69
Interest-seigniorage, 51
International Clearing Union (ICU), 177
International Monetary Fund (IMF), 12, 13–14, 176
International Tax Compact (ITC), 117
Investment agreement, 18
Investment bank, 64, 77, 85, 95–97, 109, 120, 121, 122, 127
IPCC, 116
Issuance of money, 40, 56
ITC (International Tax Compact), 117

J
Jefferson, Thomas, 53
Johnson, Simon, 112, 162
Jorberg, Thomas, vii, 73
Joób, Mark, 21
Justice Formula 2010, 169

K
Kapsch, Georg, 135
Kennedy, Margrit, 187
Keynes, John Maynard, 66, 71, 176, 177, 180, 181, 182, 184, 186
Kohl, Helmut, 157
Kramer, Ingo, 138
Krugman, Paul, 54

L
Labor market participation, 137, 138
Langenegger Talente, 187

Lao Tse, 191
Lehman Brothers, 17, 104, 108, 111
Leveraged financial speculation, 78, 79
Libor scandal, 5, 179
Lietaer, Bernard, 53, 187
Lincoln, Abraham, vii
Lisbon Treaty, 51, 57, 59, 110, 153, 156
Loan fee, 76
Location competition, 159
Lohan, Lindsay, 148
Long-Term Capital Management (LTCM), 78
LTCM (Long-Term Capital Management), 78
Luxemburg, Rosa, 172

M
Maastricht Treaty, 60, 86
Mackenroth, Gerhard, 140, 141
Mackenroth Theorem, 140–141
Macleod, Henry Dunning, vi
Macroeconomic equilibrium, 180
Malik, Fredmund, 123
Market-conformed democracy, 165–166
Markets in Financial Instruments Directive (MIFID), 18
Mass unemployment, 73
Mastronardi, Philippe, viii, 30
McKinsey, 95
McKinsey Global Institute, 44, 78, 79, 95
Means of exchange, 2, 4
Medium of payment, 2
Merton, Robert C., 120
Metallgesellschaft AG, 120
Methuselah Conspiracy, 144
MIFID II, 18
MIFID Markets in Financial Instruments Directive, 18
Minder Initiative, 23
Minimum reserve, 38, 42, 44, 47
Monetary authority, 63–64
Monetary Modernization, 63
Monetary system, 1–7, 19, 21, 22, 23, 24, 28, 32, 33, 37, 40, 53, 64, 71, 74, 79, 86, 95, 103, 117, 133, 175, 180, 186, 191, 192, 193
Monetative, 45
Money creation, 4, 5, 19, 30, 32, 37, 38, 39, 40, 43, 44, 45, 46, 48, 49, 57
Money-out of-money transaction, 72, 120, 123, 128, 179
Money supply, 3, 37, 38, 41
Money supply M1, 3, 48, 49
Monsanto, 127
Monti, Mario, 85

Morgan, John Pierpont (J. P.), 5, 6, 106
Municipal economic convention, 27, 193
Municipal monetary convention, 23, 25, 192, 193
Müller, Dirk, vi, 4, 45

N
National economic convention, 23
National monetary convention, 27
Natural monopoly, 30
Negative feedback, 161–173
Negative inheritance tax, 173
Neo-mercantilism, 184
New Deal, 173
Nietzsche, Friedrich, x
Nobel Prize, 78, 120
Non-renewable natural commodities, 133
Novartis, 58

O
Original seigniorage, 46
Ortega, Armancio, 162
Osbourne, Ozzy, 148
OTC (over the counter), 17, 120
Otte, Max, 89
Overall group tax, 158–159
Over the counter (OTC), 17, 120
Oxfam, 108, 122, 162

P
Paulson, John, 114, 162, 172
Pay as you go (PAYG), 136–140
PAYG (pay as you go), 136–140
Pension fund, 77, 143, 145
Pension scheme, 140, 142, 145
Performance-oriented society, 166
Peukert, Helge, 104, 112, 122
Pickett, Kate, 167, 168
Piketty, Thomas, 155
Plettenbacher, Tobias, 187
Porsche Piëch family, 162
Positive feedback, 165
Positive feedback system, 165
Post-democracy, 162
Pre-democracy, 105, 162
Primary market, 60, 61
Private capital levy, 92
Private capital tax, 96, 98, 141
Private equity fund, 77, 106, 107, 113, 124
Profit-oriented, 18, 47, 83, 84, 89
Project Bank for the Common Good, 145, 197
Public good, 2, 6, 24, 29–33, 39, 44, 50, 55, 56, 72, 73, 79, 91, 100, 131, 132, 133, 145, 151, 175

Public interest, 19, 54, 72, 132, 134, 172
Public service, 29, 30, 31, 32, 56, 85, 91, 94, 117, 149, 151, 199

Q
Quinn, Freddy, 148

R
Raiba Lech am Arlberg, 95
Raiffeisen, Friedrich Wilhelm, vii, 84, 198
Raiffeisen Bank, 84, 198
Rating agency, 109, 121
REACH (registration, evaluation, authorisation and restriction of chemicals), 108
Reagan, Ronald, 85
Real Effective Exchange Rates (REER), 182
Real investment, 58, 76–77, 79, 96, 145
REER (Real Effective Exchange Rates), 182
Re-feudalization, 163
Regional common good exchange, 94, 124–127, 193
Regional complementary currency, 24
Registration, evaluation, authorisation and restriction of chemicals (REACH), 108
Reich, Robert, 7, 162
Re-regulation, 1
Rescue package, 61
Reserve currency, 176, 177, 179, 180, 186
Res publica, 28, 29, 30
Rhineland capitalism, 85
Ricci, Christina, 148
Riester Pension, 142, 143, 144, 145
Risk-weighted equity capital ratio, 112
ROI, return on investment, 77, 80, 143
Rueff, Jacques, v
Rürup, Bernd, 137, 138

S
Savings bank, 84, 87, 90
Scholes, Myron S., 120
Schranne, 85
Schröder, Gerhard, 135
Schulmeister, Stephan, 58, 60, 67, 77, 78, 125, 145, 178, 181
Schultze-Delitzsch, Hermann, 84
Schumpeter, 163, 173
Schwab, Klaus, 169, 170
Schäuble, Wolfgang, viii, 105
SDR (special drawing rights), 181
SEC (Security and Exchange Commission), 123
Security and Exchange Commission (SEC), 123
Separate banking system, 90

Shadow bank, 3, 6
Share boom, 77
Siemens, 58, 124
SME, 58, 127
SMUD, San Diego Municipality District Utility, 91
Société Générale, 120
Soros, George, 169, 179
Sovereign citizens, 27, 51, 199
Sovereign debt, 49, 57, 65–70, 96, 203
Sovereign default, 57, 61, 179, 180, 186
Sovereign good, 29
Sovereign money, 19, 45, 46, 47, 48, 49, 50–51, 71
Sovereign money municipality, 191
Sovereign money reform, 30, 41–51, 65, 68, 89, 90, 202
Sovereign right, 40
Sparda Bank, 84, 95
Sparkasse Dornbirn, 95
Special drawing rights (SDR), 181
Special purpose vehicle (SPV), 106
Speculative attack, 62, 69, 70, 129, 179, 180
Speculative financial investment, 74
SPV (special purpose vehicle), 106
Stadler, Wilfried, 109, 111, 112
Starbucks, 148
Stepic, Herbert, 148
Sterntaler, 186, 187
Stiglitz, Joseph, 12, 13, 14, 18, 54, 55, 90, 116, 143, 180, 181
Stiglitz commission, 18, 117, 180, 182
Straumur Bank, 81
Stronach, Frank, viii, 164, 171
Structural irresponsibility, 109
Styrian Chamber of Commerce, 164
Super-capitalism, 162
Swiss National Bank, 55, 185
Systemic Consensus (SC principle), 25, 26, 196
Systemic instability, 62, 73, 74, 175
Systemic risk, 77, 116, 179
Systemic Risk Board, 104

T
Target system, 156
Tax haven, 3, 5, 6, 12, 15, 86, 87, 148, 149, 150, 152, 153, 155, 156, 157, 158, 159, 160
Tax Justice Network, 148, 156, 159
Tax payer, 50, 66, 87, 89, 107, 109, 129, 146
Terra, 182, 184, 186
Terra Union, 182

Index

TEU (Treaty on European Union), 57, 156
TFEU (Treaty on the functioning of the European Union), 51, 57
Thatcher, Margret, 85, 142
Too big to fail, 12, 84, 85, 87, 88, 89
Too big to jail, 88
Treaty on European Union (TEU), 57, 156
Treaty on the functioning of the European Union (TFEU), 51, 57
Triodos Bank, 94
Triple skyline, 100, 124–127
Troika, 13, 69, 183
Trump, Donald, 164
TTIP, Transatlantic Trade and Investment Partnership, 18, 85, 88, 115, 116
Turner, Adair, 103
TÜV, Technical Inspection Agency, 85, 108

U
UBS, 5, 113
UNCTAD (United Nations Conference on Trade and Development), 15, 132, 182, 183, 184
UNESCO (United Nations Educational, Scientific and Cultural Organization), 192
Unitary pension fund, 140
Unitary taxation, 117, 158–159, 160
United Nations Conference on Trade and Development (UNCTAD), 15, 132, 182, 183, 184
United Nations Educational, Scientific and Cultural Organization (UNESCO), 192
United Nations Organization (UNO), 11, 14, 15, 18, 24, 27, 89, 131, 159
UNO (United Nations Organization), 11, 14, 15, 18, 24, 27, 89, 131, 159

Uruguay Round, 85
Utilizable value, 91, 93

V
Valluga, 97, 162
Vasella, Daniel, 26
Volcker, Paul, 119
Volksbank, 84
Voralberg Talente, 186

W
Waldviertler, 126
Weidmann, Jens, 56
Werner, Richard, 79
Weseley, Snipes, 148
White, Henry Dexter, 176
Wiener Creditanstalt, 84
WIFO (Austrian Institute of Economic Research), 137, 159
Wilkinson, Richard, 167, 168
World Economic Forum (WEF), 169
World financial registry, 155
World Savings Day, 91
WTO, World Trade Organization, 3, 14–15, 85

X
Xiaochuan, Zhou, 181

Y
Youth unemployment, 69

Z
Zeise, Lucas, vi, 83, 88, 104, 105, 123, 128
Zucman, Gabriel, 155

The manufacturer's authorised representative in the EU is Springer Nature Customer Service Centre GmbH, Europaplatz 3, 69115 Heidelberg, Germany. If you have any concerns regarding our products, please contact ProductSafety@springernature.com

Printed and bound by CPI Group (UK) Ltd, Croydon, CR0 4YY
23/03/2026
02076668-0014